The Case Against Christianity

The Case Against
CHRISTIANITY

MICHAEL MARTIN

Temple University Press
Philadelphia

Temple University Press, Philadelphia 19122
Copyright © 1991 by Temple University. All rights reserved
Published 1991
Printed in the United States of America

The paper used in this publication meets the minimum requirements of American
National Standard for Information Sciences—Permanence of Paper for Printed Library
Materials, ANSI Z39.48-1984 ∞

Library of Congress Cataloging-in-Publication Data

Martin, Michael, 1932 Feb. 3–
    The case against christianity / Michael Martin.
      p. cm.
    Includes bibliographical references and index.
    ISBN 0-87722-767-5 (alk. paper)
    1. Christianity—Controversial literature.   I. Title.
BL2747.M28   1991
230—dc20   90-22000
                                                  CIP

To Bill Luckett and Larry Crull

CONTENTS

PREFACE

This book is dedicated to two people who indirectly influenced it. Without Bill Luckett who nearly thirty-five years ago first got me interested in philosophy this book would never have been written. It is fair to say that without his inspiration I would not have pursued an academic career, let alone specialized in philosophy. I have never forgotten his encouragement and help when I needed it most. Without Larry Crull with whom I first discussed the philosophical problems of Christianity over thirty years ago the idea for this book would not have been conceived. Although blind, Larry was able to see more clearly than anyone I know the philosophical difficulties of Christian belief. I regret that because of the tragic accident that took his life in the early 1960s he will not be able to read the work that his probing mind inspired.

Needless to say, many others have influenced my thoughts about Christianity. My debt to them should be clear in the pages that follow. I would like to thank Ronald Tanguay for reading Chapter 2 and making helpful suggestions. My wife, Jane Roland Martin, read the entire manuscript and her comments and suggestions enabled me to improve both its style and its content. My editor, Jane Cullen, gave me encouragement and support that, as usual, was invaluable in completing the manuscript. I am also indebted to Wanda Torres for checking notes and quotations, thus saving me from making many errors.

The Case Against Christianity

INTRODUCTION

Christianity has far more followers than any other religion in the world today. It is estimated that there are about 1.6 billion Christians in the world in comparison with about 0.8 billion Muslims, 0.6 billion Hindus, 0.3 billion Buddhists, 97 million followers of tribal religions, 17 million Jews, 16 million Sikhs, 13 million Shamanists, 5 million Confucians, 4.5 million Baha'is, 3.4 million Shintoists, and 3.3 million Jains.[1] Indeed, about one out of every three people on the surface of the earth is Christian. Furthermore, it seems clear that Christianity has had a greater influence on Western society and culture than any other religion, philosophy, or ideology. It has influenced and shaped our literature, art, music, science, law, thinking, and way of life. Indeed, it is difficult to imagine what our culture and society would be like if there had not been Christianity. This religion has not only lasted for nearly two thousand years but has grown and developed. Even today Christian missionaries are spreading the gospel of Jesus Christ in Africa and Asia; in the United States there is a resurgence of Christian fundamentalism.

However, the importance of a religion measured by the number of its followers and the scope of its influence does not make its doctrines true; 1.6 billion people can be wrong. It is well to remember that from the very start Christianity has had its critics. Some scholars believe that at the beginning of the rise of Christianity many people doubted Jesus' divinity and considered him a magician. Unfortunately, our knowledge of these early critics is limited, for when the Christian church became strong enough to gain support from the Roman Empire, it used its power to ferret out and destroy books by heretics and pagan critics.[2] This suppression lasted for many centuries.

This suppression was manifested in many ways. One of the primary ways was the church's absolute control over what was officially recognized to be the divinely inspired word of God. In the first and second centuries the teachings of the earlier Christians took the form of gospels, epistles, narratives, and prophecies. The twenty-seven canonical books of the New Testament that are used by all major Christian churches represent only a portion of this material. For example, the Book of James, the Acts of Pilate, the Acts of Paul and Thecla were not included in the official canon, that is, they were not

3

considered to be divinely inspired. The selection by the church of these twenty-seven books as canonical did not take place at once, however. The earliest canon, known as the Muratorian Canon and drawn up around A.D. 190, contained most of the books of what we know today as the New Testament with the exception of Hebrews, James, 1 and 2 Peter, and 3 John. However, there was disagreement over the divine inspiration of seven books (Hebrews, James, 2 Peter, 2 and 3 John, Jude, and Revelation) that were finally included and over others that were ultimately rejected (the epistles of Saint Ignatius, Saint Clement 1, and the Shepherd of Hermas). Athanasius published the first official list of the books of the New Testament in A.D. 365 and the church council held at Carthage in A.D. 397 confirmed it.[3] The church declared that these twenty-seven books were divinely inspired and so their infallibility was not to be questioned.

Indeed, after the suppression of early Christian critics and the official acceptance of the New Testament canon in the fourth century, the infallibility of these books was almost universally accepted until the end of the seventeenth century.[4] Then men like Voltaire, Thomas Paine, Baron D' Holbach, Johann Salamo Semler, Samuel Reimarus, J. G. Eichhorn, and G. L. Bauer began to question the historical accuracy of the Bible. As Robert Morgan and John Barton have said:

> Modern biblical scholarship arose in Western Europe as the old order crumbled in the late seventeenth and eighteenth centuries. . . . The old religious culture had centred on an unquestioned acceptance of the Judaeo-Christian understanding of God, but this was losing its self-evident character under the pressure of rationalist criticism. Enlightened human reason emancipated itself from the authority of religious traditions and no longer took for granted that the Bible spoke reliably about God and the world. The biblical picture of the world was challenged by natural science, and the biblical story further undermined by moral criticism and historical study. It was coming to be seen as a fallible human record which spoke unevenly of human religion and history.[5]

This criticism of the Bible continued with even greater sophistication into the nineteenth and twentieth centuries. Yet despite biblical criticisms of the New Testament and the growth of the spirit of scientific inquiry, it is surprising how little sustained, systematic philosophical evaluation of Christianity there has been. Perhaps the two most famous philosophical critics in modern times have been

Bertrand Russell and Friedrich Nietzsche. Yet both of their critiques are disappointing. Russell's popular, brief essay "Why I Am Not a Christian" (1927) merely provided superficial refutations of arguments for belief in God and raised questions about whether Jesus is an ideal moral teacher.[6] Yet even for a believer in God, there are serious problems with the basic doctrines of Christianity that Russell did not address. Nietzsche's sustained criticism of Christianity in *The Antichrist* (1889) in turn presupposed his controversial philosophy of the Will to Power and the Overman as well as the falsehood of many Christian doctrines.[7] Unless one has already accepted much of Nietzsche's own philosophical framework and is convinced of the falsehood of Christian doctrines, his criticisms will seem wildly irrelevant.

Although some nineteenth-[8] and twentieth-century criticisms[9] of Christianity deserve praise for raising important critical questions and for continuing the work of the earlier critics, an adequate, systematic, philosophical critique has yet to be produced. The purpose of this work is to present such a criticism. Although I have elsewhere argued at length for atheism, this view will not be presupposed in what follows.[10] Indeed, a reader can believe in God and accept everything in this book without being inconsistent.

My object in presenting the case against Christianity is theoretical, not practical. I am not so naive as to suppose that the arguments set forth here will induce many people to give up their Christian beliefs. My claim is simply that in the light of my discussion rational people should give up these beliefs.

To develop the case against Christianity it is necessary first to clarify what it is to be a Christian. How is Christianity defined? Is there a set of essential doctrines that one must hold in order to be a Christian? There are different Christian churches—Protestant, Roman Catholic, and Eastern Orthodox—and many different denominations and sects within Protestantism. As one commentator has noted:

> A stranger moving from High Mass in a Roman Catholic cathedral to a Lord's Day meeting of the Quakers might well be surprised at being told that the worshippers at the one and the other claim to be Christians; and he would be still further perplexed if he extended his observations to Christian Scientists, the Methodists, the Seventh Day Adventists, the Swendenborgians, and the Strict Baptists, without going as far afield as the Church of the Greeks, Copts, and Abyssinians.[11]

Given this great diversity it is extremely unlikely that one can distill a common set of properties that are individually necessary and jointly sufficient for being a Christian. Nevertheless, there is a set of doctrines that the majority of professing Christians believe.[12] It characterizes what I will call Basic Christianity. Other types of Christianity can be defined by adding to or subtracting from the doctrines of Basic Christianity. The doctrines that constitute Basic Christianity can be derived from an examination of the three great creeds: the Apostles', the Nicene, and the Athanasian. These are widely professed throughout Christendom and taken together summarize in a concise way the beliefs of millions of Christians.

The oldest statement of the Christian faith is the Apostles' Creed. Even today in churches throughout the world most Christians repeat the following words (or their foreign-language equivalents):

I believe in God the Father Almighty
   maker of heaven and earth;
And in Jesus Christ his only Son our Lord
   who was conceived by the Holy Spirit,
   born of the Virgin Mary,
   suffered under Pontius Pilate,
   was crucified, dead, and buried;
   he descended into hell;
   the third day he rose again from the dead;
   he ascended into heaven
   and sitteth on the right hand of God the Father Almighty;
   from thence he shall come to judge the quick and the dead.
I believe in the Holy Spirit, the holy catholic church,
   the communion of saints,
   the forgiveness of sins,
   the resurrection of the body,
   and the life everlasting. Amen.

This creed is an expansion of a formula used in baptismal rites in Rome around A.D. 150 and defines in a clear and simple way the basic principles of Christian faith for many believers.[13] According to Philip Schaff, a scholar of Christian creeds:

It is intelligible and edifying to a child, and fresh and rich to the profoundest Christian scholar, who, as he advances in age, delights to go back to primitive foundations and first principles. It has the fragrance of antiquity and the inestimable weight of universal consent. It is a bond of union between all ages and sections of Christendom.[14]

However, as Schaff notes, neither this nor any other creed is a substitute for the authority of the Bible in Protestantism and for the church in Catholicism.[15] Christians believe that the Apostles' Creed is a useful summary of important Christian doctrines that must be understood in light of the Bible and church authority. Nevertheless, for our purposes this creed helps define Basic Christianity. Although there may be great differences in doctrine and practice among different Christian churches, denominations, and sects, there is still wide agreement over the fundamentals that are captured by the Apostles' Creed.

The second great creed of Christianity, the Nicene Creed, was first framed in 325 by the council held at Nicaea under the presidency of Emperor Constantine. The main purpose of formulating this creed was to provide an explanation of the orthodox view of God the Son and thus to combat Arianism, the view that God the Son was not coeternal with God the Father. The creed affirmed that God the Son was of the same substance or nature as God the Father and not merely of like substance or nature. As the years passed, the text of this creed was expanded in two ways. It was harmonized with the Apostles' Creed by the addition of certain phrases and additions regarding the Holy Spirit. The Council of Chalcedon in 451 accepted and endorsed the expanded form of the creed. A controversy between the Western and Eastern branches of the church occurred over one phrase of the expanded version of the creed. The expanded version adopted in 451 said that the Holy Spirit proceeded from the Father. This was interpreted in the Eastern church as meaning "proceeding from the Father through the Son" while the Western church interpreted it as meaning "proceeded from the Father and from the Son." The latter interpretation, the so-called *filioque*, was officially endorsed in the West in 599.

The following Western version of the Niceno-Chalcedonian Creed is the one that is recited in the Anglican church today.[16]

> I believe in one God the Father Almighty
>> Maker of heaven and earth,
>> and of all things visible and invisible:
> And in one Lord Jesus Christ, the only-begotten Son of God;
>> begotten of his Father before all worlds,
>> God of God,
>> Light of Light,
>> Very God of Very God;
>> begotten, not made;

being of one substance with the Father;
by whom all things were made:
who for us men and for our salvation came down from heaven,
and was incarnate by the Holy Ghost of the Virgin Mary,
and was made man:
and was crucified also for us under Pontius Pilate;
He suffered and was buried;
and the third day he rose again according to Scriptures:
and ascended into heaven,
and sitteth on the right hand of the Father:
and he shall come again, with glory, to judge both the quick and the
    dead;
whose kingdom shall have no end.
And I believe in the Holy Ghost, the Lord, and Giver of Life,
who proceedeth from the Father and the Son;
who with the Father and the Son together is worshiped and
    glorified, who spake by the Prophets:
And I believe one Catholic and Apostolic Church:
I acknowledge one Baptism for the remission of sins:
And I look for the Resurrection of the dead:
and the Life of the world to come. Amen.

This creed (without the *filioque*) is, according to Schaff,

more highly honored in the Greek Church than in any other, and
occupies the same position there as the Apostles' Creed in the Latin
and Protestant Churches. It is incorporated and expounded in all the
orthodox Greek and Russian Catechisms. It is also (with the *Filioque*) in
liturgical use in the Roman (since about the sixth century), and in the
Anglican and Lutheran Churches. It was adopted by the Council of
Trent as the fundamental Symbol, and embodied in the Profession of the
Tridentine Faith by Pius IV. It is therefore more strictly an ecumenical
Creed than the Apostles' and Athanasian which have never been fully
naturalized in the Oriental Churches.[17]

The third great creed of Christianity, the Athanasian Creed, is
recited as follows:

Whosoever earnestly desires to be saved must above all hold the
Catholic Faith. Which Faith unless every one do keep whole and
undefiled, without doubt he shall perish in eternity. And the Catholic
Faith is this:
    I. That we worship one God in Trinity, and Trinity in Unity; neither
confounding the Persons: nor dividing the Substance. For there is one
Person of the Father, another of the Son: and another of the Holy Ghost.

But the Godhead of the Father, of the Son, and of the Holy Ghost is all one: the Glory equal, the Majesty coeternal. Such as the Father is, such is the Son: and such is the Holy Ghost. The Father uncreated, the Son uncreated: and the Holy Ghost uncreated. The Father incomprehensible, the Son incomprehensible: and the Holy Ghost incomprehensible. The Father eternal, the Son eternal: and the Holy Ghost eternal. And yet they are not three eternals: but one eternal. As also there are not three incomprehensibles, nor three uncreated: but one incomprehensible, and one uncreated. So likewise the Father is Almighty, the Son Almighty: and the Holy Ghost Almighty. And yet there are not three Almighties: but one Almighty. So the Father is God, the Son is God: and the Holy Ghost is God. And yet there are not three Gods: but one God. So likewise the Father is Lord, the Son Lord: and the Holy Ghost Lord. And yet not three Lords: but one Lord. For like as we are compelled by the Christian truth to acknowledge every Person by himself to be God and Lord, so are we forbidden by the Catholic Religion to say, There be three Gods or three Lords. The Father is made of none: neither created nor begotten. The Son is of the Father alone: not made, nor created, but begotten. The Holy Ghost is of the Father and of the Son: neither made, nor created, nor begotten, but proceeding. So there is one Father, not three Fathers; one Son, not three Sons: one Holy Ghost, not three Holy Ghosts. And in this Trinity none is before or after another: none is greater or less than another: but the whole three Persons are coeternal together: and coequal. So that in all things, as is aforesaid: the Unity in Trinity, and the Trinity in Unity is to be worshiped. He, therefore, who will be saved must thus think of the Trinity. II. Furthermore, it is necessary to everlasting salvation: that he also believe rightly in the incarnation of our Lord Jesus Christ. For the right Faith is, that we believe and confess: that our Lord Jesus Christ, Son of God, is God and Man; God, of the Substance of the Father, begotten before the worlds: and Man, of the Substance of his Mother, born in the world: perfect God and perfect Man: of a reasonable soul and human flesh subsisting; equal to the Father, as touching His Godhead: and inferior to the Father, as touching his Manhood. Who, although he be God and Man, yet he is not two but one Christ; one, not by conversion of the Godhead into flesh, but by taking of the Manhood into God; one altogether; not by confusion of Substance: but by unity of Person. For as the reasonable soul and flesh is one Man, so God and Man is one Christ: who suffered for our salvation, descended into Hades, rose again the third day from the dead. He ascended into heaven, he sitteth on the right hand of the Father, God Almighty: from whence he shall come to judge the quick and the dead. At whose coming all men shall rise again with their bodies: and shall give account for their own works. And they that have done good shall go into life everlasting: and they that have done evil into everlasting fire.

This is the Catholic Faith: which except a man believe faithfully he cannot be saved. Glory be to the Father, and to the Son: and to the Holy Ghost; as it was in the beginning, is now, and ever shall be: world without end. Amen.[18]

Although the origins of this creed are obscure, the first clear mention of it is between 659 and 670.[19] Although initially attributed to Athanasius, bishop of Alexandria (d. 373), this belief about the source of the creed was abandoned in the seventeenth century. Although it has had great authority in Roman Catholicism and has been adopted by the Lutheran and several Reformed churches, unlike the Nicene Creed, it has never obtained ecclesiastical sanction in the Greek Orthodox church.[20]

An examination of the contents of the three creeds reveals several theological, historical, and eschatological assumptions.

1. Theism

All three creeds assume that God exists. Although it is possible to interpret God in many ways, traditionally Christians who profess these creeds have been theists; that is, they have believed in an all-powerful, all-good, and all-knowing Being who created the Universe.

2. The Existence of a Historical Jesus in Pilate's Time

It is obvious that the Apostles' and the Nicene Creed assume that Jesus was a human being who lived in or around the time of Pontius Pilate. The Athanasian Creed certainly assumes that Jesus was a human being but does not explicitly say when he lived.

3. The Incarnation

All three creeds assume that Jesus is the Son of God. The second part of the Athanasian Creed is the most explicit and detailed on this point: According to it, Jesus is *both* human and divine. Even the least explicit, the Apostles' Creed, affirms that Jesus is the Son of God. Both the Nicene and the Athanasian Creed can be interpreted as giving definite content to these assumptions. The Nicene Creed rules out the Arian interpretation of the relation between Jesus and God, and the Athanasian Creed rules out others.[21]

4. The Trinity

The relationship obtaining among Jesus the Son of God, God the Father, and the Holy Ghost is not clearly stated in either the Apostles' or the Nicene Creed. Indeed, it is possible in relation to these two creeds to understand God the Son and the Holy Spirit as being subordinate to God the Father. This interpretation is ruled out, however, by the Athanasian Creed, where it clearly states that God is three persons in one.

5. The Virgin Birth

According to both the Apostles' and the Nicene Creed, Jesus was born of a virgin. This view is not assumed explicitly in the Athanasian Creed but is only suggested by its more metaphysical language.

6. The Crucifixion by Pilate

Both the Apostles' and the Nicene Creed assume that Jesus was sentenced to death and crucified by the order of Pontius Pilate. The Athanasian Creed makes no such assumption.

7. The Resurrection on the Third Day

All three creeds assume that Jesus was resurrected from the dead on the third day after his death.

8. Salvation through Faith in Jesus

The Nicene Creed certainly suggests that salvation comes through belief in one Lord Jesus Christ, the only-begotten Son of God, "who for us men and our salvation came down from heaven," who died on the cross, was resurrected, ascended to heaven, and will come in glory and in judgment. The creed does not explicitly say in what this belief consists, although it is natural to infer that a necessary condition for salvation through belief in Jesus is belief in the content of the creed itself. The Athanasian Creed is more explicit. It says explicitly that "whosoever who earnestly desires to be saved must above all hold the Catholic Faith," and it further affirms that unless one does keep this faith whole and undefiled "he shall perish in eternity." The Catholic Faith, according to the creed, is the content of the creed itself. The Apostles' Creed says nothing explicit about salvation. However, given what we understand of the use of the creed by Christian churches it is natural to suppose that holding it is considered by most Christians to be at least a necessary condition for salvation through Jesus Christ.

9. The Second Coming

All three creeds assume that Jesus will come again to judge both those living and the dead. Furthermore, all three creeds assume that this will involve the resurrection of the dead.

There is one aspect of Christianity that is conspicuously absent in all three creeds. Nothing is said about the ethical teachings of Jesus, although the Athanasian Creed speaks vaguely about doing good works. This lack of ethical content in the great creeds of Christianity can perhaps be explained by the fact that Christians believe that if one accepts Jesus as the Son of God then one will accept his ethical teachings. Nevertheless, since ethics plays such a large role in discussions of Christianity, it seems useful to make it explicit. Let us then introduce a final assumption of the Christian faith.

10. Jesus as the Model of Ethical Behavior

Jesus' life provides a model of ethical behavior that should be emulated and his ethical teachings provide rules of conduct that should be followed.

Given these assumptions it is now possible to define Basic Christianity and other types as well. The assumptions of theism, the historicity of Jesus, the Incarnation, salvation through faith in Jesus, and Jesus as the model of ethical behavior seem more central to most Christian's thinking than the other assumptions. Let us then define Basic Christianity by these assumptions. Thus:

> Person P is a Basic Christian if and only if P believes that a theistic God exists, that Jesus lived at the time of Pilate, that Jesus is the Incarnation of God, that one is saved through faith in Jesus, and that Jesus is the model of ethical behavior.

Orthodox Christianity can be defined in terms of Basic Christianity plus the other assumptions. Thus:

> Person P is an Orthodox Christian if and only if P is a Basic Christian and P believes in the Trinity, the Virgin Birth, the Crucifixion by Pilate, the Resurrection, and the Second Coming.

Various forms of Liberal Christianity can in turn be defined by subtracting elements from Basic Christianity. One form of Liberal Christianity can be defined in terms of belief in a theistic God and the acceptance of Jesus as a model of ethical behavior combined with a rejection of all of the remaining assumptions except the historicity of Jesus. An extreme form of Liberal Christianity can be characterized by the acceptance of Jesus as a model of ethical behavior combined with a rejection of the other assumptions including even the assumption of theism. In this extreme form the only element that remains of Christianity is its ethics. Many Christians would not consider either type of Liberal Christianity to be Christianity at all.

One obvious problem arises with this attempt to define Christianity purely in terms of belief. For it may be objected that being a Christian involves more than belief; that it also involves following, or at least attempting to follow, the ethical teaching of Jesus. Consequently, it will be said that my definitions are too narrow. This objection can easily be met by saying that the above definitions provide only an analysis of the intellectual content of Christianity and not its other aspects. Consequently, they provide only necessary conditions for being a Christian and should therefore be stated in terms of "only if" rather than "if and only if." Amended in this way they are perfectly adequate. In order to provide a sufficient condition, one would have to add that person P follows, or at least attempts to follow, the ethical teaching of Jesus. Thus on the revised definition:

> Person P is a Basic Christian if and only if P believes that a theistic God exists, that Jesus lived at the time of Pilate, that Jesus is the Incarnation of God, and that Jesus is the model of ethical behavior *and* P follows or attempts to follow the ethical teachings of Jesus.

The definitions of Orthodox Christianity and Liberal Christianity could be amended in a similar way.[22]

The assumptions considered above fall roughly into three categories—historical, theological, and ethical—and their evaluation raises different questions. The existence of Jesus, the Virgin Birth, the Crucifixion by Pilate, and the Resurrection of Jesus on the third day seem clearly to be historical theses. Thus, it seems possible in principle to gather evidence about whether there was a person Jesus who lived at the time of Pilate, and whether this man, if he did live at that time, was crucified on the order of Pilate. Although it may seem more difficult to determine if Jesus was born of a virgin and was resurrected from the dead on the third day by historical methods, they are clearly relevant in determining the truth of these assumptions, just as historical research is relevant to the determination of the truth of the Second Coming. Moreover, historical evidence seems relevant in deciding whether Jesus was the Son of God and not a mere man and what Jesus taught about salvation and ethics.

However, the assumptions of the Virgin Birth, the Incarnation, and salvation through faith in Jesus raise not only historical issues but theological ones. For example, is the doctrine of the Virgin Birth compatible with Jesus' being the Messiah? How could an entity with the properties of a human being be identical to an entity with the properties of the Son of God? Is salvation through faith in Jesus compatible with belief in an all-good God?

The assumption of Jesus as the model of ethical behavior also raises ethical concerns. For example, are his ethical views plausible? Should they be a model of ethical behavior?

In this work I will not evaluate either the assumption of theism or the assumption of the Trinity. Although I have evaluated the former assumption elsewhere, here I will not assume either its truth or falsehood. The doctrine of the Trinity has been critically evaluated at great length and with great subtlety by Michael Durrant and I have nothing significant to add to his conclusion that "no intelligible account can be offered of the Trinitarian formula and hence of the doctrine of the Trinity."[23] However, I will not be assuming the falsehood of the Trinity in this work. There is no need to if my argument against the Incarnation is correct. Although one can perhaps consistently hold a doctrine of the Trinity and give up the doctrine of the Incarnation by supposing that Jesus is not the Incarnation of the Son of God, this would be tantamount to giving up the *Christian* doctrine of the Trinity. As the Athanasian Creed makes abundantly clear, one member of the Trinity is the Son of God and the Son of God is Jesus. So undermining the Incarnation will indirectly undermine the Christian Trinity.

The other assumptions of Christianity—the historicity of Jesus, the Incarnation, the Virgin Birth, the Resurrection, salvation through faith in Jesus, the Second Coming, and Jesus as a model of ethical behavior—are evaluated in the chapters that follow. In Chapter 1 I consider the basis of Christian belief and argue that Christians should base their beliefs on epistemic reasons and not pragmatic or what I call beneficial reasons. In addition, I maintain that they should not base their beliefs on faith or maintain that Christian doctrines are basic beliefs, that is, beliefs that one does not need reasons to hold. In Chapter 2 I consider the historicity of Jesus. I argue that a good case can be made that Jesus did not live in the first century and that recent attempts to refute this thesis fail. In Chapter 3 I argue against the truth of the Resurrection. I maintain that even if Jesus did exist, there is good reason to suppose that he did not rise from the dead. In Chapter 4 I evaluate the doctrines of the Virgin Birth and the Second Coming. I maintain that there are good reasons to suppose that even if Jesus did exist, he was not born of a virgin, and that despite what he might have proclaimed, he did not come again in glory and it is unlikely that he ever will. In Chapter 5 I critically consider the doctrine of the Incarnation. I argue first that there are conceptual problems with the concept of the Incarnation and second, that even if there were not, there is no good reason to suppose that Jesus was the

Incarnation of the Son of God. In Chapter 6 I evaluate the ethical views presented by Jesus in the Gospels and some recent representative theories of Christian ethics. I conclude that many of Jesus' ethical views are unacceptable and that some of his behavior is questionable from a moral point of view. I show that even if recent Christian ethical theorists capture the essence of Christian ethics, it is unclear what of significance they add to secular ethics. In Chapter 7 I argue that the New Testament has at least four different accounts of salvation and that all of them conflict with a belief in an all-good God. In Chapter 8 I consider some critical responses to my argument. Finally, I evaluate the Divine Command theory of ethics, a well-known religious metaethical view, and some historically important theories of the Atonement in two appendices. I do so because these doctrines are not part of the definition of Christianity that I have constructed. The chapters of this book are meant to cover the major doctrines that define Christianity. Unlike the doctrines of the Incarnation, Virgin Birth, and so forth, the doctrine of the Atonement is not part of any of the Christian creeds and there has never been an official doctrine of the Atonement. Similarly, although the Divine Command Theory is often associated with Christianity, it is not the official Christian metaethical view.

NOTES

1. *The 1988 Information Please Almanac* (Boston: Houghton Mifflin, 1988), p. 400.

2. See Morton Smith, *Jesus the Magician* (San Francisco: Harper and Row, 1978), p. 1.

3. E. Royston Pike, *Encyclopaedia of Religion and Religions* (New York: Meridian Books, 1958), pp. 24, 55; *New Columbia Encyclopedia*, 4th ed., s.vv. "New Testament," "Pseudepigrapha."

4. R. W. Brockway, "Unbelief in Revelation," *Encyclopedia of Unbelief* (Buffalo, N.Y.: Prometheus, 1985), vol. 2, pp. 554–59.

5. Robert Morgan and John Barton, *Biblical Interpretation* (Oxford: Oxford University Press, 1988), p. 17.

6. Reprinted in Bertrand Russell, *Why I Am Not a Christian and Other Essays on Religion and Related Subjects* (New York: Simon and Schuster, 1957), pp. 3–23.

7. See Walter Kaufman, *The Portable Nietzsche* (New York: Penguin Books, 1978). See also Walter Kaufman, *Nietzsche—Philosopher, Psychologist, Antichrist* (Princeton, N.J.: Princeton University Press, 1974), chap. 12.

8. For example, W. S. Ross ("Saladin") wrote many attacks on Christianity including a pamphlet first published in 1887, *Did Jesus Christ Rise from the Dead?* (London: W. Stewart and Co., n.d.); Charles Watts, a rationalist publisher and author, wrote and published many criticisms of Christianity including a pamphlet entitled *The Death of Christ* (London: Watts and Co., 1896). Ross's and Watts's pamphlets are reprinted in Gordon Stein, ed., *An Anthology of Atheism and Rationalism* (Buffalo, N.Y.: Prometheus, 1980). Ludwig Feuerbach in *The Essence of Christianity* (1841) assumes that God is simply the projection of human ideals onto nature and the Incarnation is the practical, material embodiment of these ideals. Although Feuerbach attempts to show many contradictions in the concepts connected with Christianity, he provides little in the way of systematic evaluation of the evidence for its major doctrines.

9. For example, John M. Robertson wrote several books arguing that Jesus was a myth. For instance, see his *The Historical Jesus: A Survey of Positions* (London: Watts and Co., 1916). Edward Greenly carefully considers the evidence for the existence of Jesus in *The Historical Reality of Jesus* (London: Watts and Co., 1927). Hypatia Bradlaugh Bonner wrote several books critical of Christianity. See, for example, her *Christianity and Conduct* (London: Watts and Co., 1919). For important recent criticisms see Paul Kurtz, *The Transcendental Temptation* (Buffalo, N.Y.: Prometheus, 1986), chap. 7; and Michael Arheim, *Is Christianity True?* (Buffalo, N.Y.: Prometheus, 1984).

10. Michael Martin, *Atheism: A Philosophical Justification* (Philadelphia: Temple University Press, 1990).

11. Pike, *Encyclopaedia of Religion and Religions*, p. 95.

12. For other attempts to capture the essence of Christianity see Jaroslav Pelikan, "Christianity: An Overview," *The Encyclopedia of Religion* (New York: Macmillan, 1987), vol. 3, pp. 354–62; John Hick, "Christianity," *The Encyclopedia of Philosophy*, ed. Paul Edwards (New York: Macmillan and Free Press, 1967), vol. 2, pp. 104–8.

13. Paul T. Fuhrman, *An Introduction to the Great Creeds of the Church* (Philadelphia: Westminster Press, 1960), p. 26.

14. Philip Schaff, *The Creeds of Christendom* (New York: Harper and Brothers, 1877), vol. 1, p. 15.

15. Ibid., pp. 7–8.

16. Fuhrman, *An Introduction to the Great Creeds of the Church*, pp. 46–47.

17. Schaff, *The Creeds of Christendom*, vol. 1, p. 27.

18. Fuhrman, *An Introduction to the Great Creeds of the Church*, pp. 49–51.

19. Ibid., p. 51.
20. Schaff, *The Creeds of Christendom*, pp. 40–42.
21. Ibid., p. 39.
22. Others may maintain that an essential aspect of Orthodox Christianity is performing certain rituals or sacraments such as baptism. Whether performing such rituals is necessary for being an Orthodox Christian is at least debatable, but if it is, this could be added to the definition. Without this addition, the definition of Orthodox Christianity can be understood to specify only necessary conditions for being an Orthodox Christian.
23. Michael Durrant, *Theology and Intelligibility* (London and Boston: Routledge and Kegan Paul, 1973), p. 195.

1

The Basis
of Christian Belief

What is the relationship between the evaluation of the assumptions of Christianity outlined in the Introduction and Christian belief? Suppose that these doctrines are not supported by evidence or argument. Suppose, what is worse, that the weight of the evidence is against them. Should Christians still believe them? Should the doctrines be believed on pragmatic rather than evidential grounds? For example, should one believe Christian doctrines if they make one happy? On the other hand, perhaps it is permissible to believe Christian doctrines without evidence and argument or even without a pragmatic basis. Can Christianity be based on pure faith? Indeed, why does one need a basis for Christian belief? Perhaps Christian doctrines are basic beliefs that need no justification.

Christian Belief and Epistemic Reasons

Under what conditions should one believe Christian doctrines? Surely the answer that recommends itself to reason and common sense is: Other things being equal, one should believe them only if there are good reasons to do so. However, this answer can be interpreted broadly or narrowly. In the broad interpretation we can understand having good reason for believing that the doctrines are true to include reasons that make the doctrines likely as well as ones that benefit the believer and others. Let us call the first sort *epistemic reasons* and an argument based on these an *epistemic argument*. Let us call the second sort *beneficial reasons* and an argument based on these a *beneficial argument*. Beneficial reasons can, in turn, be either moral or prudential. In the narrow interpretation we can understand having good reasons for believing that the doctrines are true to include only epistemic reasons.

There is a strong presumption that one should believe Christian doctrines only on epistemic reasons.[1] First, there are good utilitarian arguments for believing them only when there is good evidence for them. William K. Clifford, in his famous essay "The Ethics of Belief," argued that "it is wrong always, everywhere, and for anyone, to believe anything on insufficient evidence."[2] Clifford maintains that believing on insufficient evidence has a variety of harmful consequences: It corrupts our character, undermines public confidence, leads to irresponsible action, and fosters self-deception. Although Clifford's fears may have been exaggerated, there is surely a great deal of truth in what he says—there are indeed great dangers in believing Christian doctrines, or anything else, on insufficient evidence. However, Clifford was talking primarily about believing something on insufficient evidence, not about believing something that is contrary to the evidence. If there is anything to Clifford's utilitarian arguments when Christian doctrines are based on insufficient evidence, there is even more to them when belief in such doctrines goes against the evidence. Although believing in Christian doctrines that are in conflict with the evidence is not necessarily morally wrong, as apparently Clifford thought, there are certainly moral dangers in doing so, and as a general social policy believing something that is in conflict with the evidence should be avoided.

Moreover, Clifford overlooked an important point. His argument for basing belief only on epistemic reasons was itself a moral one. Thus, ironically, his reason for not using beneficial reasons in justifying belief was apparently based on one type of beneficial reason: the undesirable *moral* consequences of doing so. In addition, Clifford should have argued that there is an independent epistemological duty to base one's beliefs on purely epistemic reasons. If one does not so base them, one is epistemologically irresponsible. To be sure, under some circumstances this epistemological duty may have to give way to moral considerations.[3] But this does not mean that there is not an epistemological duty that must be outweighed by moral considerations. Although Clifford gives strong *moral* reasons why in general this suspension is impermissible, he does not consider the initial *epistemological* duty that these reasons must outweigh.

Taking these points into account one can say that there is both a moral duty *and* an epistemic duty not to believe Christian doctrines unless there are good epistemic reasons to believe them.

Christian Belief and Beneficial Reasons

Although there is a strong presumption that epistemic reasons should prevail, there are some conditions under which it is permissible to believe Christian doctrines on the basis of beneficial reasons. One special case in which beneficial reasons may be used to decide whether to believe some Christian doctrine p or to believe ~p is when there are equally strong epistemic reasons for p and ~p. Indeed, there is a presumption that beneficial reasons should only be used in such cases.[4] One supposes that beneficial reasons should normally be used only as tiebreakers.

It should be noted that both presumptions—that only epistemic reasons should be used and that beneficial reasons should only be used when epistemic reasons are evenly balanced for and against—allow that in special circumstances it is morally permissible for people to believe Christian doctrines because of beneficial reasons and without adequate epistemic reasons and that in *very* special circumstances it is morally permissible for people to believe Christian doctrines for beneficial reasons even when there are strong epistemic reasons to believe the opposite.[5] Clearly, however, candidates for these special circumstances must be scrutinized carefully for both the likely benefits that will result from belief in terms of beneficial reasons and the possible long-term adverse effects on society, its institutions, and human personality and character.

Our presumptions could be defeated by special circumstances. For example, suppose you are a non-Christian and are kidnapped by a religious fanatic with access to nuclear weapons who will kill you and blow up New York City, London, Paris, and Tokyo unless you accept the Apostles' Creed. You have good reason to suppose that if you undergo two months of rigorous Christian indoctrination, you will accept the creed. To make the case crystal clear, let us suppose that very few people will know of your conversion, that the fanatic will die in three months, that he has no disciples to carry on his work, and that the effects of the indoctrination will disappear in four months. Presumably, in such a case there would be good grounds for undergoing the religious indoctrination. Even the most militant anti-Christian would perhaps admit that under this circumstance refusing to convert would serve no purpose; indeed, would be an act of insanity.

Let us now consider a more realistic case in which the question arises of whether beneficial reasons for believing in God should count. On her death bed Mrs. Smith, an eighty-nine-year-old Black Muslim and former Catholic, is not completely convinced that she will see her dead husband again unless she returns to the Catholic church. It is clear that her mental state is such that with only a little encouragement from a priest she will embrace her old faith once again. Should we ask a priest to visit her? The answer may seem obvious but it is not until many questions are resolved. For example, given her present situation, is she competent to make the choice? Will this case set a precedent for other cases? Will other people know of her return to the fold and be encouraged to do the same? To simplify the case, let us assume that there are no more epistemic reasons to believe in the doctrines of the Black Muslims than in the teachings of the Catholic church, her return to Catholicism would set no precedent, that she has only a few days to live, that she would be much happier if she did believe, that very few people would ever know about her return, and that her choice to return was competent, rational, and uncoerced. We may conclude that under these assumptions we should send for a priest. But these are big assumptions to make and cannot simply be taken for granted.

It may be asked: If we grant these two presumptions, is there not still a presumption that in those rare cases in which it is legitimate to use beneficial reasons to decide what to believe or not to believe, the Christian doctrine is to be preferred? It is hard to see why this would be true. General beneficial arguments for the existence of God such as Pascal's and William James's provide no unique reason for accepting the Christian God over other supernatural beings.[6] Furthermore, whether someone would be happier believing in the Christian doctrines rather than, say, the doctrines of Islam or Judaism is an individual matter that must be decided with respect to the particular person's background.

Christian Doctrines and Faith

But why do Christians have to believe on either epistemic or beneficial reasons? Cannot Christian doctrines be based on faith? Let us take a look at some theories of faith in order to see the problems of believing on faith.[7]

Thomas Aquinas's theory is representative of a traditional conception of faith.[8] In his view, faith is not only not opposed to reason but is in some respects guided by it. In contrast to Aquinas some religious thinkers have maintained that faith needs no rational guidance. Søren Kierkegaard, for example, argued that there is great merit in Christian belief that not only goes beyond the evidence but even against it.[9] Maintaining that religious faith was more important than reason in achieving human happiness[10] and interpreting religious faith as a total and passionate commitment to God, he argued that people with this faith completely disregard any doubts that they may have. If there are serious problems with both of these theories, it is likely that there will be ones with other theories that are based on similar ideas.

According to Aquinas's theory, religious truths are divided into those of reason and those of faith. On his view, the truths of reason include the proposition that an all-powerful, all-knowing, all-good God exists. However, particular Christian doctrines such as that there are three persons in one God and that Jesus was born of a virgin cannot be known by reason. Aquinas nevertheless maintained that these truths can be known because they are revealed by God to human beings through the Bible or the church.

On Aquinas's view, although a truth of faith, P, is not capable of rational demonstration, the proposition Q—God has revealed P—can be believed on rational grounds.[11] He used three kinds of arguments to show that Q is true: scriptural prophesies have been fulfilled; the Christian church has succeeded without any promise of carnal pleasure in an afterlife or without any resort to violence in this life; and miracles have occurred within the Christian tradition.[12] On his theory of faith, therefore, one must assume that God exists. Otherwise it would make no sense to suppose that God revealed truths through the Bible or through the church. Consequently, belief in God is not *based* on faith, but is a *precondition* of faith in such Christian doctrines as that there are three persons in one God and that Jesus was born of a virgin.[13]

Because in Aquinas's theory there is an attempt to guide faith by reason, his view of faith has decided advantages over some more recent ones. Indeed, according to Aquinas, a Christian who believes, for example, in the Virgin Birth has very good reason to suppose that his or her belief is true. Nevertheless, Aquinas's view is unacceptable.

Even if the existence of God is assumed, the reasons that Aquinas gives to suppose that God revealed certain truths through the Bible and the church have little merit. As we have seen, Aquinas appeals to the existence of miracles within the Christian tradition as support for his view that it is rational to believe that God revealed particular Christian doctrines. However, there are difficult general obstacles that must be overcome for anyone who claims that a miracle has occurred and, as I argue in Chapter 2, these have not been overcome in the standard defense of miracles.[14] Further, an appeal to Christian miracles has special problems such as ones connected with Jesus' life and death—the Virgin Birth and the Resurrection—since these are among the assumptions of Christianity. But surely we cannot appeal to the Virgin Birth or the Resurrection to support the truth of Christianity without begging the question.

Aquinas's appeal to the success of the Christian church to justify his belief in the rationality of Christian revelation faces the problem that many different churches or similar institutions outside the Christian tradition have been successful in the way he specifies.[15] If this sort of success shows that God revealed truths in the religious traditions dominated by these different churches or their equivalents, then conflicting "truths" were revealed. But conflicting propositions cannot both be true.

Further, Aquinas's appeal to fulfilled biblical prophecy to justify the rationality of believing the assumptions of Christianity on faith is plagued by the problem of unfulfilled prophecies. One of the most notorious of these is Jesus' false prophecy of the imminence of his Second Coming.

There is still another problem with Aquinas's view, however. According to Aquinas the truths of faith are certain and are supposed to be believed without any doubt. But not all the historical events that are supposed to provide the evidence for God's revelation can be known with certainty. Indeed, the evidence for some of the historical assumptions of Christianity is weak. It is difficult to see how one can claim certainty for revelations that are based on historical events that are not known with certainty, however. Such a high degree of belief seems irrational in the light of the historical evidence.

According to Kierkegaard, the person with faith or, in his words, "the knight of faith," is not unaware of the possibility of error in such a commitment but is not anxious because of this possibility. The knight of faith keeps well in mind that according to objective reasoning—that is, reasoning that would be accepted by all (or almost all) intelligent, fair-minded, and sufficiently informed persons to have established its conclusion as true or probably true—belief in God is not justified.

Nevertheless, it is precisely because it is not based on objective reasoning that faith is the highest virtue. Kierkegaard maintains that with objective certainty comes lack of personal growth and spiritual stagnation. But with faith there is risk, danger, and adventure—all essential for spiritual growth and transcendence. Kierkegaard argues that even when the Christian God seems paradoxical and absurd, total and passionate commitment to God without adequate evidence for such commitment is necessary for human salvation and ultimately for human happiness. He not only rejects as being irrelevant to Christian faith any appeal to the traditional arguments for the existence of God but any recourse to historical evidence to substantiate the claims of Scripture.

There are many problems with this theory of faith. First of all, religious faith as Kierkegaard conceives of it can be condemned on ethical grounds. It is dangerous to be guided by blind, passionate faith, yet this is precisely what Kierkegaard recommends. His knight of faith is simply a fanatic. Indeed, his model of a knight of faith is Abraham, who was willing to sacrifice his son, Isaac.[16] We know from history the incalculable harm that can be done by fanaticism. Indeed, Walter Kaufmann was certainly correct when he called fanaticism "one of the scourges of humanity."[17] Consider, for example, the many religious wars waged by opposing sides who both believed blindly that their cause was right. Since its furtherance tends to result in great social harm, faith as Kierkegaard conceives of it is not a virtue but a vice.

Moreover, it is unclear how Kierkegaard's view of faith can be reconciled with a view of an all-good God.[18] How could an all-good God want his creatures to have blind faith in him despite adequate evidence let alone with negative evidence? Surely an all-good God would not want his creatures to be fanatics especially when there is good reason to suppose that fanaticism leads to great human suffering. It would seem that if God is good in any sense of the term that is analogous to our standard sense, faith on Kierkegaard's model would not be something that God could desire and reward.

There is another reason why God would not want his creatures to have faith in Kierkegaard's sense, however. According to Kierkegaard, since one should have faith in improbabilities and absurdities and Christianity is absurd and paradoxical, one should have faith in the Christian God. But there may well be other religious beliefs that are even *more* absurd and improbable than those of Christianity.[19]

So far we have considered a traditional view of faith of Aquinas— a view that purports to be guided by reason—and the irrational faith of Kierkegaard. However, faith can be approached from the point of view of philosophy of language. From this perspective religious faith must be understood in terms of the function of religious language. A conception known as "Wittgensteinian fideism" has been developed from the views of Ludwig Wittgenstein[20] by his followers such as Norman Malcolm, D. Z. Phillips, and Peter Winch.[21] Perhaps this view is less problematic than the other two theories we have considered.

According to this theory religious discourse is embedded in a form of life and has its own rules and logic.[22] It can only be understood and evaluated on its own terms and any attempt to impose standards on such discourse from the outside, for example from science, is quite inappropriate. Since religious discourse is a separate, unique language game different from that of science, religious statements, unlike scientific ones, are not empirically testable. To demand that they be is a serious misunderstanding of that form of discourse. On this view of the language game of religion, religious discourse is rational and intelligible when judged on its own terms, which are the only appropriate ones. Because the meaning of a term varies from one langauge game to another, to understand religious language one must see it from within the religious language game itself. In general, a philosopher's task is not to criticize a form of life or its language but to describe both of these and, where necessary, to eliminate philosophical puzzlement concerning the operation of the language. In particular, the job of a philosopher of religion is to describe the use of religious discourse and eliminate any perplexities that may result from it.

Once again, however, there are serious problems with this view. First, the basis for distinguishing one form of life from another, one language game from another, is unclear. For example, consider the practices of astrology and fortune-telling by reading palms, tea leaves, and so on. Do these constitute forms of life with their own language games? In religion, is there only one religious language game or form of life, or are there many? Is there one for each religion? Is there one for each religion? Is there one for each denomination or sect within each religion? The differences between Buddhism and Christianity are so vast that one strongly suspects that the Wittgensteinian fideist would have to say that these constitute different forms of life involving different language games. If this is granted, must one not also admit that the practices of different Christian denominations differ in fundamental ways? If one goes this far, would not one have to say that different Protestant denominations, for example, the Methodist and the Baptist denominations, and even different sects within them, have different religious language games? Yet since for Wittgensteinian fideism the same terms in different language games have different meanings, this seems to have the absurd consequence that members of one Baptist sect would not be able to understand members of another.

In addition, since each form of life is governed by its own standards, there can be no external criticism. Yet this has unacceptable consequences. Suppose that astrology and fortune-telling by reading palms or tea leaves constitute separate forms of life. It would follow that these practices must not be judged by outside standards despite the fact that they seem to be based on false or at least dubious assumptions. Suppose each religious form of life is governed by its own standards. Then there could be no external standards that could be used in criticizing a religious form of life. However, this has unfortunate consequences. For example, some religious denominations practice sexual and racial discrimination—the Mormon church at one time excluded blacks from positions in the church hierarchy and it still excludes women. It is not implausible to suppose that most enlightened people today believe that this practice and the beliefs on which it rests are wrong, yet if Mormonism is a separate form of life, there can be no external criticism of its practices.

Despite what Wittgensteinian fideists say, external criticism is not only possible but essential. If their position is correct, there would be something contradictory or incoherent in the claim, "This is an ongoing religious form of life and it is irrational." But there is not. Indeed, even participants in a religion sometimes find its doctrines incoherent, its major arguments resting on dubious premises, and some of its practices morally questionable. In fact, there seems to be no good reason why a religious form of life or, for that matter, any form of life could not be evaluated externally and found wanting. Although insight into a form of life may be gained by taking the participant's perspective, one cannot rest content with this because the participants may be blind to the problems inherent in their own practices and beliefs and the perspective of an outsider may be necessary if these are to be detected.

Wittgensteinian fideism also has paradoxical implications concerning the truth of religious utterances within a language game. If

Jones says "Jesus is not the Son of God" within the Muslim language game and Smith says "Jesus is the Son of God" within the Christian language game, the Wittgensteinian fideist would seem to be holding that both statements are true. Since they seem to contradict one another how can that be? The answer a Wittgensteinian fideist would give is that the meaning of a religious utterance is relative to the language game to which it belongs. So, despite appearances to the contrary, what Jones denies in our example is not what Smith affirms. One tends to think otherwise because one does not realize that the meaning of religious utterances is relative to different language games.

But why should we accept the theory of language and meaning presupposed by this view? There seems to be no good reason to believe the thesis that the meaning of language is radically contextual and that it is impossible to communicate across practices or ways of life. Indeed, it makes nonsense of the debates not only between Christians and non-Christians, but between defenders of different Christian denominations. For on this view, despite the long and bitter arguments, there is no real disagreement; the debating parties are on different tracks talking past one another. Such a view, although perhaps not impossible, seems highly unlikely.

A more plausible way to understand these examples is that the Christian and non-Christian are really disagreeing and that there is a common language and common categories. Surely, religious language is not completely compartmentalized from other languages and the language of one religion, denomination, or sect is not completely compartmentalized from the language of others.

Christian Doctrines as Basic Beliefs

Instead of basing Christian doctrines on faith one might argue that they are basic beliefs; that is to say, beliefs that form the foundation of other beliefs.[23] Such an approach to Christian doctrine has its source in a critique of the classical foundational approach to epistemology.

Foundationalism was once a widely accepted view in epistemology and, although it has undergone modification, it still has many advocates. The motivation for the view seems compelling. All of our beliefs cannot be justified in terms of other beliefs without the justification generating an infinite regress or vicious circularity. Therefore, there must be some beliefs that do not need to be justified by other beliefs. Because they form the foundation of all knowledge, these are called basic and the statements expressing them are called basic statements.

Classical foundationalism considered only two types of basic statements: certain simple and true statements of mathematics, for example, "2 + 2 = 4," and logic, for example, "Either p or ~p," and those statements that are evident to the senses. Some foundationalists have included in the class of statements that are evident to the senses ones about observed physical objects, for example, "There is a blue bird in the tree." However, in modern times it has been more common to restrict statements that are evident to the senses to ones about the author's immediate sense impressions, for example, "I seem to see a blue bird in the tree," or "I am being appeared to bluely," or perhaps "Here now blue sense datum."

The most important representative of this point of view in contemporary philosophers of religion, Alvin Plantinga, has argued against classical foundationalism maintaining that belief in God should be considered a basic belief.[24] Although Plantinga has not to my knowledge held that all the fundamental doctrines of Christianity are basic beliefs this idea would certainly be in keeping with his general approach.

Following in a long line of Reformed thinkers, that is, thinkers influenced by the doctrines of John Calvin, Plantinga argues that traditional arguments for the existence of God are not needed for rational belief. He cites with approval Calvin's claim that God created humans in such a way that they have a strong tendency to believe in God. Although this natural tendency to believe in God may be partially suppressed, Plantinga argues that it is triggered by "a widely realizable condition"[25] such as "upon beholding the starry heavens, or the splendid majesty of the mountains, or the intricate, articulate beauty of a tiny flower."[26] This natural tendency to accept God in these circumstances is perfectly rational, he says. No argument is needed. He maintains that the best interpretation of Calvin's views, as well as of the other Reformed thinkers he cites, is that they rejected classical foundationalism and maintained that belief in God can itself be a properly basic belief.

Surprisingly, Plantinga insists that although belief in God and beliefs about God's attributes and actions are basic, for Reformed epistemologists this does not mean that there are no justifying circumstances or that they are without grounds. The circumstances that trigger the natural tendency to believe in God and to believe certain things about God provide the justifying circumstances for belief. So although beliefs about God are properly basic, they are not groundless.[27]

How are we to understand this claim that religious beliefs are basic but not groundless? This seems initially puzzling since one would normally suppose that basic beliefs by definition are groundless. Plantinga draws an analogy between basic statements of religion and basic statements of perception and memory. A perceptual belief, he says, is taken as properly basic only under certain circumstances. For example, if I know that I am wearing rose-tinted glasses, then I am not justified in taking the statement "I see a rose-colored wall before me" as properly basic; if I know that my memory is unreliable, I am not justified in taking the statement "I remember that I had breakfast" as properly basic. Although he admits that these conditions may be hard to specify, he maintains that their presence is necessary in order to claim that a perceptual or memory statement is basic. Similarly, he maintains that not every statement about God that is not based on argument or evidence should be considered properly basic. A statement is properly basic only in the right circumstances. What circumstances are right? Plantinga gives no general account, but in addition to the triggering conditions mentioned above, the right circumstances include reading the Bible, having done something wrong, and being in grave danger. Thus if a person is reading the Bible and believes that God is speaking to him or her, his or her belief is properly basic.

Furthermore, Plantinga insists that although Reformed epistemologists allow belief in God to be a properly basic belief, this does not mean that they must allow that anything at all can be a basic belief. To be sure, he admits that he and other Reformed epistemologists have not supplied us with a criterion of what is properly basic. He argues, however, that this is not necessary. One can know that some beliefs in some circumstances are not properly basic without having an explicitly formulated criterion of basicness. Thus, Plantinga says that Reformed epistemologists can correctly maintain that belief in voodoo or astrology or the Great Pumpkin are not basic beliefs.

How is one to arrive at a criterion of being properly basic? According to Plantinga the route is "broadly speaking, *inductive*." "We must assemble examples of beliefs and conditions such that the former are obviously properly basic in the latter. . . . We must frame hypotheses as to the necessary and sufficient conditions of proper basicality and test these hypotheses by reference to those examples.[28] He argues that, using this procedure,

> The Christian will of course suppose that belief in God is entirely proper and rational; if he does not accept this belief on the basis of other propositions, he will conclude that it is basic for him and quite properly so. Followers of Russell and Madelyn Murray O'Hare [sic] may disagree; but how is that relevant? Must my criteria, or those of the Christian community, conform to their examples? Surely not. The Christian community is responsible to *its* set of examples, not to theirs.[29]

The problems with Plantinga's defense of the thesis that belief in God is basic can only be summarized here.[30] First, to consider belief in God as a basic belief seems completely out of keeping with the spirit and intention of foundationalism. Whatever else it was and whatever its problems, foundationalism was an attempt to provide critical tools for objectively appraising knowledge claims and to give knowledge a nonrelativistic basis. Paradoxically, Plantinga's foundationalism is radically relativistic and puts any belief beyond rational appraisal once it is declared basic.

Second, Plantinga's claim that his proposal would not allow any belief to become a basic belief is misleading. It is true that it would not allow any belief to become a basic belief *from the point of view of Reformed epistemologists.* However, it would seem to allow any belief at all to become basic from the point of view of *some* community.[31] Although Reformed epistemologists would not have to accept voodoo beliefs as rational, voodoo followers would be able to claim that insofar as they are basic in the voodoo community they are rational, and moreover, that Reformed thought was irrational in this community.

Third, on this view the rationality of any belief is absurdly easy to obtain. The cherished belief that is held without reason by *any* group could be considered properly basic by the group's members. There would be no way to evaluate critically any beliefs so considered. The community's most cherished beliefs and the conditions that, according to the community, correctly triggered such beliefs would be accepted uncritically by the members of the community as just so many more examples of basic beliefs and justifying conditions.

Fourth, Plantinga seems to suppose that there is a consensus in the Christian community about what beliefs are basic and what conditions justify these. But this is not so for some Christians believe in God on the basis of the traditional arguments or on the basis of religious experiences; their belief in God is not basic. More important, there would be no agreement on whether certain doctrinal beliefs, for example, ones concerning the authority of the pope, the composition of the Trinity, the nature of Christ, or the means of salvation, were true, let alone basic.

Fifth, although there may not at present be any clear criterion for what can be a basic belief, belief in God seems peculiarly inappropriate for inclusion in the class since there are clear disanalogies between it and the basic beliefs allowable by classical foundationalism.[32] In his critique of classical foundationalism, Plantinga has suggested that belief in other minds and the external world should be considered basic. There are, however, many plausible alternatives to belief in an all-good, all-powerful, all-knowing God, but there are few, if any, plausible alternatives to belief in other minds and the external world. Although there are many skeptical arguments against belief in other minds and the external world, there are no arguments that are taken seriously that purport to show that there are no other minds or that there is no external world. In this world atheism and agnosticism are live options for many intelligent people; solipsism is an option only for the mentally ill.

Sixth, as we have seen, Plantinga, following Calvin, says that some conditions that trigger belief in God or particular beliefs about God also justify these beliefs so that although these beliefs concerning God are basic, they are not groundless. Although Plantinga gives no general account of what these justifying conditions are, he presents some examples of what he means and likens these justifying conditions to those of properly basic perceptual and memory statements.[33] The problem here is, however, the weakness of the analogy. As Plantinga points out, before we take a perceptual or memory belief as properly basic we must have evidence that one's perception or memory is not faulty. Part of one's justification for believing that one's perception or memory is not faulty is that in general it agrees with the perception or memory of our epistemological peers; that is, our equals in intelligence, perspicacity, honesty, thoroughness, and other relevant epistemic virtues[34] and also with one's other experiences.[35]

We have already seen that lack of agreement is commonplace in religious contexts. Different beliefs are triggered in different people when they behold the starry heavens or read the Bible. Beholding the starry heavens can trigger a pantheistic belief or a purely aesthetic response without any religious component; sometimes no particular response or belief at all is triggered. From what we know about the variations of religious belief, it is likely that people would not have theistic beliefs when they behold the starry heavens if they had been raised in nontheistic environments. In short, there is no consensus in the Christian community, let alone among Bible readers generally. So, unlike perception and memory, there are no grounds for claiming that a belief about God is properly basic since the conditions that trigger it yield widespread disagreement among epistemological peers.[36]

Besides these general problems there are particular difficulties in making fundamental doctrines of Christianity basic beliefs. Such doctrines as the existence of Jesus, the Resurrection, and the Virgin Birth are inferred from controversial historical facts that scholars have debated and are still debating. To suppose that they are basic beliefs would mean that these debates are futile and unnecessary. Moreover, although one might somewhat plausibly suppose, as Calvin did, that people have a natural tendency to believe in God, surely no one supposes that there is natural tendency to believe that Jesus was resurrected or born of a virgin. These are surely learned beliefs and are hardly naturally triggered by widely realizable conditions such as beholding the starry heavens.

Conclusion

There is strong presumption that Christian doctrines should be based on epistemic reasons and not, except in rare and special circumstances, on beneficial reasons. Nor should they be based on faith or considered to be basic beliefs. But this means that the evidence for and against them must be examined and belief in them must be based on this examination.

NOTES

1. See Michael Martin, *Atheism: A Philosophical Justification* (Philadelphia: Temple University Press, 1990), chaps. 1, 10.

2. William K. Clifford, "The Ethics of Belief," in *Philosophy of Religion*, ed. Louis P. Pojman (Belmont, Calif.: Wadsworth, 1987), p. 387.

3. Lorraine Code, *Epistemic Responsibility* (Hanover and London: University Press of New England, 1987), p. 78.

4. Martin, *Atheism: A Philosophical Justification*, chap. 1.

5. Mackie, for example, has suggested that it is reasonable in science to give tentative acceptance to a hypothesis that is only plausible and yet without adequate evidential support and it is reasonable in social contexts to trust others before there is adequate evidence that trust is justified since such trust is necessary for cooperation. See J. L. Mackie, *The Miracle of Theism* (Oxford: Clarendon Press, 1982), p. 206.

6. Martin, *Atheism: A Philosophical Justification*, chap. 9.

7. Ibid., chap. 10.

8. See, for example, *Summa Contra Gentiles*, trans. Vernon J. Bourke (New York: Doubleday, 1953), Book 1.

9. Cf. J. Kellenberger, "Three Models of Faith," *International Journal for the Philosophy of Religion* 12 (1981): 219.

10. See Søren Kierkegaard, *Concluding Unscientific Postscript*, trans. David F. Swenson; introduction, notes, and completion of translation by Walter Lowrie (Princeton, N.J.: Princeton University Press, 1941).

11. See William L. Rowe, *Philosophy of Religion* (Belmont, Calif.: Wadsworth, 1978), p. 172.

12. *Summa Contra Gentiles*, Book 1, chap. 7.

13. Anthony Kenny, *Faith and Reason* (New York: Columbia University Press, 1983), p. 75.

14. Martin, *Atheism: A Philosophical Justification*, chap. 7.

15. The only other religious tradition that Aquinas considers is Islam. He dismisses this religion's success as based on promises of carnal pleasure and force of arms. That this is at least too simple a view of the success of Islam seems clear. Further, Aquinas's thesis that the success of Christianity is a miracle not explainable in naturalistic terms is surely dubious.

16. See Walter Kaufmann, *From Shakespeare to Existentialism* (Garden City, N.Y.: Doubleday, 1959), p. 177.

17. Ibid., p. 178.

18. Mackie, *The Miracle of Theism*, p. 216.

19. Some scholars have suggested that some of the teachings of the Koran are more absurd than some teachings of Christianity and that the claim that Nero is God incarnate is more absurd than the same claim about Jesus. See Kaufmann, *From Shakespeare to Existentialism*, p. 198.

20. See Ludwig Wittgenstein, *Lectures and Conversations on Aesthetics, Psychology, and Religious Belief*, ed. Cyril Barrett (Oxford: Blackwell, 1966).

21. See, for example, Norman Malcolm, "The Groundlessness of Belief," in *The Philosophy of Religion*, ed. Pojman, pp. 422–30. See also D. Z. Phillips, *Concept of Prayer* (London: Routledge and Kegan Paul, 1970), and

Peter Winch, *The Idea of a Social Science* (London: Routledge and Kegan Paul, 1958).

22. For an excellent analysis and evaluation of this approach see Kai Nielsen, *An Introduction to the Philosophy of Religion* (New York: St. Martin's Press, 1982), chaps. 3–5. See also Gary Gutting, *Religious Belief and Religious Skepticism* (Notre Dame, Ind.: University of Notre Dame Press, 1982), chap. 1.

23. For an extended discussion of this view see Martin, *Atheism: A Philosophical Justification*, chap. 10.

24. See Alvin Plantinga, "Religious Belief Without Evidence," in *Philosophy of Religion*, ed. Pojman, pp. 454–68; Alvin Plantinga, "Is Belief in God Properly Basic?" *Nous* 15 (1981): 41–51; Alvin Plantinga, "Is Belief in God Rational?" *Rationality and Religious Belief*, ed. C. F. Delaney (Notre Dame, Ind.: University of Notre Dame Press, 1979), pp. 7–27. For a similar position see Nicholas Wolterstorff, "Can Belief in God Be Rational If It Has No Foundations?" in *Faith and Rationality*, ed. Alvin Plantinga and Nicholas Wolterstorff (Notre Dame, Ind.: University of Notre Dame Press, 1983).

25. Plantinga, "Religious Belief Without Evidence," p. 464.

26. Ibid., p. 465.

27. Plantinga, "Is Belief in God Properly Basic?" p. 46.

28. Plantinga, "Religious Belief Without Evidence," p. 468.

29. Ibid.

30. There are also problems with his critique of classical foundationalism. See Martin, *Atheism: A Philosophical Justification*, chap. 10.

31. Cf. Kenny, *Faith and Reason*, p. 16; William J. Abraham, *An Introduction to the Philosophy of Religion* (Englewood Cliffs, N.J.: Prentice-Hall, 1985), pp. 93–96; Philip Quinn, "In Search of the Foundations of Theism," in *Philosophy of Religion*, ed. Pojman, p. 472; Louis Pojman, "Can Religious Belief Be Rational?" in *Philosophy of Religion*, ed. Pojman, p. 481; J. Wesley Robbins, "Is Belief in God Properly Basic?" *International Journal for the Philosophy of Religion* 14 (1983): 241–48.

32. See Abraham, *An Introduction to the Philosophy of Religion*, p. 95.

33. In his most recent writings Plantinga has begun to relate epistemic justification to proper cognitive functioning and the latter to God's designing human beings in such a way that they tend to have true beliefs under certain circumstances. See Alvin Plantinga, "Epistemic Justification," *Nous* 20 (1986): 15.

34. Cf. Gutting, *Religious Belief and Religious Skepticism*, p. 83.

35. See Richard Grigg, "Theism and Properly Basicality: A Response to Plantinga," *International Journal for the Philosophy of Religion* 14 (1983): 126.

36. Further, given Plantinga's latest attempt to relate epistemic justification to God's designing human beings in such a way that they tend to have true beliefs under certain circumstances, the problem arises how to account

for this lack of uniformity. How can the human cognitive apparatus be working properly in the area of religious belief when there is so little agreement among people about such beliefs? And if the human cognitive apparatus is not working properly in the area of religious belief, how can one claim that God designed the apparatus?

2

The Historicity
of Jesus

*T*he assumption that Jesus was an actual historical figure is basic to all forms of Christianity. Although Liberal Christianity denies Jesus' divinity, it is still committed to his historicity, namely, that he was a human being who lived in or around the time of Pontius Pilate. Orthodox Christianity, in addition to assuming Jesus' historicity, makes several assumptions that presuppose it. The beliefs that Jesus was born of a virgin at the beginning of the first century, was crucified under orders from Pontius Pilate, was resurrected, and will return again in glory to judge the living and the dead all assume the historicity of Jesus.

Indeed, the historicity of Jesus is not only taken for granted by Christians but is assumed by the vast majority of non-Christians and anti-Christians. Muslims, for example, although denying that Jesus was the Son of God, maintain that he was the greatest of all prophets.[1] Assuming without question Jesus' historicity, famous critics of Christianity such as Russell and Nietzsche evaluated his moral example and teachings. The very idea that Jesus is a myth is seldom entertained, let alone seriously considered. As Gordon Stein, an authority on free thought and rationalism, has noted: "For anyone to question today whether Jesus Christ ever lived may seem strange and shocking to the average person."[2]

But can Jesus' historicity be questioned? Stein argues, "In reality, it is a legitimate question to ask whether a person was historical or mythical. True, at one point in time, the question of Jesus' historicity was a much more popular one for discussion than it is now, but the issue is far from resolved today."[3]

But why would anyone not believe that there was a man called Jesus who lived in or around the time of Pontius Pilate? The Gospels certainly teach that Jesus lived in this time. How then can anyone doubt it? The belief that Jesus was an actual historical figure is usually based on the assumption that the Gospels are historically accurate and trustworthy. Are they? If the historical accuracy and trustworthiness of the Gospels are called into question, then the historicity of Jesus is called into question as well. And if this assumption is called into question, then so are the historical assumptions of Orthodox Christianity that presuppose it.

It is important to realize that the historicity of Jesus is not something that has seemed to be an established truth to all biblical scholars and historians. For example, in 1850 Bruno Bauer, a German theologian and historian, denied the historicity of Jesus.[4] At the turn of this century there was a fierce debate on the subject. John M. Robertson, the ablest critic of Jesus' historicity writing at the time, wrote several books on the subject.[5] In the last thirty years, Guy Fau,[6] Prosper Alfaric,[7] W. B. Smith,[8] John Allegro,[9] and G. A. Wells[10] have all denied the historicity of Jesus.

This chapter, then, considers the question of whether there is reliable historical evidence for the assumption of the historicity of Jesus. It will also ask if there is any historical evidence against this assumption.

The Problem

SKEPTICISM AND THE HISTORICAL JESUS

Although the historicity of Jesus is so much taken for granted today that one who dares to question this assumption is often thought to be a crank or worse, a strong prima facie case challenging the historicity of Jesus can be constructed. Modern critical methods of biblical scholarship have called into question the historical accuracy of the Bible and, in particular, the New Testament.[11] In the light of this critical approach to the New Testament many theologians have argued that not much is known about Jesus. For example, W. Trilling argues that "not a single date of his life" can be established with certainty[12] and J. Kahl maintains that the only thing that is known about him is that he "existed at a date and place which can be established approximately."[13] Other scholars argue that the quest for the historical Jesus is hopeless.[14] Given these admissions the question can be raised of whether a single date in his life can be established even with probability and if we know he existed at a date and place that can be established even approximately. Skepticism about the details of Jesus' life can generate skepticism about his very existence.

But how precisely can a skeptical argument against the historicity of Jesus be developed? Who of the various critics of the existence of Jesus should be taken seriously?

WELLS'S ARGUMENT IN BRIEF

The most respected contemporary critic of the historicity of Jesus is G. A. Wells. His books on the subject are the best known in contemporary literature and contemporary apologists for the historicity of Jesus single out his position for special attention. Let us begin by considering a brief version of his argument.[15] Wells stresses that his skepticism concerning the historicity of Jesus is based in large part on the views of Christian theologians and biblical scholars[16] who admit that the canonical Gospels were written by unknown authors not personally acquainted with Jesus, between forty and eighty years after Jesus' supposed lifetime. According to Wells they also admit that there is much in these accounts that is legend and that the Gospel stories are shaped by the writers' theological motives. Furthermore, the evidence provided by the Gospels is exclusively Christian.

Given this situation, Wells says, a rational person should believe the accounts of the Gospels only if they are independently confirmed. But he maintains that even many Christian scholars have conceded that non-Christian evidence is not helpful here.[17] Furthermore, he argues that the earliest Christian writers do not support the thesis that Jesus lived early in the first century. He points out that it is acknowledged by all biblical scholars that the earliest Christian writers—Paul and other epistle writers—wrote before the Gospels were composed. Although these earliest writers certainly believed that Jesus lived and died, Wells maintains that they do not provide any support for the thesis that he lived early in the first century. Thus, those Pauline letters now admitted to be genuine by most scholars, and those letters that are considered probably or possibly authentic, are silent about the parents of Jesus, the place of his birth, his trial before Pilate, the place of his crucifixion, and his ethical teachings. Yet it is precisely these facts that would lend credibility to the claim that Jesus was a first-century, historical figure.

What is particularly surprising about this silence, Wells argues, is that there is a great deal in the Gospel story of Jesus' life and teachings that would be relevant to the disputes that Paul was engaged in. For example, one of the issues facing Paul was: Should gentiles be admitted to Christianity and if so, should they be required to keep the Jewish law? Yet Paul does not cite Jesus' teachings on this matter. Furthermore, when Paul does make such ethical pronouncements as "Bless those that persecute you" he does not cite the authority of Jesus. It seems likely then that Paul simply did not know what Jesus was supposed to have taught according to the Gospels.

Other Christian writers who are likely to have written before the end of the first century are also silent about Jesus' ethical teachings, his miracle workings, and the historical setting of his crucifixion. Thus, the early post-Pauline epistles (2 Thessalonians, Ephesians, Hebrews, 1 Peter, and possibly also the letters of James and 1, 2, and 3 John) provide no support for the thesis that Jesus lived in the early part of the first century. As Wells puts it: "Can these writers, independent of each other as they mainly are, all have believed that Jesus lived the kind of life portrayed in the Gospels and yet have remained silent even about the where and when of his life?"[18]

Wells argues that scholars agree that the first Christian epistles to characterize Jesus in a way that roughly corresponds to the Gospel accounts (1 and 2 Timothy, Titus, 2 Peter, 1 Clement, seven letters of Ignatius of Antioch) were written somewhere between A.D. 90 and A.D. 110. Maintaining that it is difficult to explain this fact on the assumptions of the historicity of Jesus, he concludes:

> Since, then, these later epistles do give biographical references to Jesus, it cannot be argued that epistle writers generally were disinterested in his biography, and it becomes necessary to explain why only the earlier ones (and not only Paul) give the historical Jesus such short shrift. The change in the manner of referring to him after A.D. 90 becomes intelligible if we accept that his earthly life in the 1st-century Palestine was *invented* late in the 1st century. But it remains very puzzling if we take his existence then for historical fact.[19]

Wells admits that there are a few statements in Paul's epistles that can be interpreted as corroborating the Gospel accounts of Jesus as someone who lived in the early part of the first century. For example, Paul refers to James, the leader of the Jerusalem Christians whom he knew personally, in a way that suggests that Jesus and James were brothers. This would indicate that Jesus was a contemporary of Paul. But Wells suggests another interpretation of the passage[20] arguing that if Jesus was Paul's contemporary "then not only what Paul says about him but also the whole treatment of him in the earliest Christian literature is—to say the least—not what one might reasonably expect; and that the real question is: Which view does better justice to the evidence as a whole?"[21]

If the earliest Christian writers did not think that Jesus was a person who lived in the first part of the first century, on what was their belief in the existence of Jesus based? Wells argues that Jewish Wisdom literature provides a ready source and inspiration for many aspects of Christianity:[22]

> The book of Proverbs represents Wisdom as a supernatural personage, created by God before he created heaven or earth, who then mediated in this creation and is to lead man into the path of truth. In the Wisdom of Solomon, Wisdom is the sustainer and governor of the universe who comes to dwell among men and bestows her gifts on them, but most of them reject her. It is told in 1 Enoch that, after being humiliated on earth, Wisdom returned to heaven.[23]

Moreover, although the Wisdom literature does not state explicitly that Wisdom lived on Earth as a human being or was crucified, Wells argues that these ideas are suggested by some passages in the Wisdom literature or in other Jewish literature. Furthermore, there was a tradition of the crucifixion of holy men in Palestine in the first and second centuries B.C. that alluded to Dead Sea Scrolls and other literature and was recorded by the historian Josephus. Indeed, the Talmud speaks of Jesus living somewhere in the second century B.C. The alleged eyewitness reports of Jesus' postresurrection appearances to Paul and others (1 Cor. 15:3–8) can be interpreted in the light of Jewish literature and tradition. Thus, Wells argues:

> Historical tradition about crucifixions some two centuries before may, then, have confirmed in Paul's mind the suggestions of the Wisdom literature. Paul (and his contemporaries) would have been more readily persuaded by a new interpretation of familiar scriptures and prophecies—an interpretation that seemed to elucidate historical remote events of which he had some (albeit sketchy) knowledge—than by the kind of historical evidence that might impress a modern skeptic.[24]

The question remains on Wells's account of why Christians started to believe by the end of the first century that Christ had lived in the first part of that century. He argues that one factor that may have caused a radical change in Christian belief was the Jewish war with Rome. Beginning in A.D. 66 and ending with the destruction of

Jerusalem in A.D. 70, it resulted in the dispersion of Palestine Christians and the reduction of their importance. Because of this break in continuity it would have been difficult for Christian writers to have reliable information about Palestinian Christianity at the beginning of the century.

Wells argues that the first writers to connect Jesus with Pontius Pilate were active in gentile Christian communities and had only hazy ideas about Palestine. Although these Christians lacked knowledge about Palestine he argues that they would have naturally placed Jesus in the beginning of the first century. Why? Wells reconstructs their reasoning in the following way. Paul taught that God sent Jesus to earth to begin a new era. But what does this mean? This could mean that Jesus' life and death had begun "the final epoch (however long) of human history (prior to his second coming)."[25] However, this idea could have been further interpreted as it was in Hebrews and 1 Peter to mean that Jesus lived and died "in the last days." But what are the last days? This would have naturally been interpreted to mean the relatively recent past.

But why would this interpretation have seemed justified to Christians of the last part of the first century? According to Wells they would naturally have assumed that since Palestine was under Roman rule (after A.D. 6), Jesus' crucifixion was a Roman punishment. Further, since there was no one who claimed to have had firsthand acquaintance of Jesus at the end of the first century, it would have been natural to suppose that he had not lived recently. Consequently, it would have been natural for them to place Jesus somewhere at the beginning of the first century. But why would these Christians have assumed that Pontius Pilate was Jesus' murderer? Wells argues that he was infamous for his ruthless rule of Judea between A.D. 6 and A.D. 41. Hence, he would have naturally come to mind as Jesus' murderer. In this way, Wells argues, Christians of the last part of the first century would come to assume that Jesus died under the orders of Pilate at the beginning of the first century.

Wells concludes his argument by saying:

> This argument does not impute fraud to the Christians of the late 1st century. Those who lack understanding of the process whereby myths are formed are apt to argue that either a tradition is true or else it must have been maliciously invented by cynics who knew the facts to be otherwise available. The preceding argument suggests no such process but simply honest reasoning from the data.[26]

THE ARGUMENT EXPANDED AND DEFENDED

Although Wells puts forward his argument as a critique of the historicity of Jesus, the principles of evaluation of historical evidence on which it is based have much wider relevance. Let us try to understand the argument's structure. Suppose that documents D_1, D_2, . . . D_n, tell the story of the life of a person P who allegedly lived at some remote time t. Should one believe that P is an actual historical person? Only under certain circumstances, Wells says. First of all, one would want to know if D_1, D_2, . . . D_n are based on the reports of people who lived at t and if they are reliable reporters. Suppose one discovers that D_1, D_2, . . . D_n were written several decades after t. Further, suppose one notices that D_1, D_2, . . . D_n contradict one another at any many points and that P is reported in the documents to have performed acts that are improbable. Let us also suppose that there is good reason to think that the writers of D_1, D_2, . . . D_n were devoted followers of what they took to be the teachings of P.

Under these circumstances, before it is rational for one to believe that P existed at t, one would want evidence that would independently confirm P's existence at t from documents written by people who lived at t but who were not devoted followers of P's teachings. Furthermore, one would want P's existence at t independently confirmed by other devoted followers who wrote at a time closer to t than the time that D_1, D_2, . . . D_n were written. If this independent confirmation is not forthcoming, then a rational person surely would have good grounds for being skeptical about the historicity of P. Let us suppose further that the major elements in the story of P that are given by D_1, D_2, . . . D_n could be accounted for in terms of the literary tradition T in which D_1, D_2, . . . D_n was written without supposing that P existed at t. This should reinforce one's skepticism and provide further justification for not believing that P existed at t.

This general and abstract account of the Wellsian argument can be given substance by supposing that P is Jesus, that documents D_1, D_2, . . . D_n are the Gospels of Matthew, Mark, Luke, and John, that the documents based on the writings of people who lived at t and who were not devoted followers of P's teachings are Jewish and pagan historical sources, that the documents from devoted followers who wrote closer to the time of Jesus' alleged life are Pauline and early non-Pauline epistles, and that the tradition T is the tradition of Jewish Wisdom literature.

Put in this way the general evidential principles that control

Wells's scepticism about the historicity of Jesus seem reasonable and plausible. The primary historical sources for an existence claim about an individual become doubtful if they are contradictory, report events that are intrinsically improbable, and are based on clearly biased writers who wrote long after the individual was supposed to have died *and* this claim is not independently confirmed either by other writers both biased and unbiased who wrote earlier than the primary source. Such doubts increase when the major aspect of this individual's life can be accounted for without making any existence assumption, that is by supposing that the individual's life and existence is a myth.

Let us discuss these points in more detail.

The Dates of the Gospels

Most biblical scholars and historians agree that Mark was the earliest Gospel and was written between A.D. 70 and A.D. 135. They agree that it is unlikely that it was written before A.D. 70. Although Mark was not mentioned by other authors until the middle of the second century, it very probably existed earlier than this. Biblical scholars maintain that Matthew and Luke used it as one of their sources. So Matthew was written after Mark. But when was Matthew written? Matthew was unknown to all writers of Christian epistles of the first century and probably was unknown to both Clement of Rome, who wrote at the beginning of the second century, and Ignatius, who wrote around A.D. 110. However, it was known by Polycarp who wrote somewhere between A.D. 120 and A.D. 135.[27] Because of this Wells argues that Matthew was written at the beginning of the second century. Since Mark was not mentioned by first century epistle writers and is presupposed by Matthew, he maintains that it also was not written until around the second century.[28] However, most biblical scholars date Mark around A.D. 80 and Matthew around A.D. 90.

Scholars agree that Luke was written after Mark since it took material from Mark. They also widely agree that Luke was written after Matthew. However, it could not have been written much after it since it shows no knowledge of Matthew. Since most scholars believe that Matthew was written about A.D. 90, they maintain that Luke was written about A.D. 100. Again, it was not known to Clement of Rome or Ignatius, but it was known to Polycarp. Because of this Wells prefers a later date.

Biblical scholars widely agree that John was written later than the other three Gospels and many believe that it reached its present form about A.D. 110. It could not have been written much later than the other Gospels since a papyrus fragment of John dated A.D. 125 was found in Egypt. This is the earliest preserved fragment of the New Testament.[29] One reason for believing that it was written at a later date is that it was not cited or referred to by the earlier Christian writers who quoted the other Gospels. However, this failure to refer to John could instead be due to their hostility to the theological views expressed in the Gospel or to the fact that John was only known in certain geographical regions. Perhaps a better reason for postulating a later date is that John's theology is more advanced and sophisticated than that of the other Gospels. For example, it eliminates the literal doctrine of a Second Coming.

In conclusion, the major historical sources for the life of Jesus are the four Gospels—Mark, Matthew, Luke, and John—which were probably written somewhere between A.D. 70 and A.D. 125, that is, about forty to eighty-five years after the alleged death of Jesus. Given the ignorance of the first century Christian epistle writers about these Gospels, it is possible that the earliest one was not written until the beginning of the second century or about seventy years after the alleged death of Jesus.

The Difficulty of Accepting the Gospel Stories

The mere fact that the earliest Gospels were probably written between forty to seventy years after the alleged death of Jesus should not by itself make us skeptical about his historicity. However, this evidence does suggest that the Gospel stories can hardly be based on eyewitness reports. Indeed, we have good independent reason to suppose that Mark, the earliest Gospel, was not written by someone who lived in Palestine between Jesus' supposed death and the writing of Mark. The writer shows ignorance of Palestine geography that seems incompatible with the assumption that he lived in the region.[30]

Skepticism should develop, however, when the fact that the Gospels are not written by eyewitnesses is combined with the various contradictions in them and with the miracles that are attributed to Jesus. The contradictions show that not all of the Gospel stories could be true. To cite two obvious examples that we will consider in detail in Chapter 3 and Chapter 4, the accounts that the four Gospels give of what happened at the empty tomb cannot be reconciled and the genealogies of Jesus given in Matthew and Luke are in conflict. The various reports of miracles connected with Jesus' life may be true but a rational person will surely demand better evidence than the conflicting reports of four unknown authors writing decades after the events.

Since the Gospels are not written by eyewitnesses and since they contain contradictions and prima facie unbelievable stories, one must ask if there is any independent evidence for their truth. Ideally, one would like to have independent evidence that is contemporary with the time of Jesus' supposed existence and have independent sources that are in agreement. That this is not an overly cautious policy becomes clear from other cases.

We know from other historical research that accounts given of events that supposedly happened many years before sometimes turn out to be myths bearing little correspondence to reality.[31] For example, as Wells has pointed out, although for centuries William Tell was believed to have founded the Swiss Confederation he is now believed to have no historical existence and to simply be a legendary figure.[32] Indeed, the parallels between the legend of William Tell and the supposed historicity of Jesus are striking. Some of the deeds attributed to both have been attributed to previous heroes. For example, the apple episode had been told of the Danish folk hero, Toki, before Tell's alleged time; the story of the resurrection from the dead of the god–man Osiris was part of the religion of the ancient Egyptians long before the story of the resurrection from the dead of the god–man Jesus. The earlier documents make no mention of many of the events connected with the life of Tell. The earliest Jewish and pagan sources make no mention of important events connected with the life of Jesus; even Paul and other earlier writers seem ignorant of the details of his life. Later documents give more details (precise names and dates) many years after the life of Tell; the Gospels give details (precise names and dates) many years after Jesus' life. Once Tell's existence was accepted, some of the earlier documents that did not mention him were improved by forgeries and interpolations. For example, his name was forged in the register of deaths at Schattorf. Once Jesus' existence was accepted some earlier documents were also improved by forgeries and interpolations. For example, as we shall soon see, there is good reason to suppose that a well-known passage in Flavius Josephus's *Antiquities* mentioning Jesus was interpolated by later Christian copyists. These parallels do not prove that Jesus did not exist but they should give us serious pause. They also suggest the importance of evidence from the time when the hero allegedly lived that lends support to the hypothesis that he actually existed.[33]

When Failure to Confirm Is to Disconfirm

To accept the historicity of Jesus one must have independent historical evidence, but this evidence is not forthcoming. What can we conclude? It might be argued that what we *cannot* conclude is that Jesus did not exist; that from this, we are not entitled to draw any conclusion concerning his historicity on rational grounds.

But is there no evidence against the historicity of Jesus? Sometimes the lack of evidence for a hypothesis is evidence against it. To be sure, it is not true in general that if a hypothesis is not supported by the available evidence it is disconfirmed. For example, if Jones's fingerprints are not found on the murder weapon, this does not disconfirm the hypothesis that Jones is the murderer unless one has good reason to suppose that if Jones was the murderer, his fingerprints would be found on the weapon. If, however, we have reason to suppose that the murderer did not have time to wipe fingerprints from the weapon and did not wear gloves, and so on, the lack of Jones's prints on the weapon would tend to disconfirm the hypothesis that Jones was the murderer.

In the light of this insight, let us formulate a principle of justified belief called the Negative Evidence Principle (NEP).

> A person is justified in believing that p is false if (1) all the available evidence used to support the view that p is true is shown to be inadequate and (2) p is the sort of claim such that if p were true, there would be available evidence that would be adequate to support the view that p is true and (3) the area where evidence would appear, if there were any, has been comprehensively examined. [34]

NEP is justified in terms of our ordinary and scientific practice. Consider the following example. A man dies apparently leaving no will. One normally supposes that a person's will is the sort of entity that would be discovered through investigation if it existed. So there is a presumption that if a will exists, there should be evidence of its existence. Although the man's son claims that there is a will, none of the available evidence gives support to the hypothesis that a will exists. For example, the man said he would not make a will and all his records, papers, and so on have been comprehensively examined without one being found. However, the son claims that although a will exists there are good reasons why it has not been found. He claims that his father had good reasons for saying that he would not make a will and that there are good reasons why there is no evidence of a will among his father's records, papers, and so on. Thus, the son attempts to defeat the presumptive grounds for disbelief in the existence of his father's will. However, the reasons the son gives for his contention are inadequate and so are the reasons given by the best legal and psychological experts that he can hire. The presumptive grounds, then, are not defeated. We would surely be justified in this case not simply in having no belief that a will exists but in disbelieving that it exists.

This example and others like it indicate that NEP is an accepted principle of justification in ordinary life and science. It would be quite arbitrary, therefore, not to use NEP in the context of biblical scholarship. One cannot infer that because the assumption of the historicity of Jesus is not supported by the available historical evidence that it is false. But the situation is quite different if we have reason to expect that if this assumption is true, then certain evidence would be available that is not. In this case, we should believe that it is false.

Is there evidence one would expect to be available that would support the hypothesis of the existence of Jesus that is not available?

Jesus as a Public Figure

According to the Gospels, Jesus and the events that surrounded his ministry were supposed to be well known in his own time. The Gospels teach that Jesus was a public figure known throughout the regions of Judea and Galilee. For example, in Mark it is written:

> And they cast out many demons, and anointed with oil many that were sick and healed them. King Herod heard of it: for Jesus' name had become known. Some said "John the baptizer has been raised from the dead; that is why these powers are at work in him." (Mark 6:13–14) [The Revised Standard Version of the Bible has been used throughout this work.]

According to the Gospel of Luke:

> And he came and touched the bier, and the bearers sat still. And he said, "Young man, I say to you arise." And the dead man stood up, and began to speak. And he gave him to his mother. Fear seized them all; and they glorified God, saying, "A great prophet has arisen among us!" and "God has visited his people!" And this report concerning him spread through the whole of Judea and all the surrounding country. (Luke 7:14–17)

Given the fact that Jesus was supposed to be a public figure throughout the land one would expect that he would be mentioned by contemporary historians and referred to in documents of the times. If he was not, then it would seem that NEP would apply and one should disbelieve that Jesus existed. Is there such independent confirmation?

The Jewish Historian Flavius Josephus

One of the best-known historians living in Judea close to the time Jesus was supposed to have lived was the Jewish historian Flavius Josephus. In his major works, *History of the Jewish War* and *Antiquities of the Jews*, Jesus is mentioned only twice. In Book 18 of the *Antiquities* the following passage, known in scholarly literature as Testimonium Flavianum, appears:

> About this time there lived Jesus, a wise man, if indeed one ought to call him a man. For he was one who wrought surprising feats and was a teacher of such people as accept the truth of the Messiah. When Pilate, upon hearing him accused by men of the highest standing amongst us, had condemned him to be crucified, those who had in the first place come to love him did not give up their affection for him. On the third day he appeared to them restored to life, for the prophets of God had prophesied these and countless other marvelous things about him. And the tribe of the Christians, so called after him, has still to this day not disappeared. (*Antiquities* 18:63–64)

It would seem that far from disconfirming the historical assumptions of Christianity this passage confirms them. But this is not so. Biblical scholars are almost in uniform agreement that this passage is spurious—a Christian interpolation—and, consequently, that it cannot be taken seriously as independent confirmation of the historicity of Jesus.[35]

What are the reasons for supposing this passage is a later Christian interpolation?[36] First, it appears out of context, thereby breaking the flow of the narrative. Furthermore, earlier Christian writers, such as Origen, who were well acquainted with Josephus's writings seemed to be unaware of this passage.[37] Moreover, the passage is written as if Josephus were a Christian and not a Pharisaic Jew and therefore it is unlike anything else in the *Antiquities*.

The other passage in *Antiquities* in which Jesus is mentioned tells how Ananus, son of Ananus the high priest, thought he now had a proper opportunity (to exercise his authority). Festus was now dead and Albinus was but upon the road; so he assembled the sanhedrim of judges, and brought before him the brother of Jesus, who was called Christ, whose name was James, and some others (or some of his companions) and when he had formed an accusation against them, he delivered them to be stoned. (*Antiquities* 20.9.1)

Scholarly opinion is divided over whether this passage is a Christian interpolation.[38] However, if Jesus did exist, one would have expected Josephus to have mentioned Jesus more than once in his histories and to have said more about him.[39] Moreover, as J. C. O'Neill has shown, Josephus mentions other leaders of Messianic proportions, ones with large followings who might have been considered Messiahs by people who were looking for a Messiah.[40] Furthermore, in the *Antiquities* more space is given to John the Baptist than to Jesus, and, indeed, Josephus describes John as one would expect him to have described Jesus. For example:

Now, when (many) others came in crowds about him, for they were greatly moved (or pleased) by hearing his words, Herod, who feared lest the great influence John had over the people might put into his power an inclination to raise a rebellion (for they seemed ready to do anything he should advise), thought it best, by putting him to death, to prevent any mischief he might cause. (*Antiquities* 18.5.2)

Given the alleged fact that Jesus was a public figure known throughout the land, it is unexpected that Josephus mentioned him at most once in passing while mentioning other Messianic figures and John the Baptist in greater detail. Thus, NEP applies.

The Talmud and the Tol'doth Jeshu

Josephus is not the only Jewish historical source outside the Gospels. Two others—the Talmud and the Tol'doth Jeshu—should be briefly considered.

Most biblical scholars argue that the earliest references to Jesus in rabbinical literature occur no earlier than the second century. Consequently, they say that the Talmud tells us "what the 'Sages of Israel' thought of his origin and teaching some seventy years after he was crucified."[41] Moreover, it has seemed clear to such scholars that the rabbis of the second century had no independent knowledge of the historical assumptions of Christianity but were simply reacting to the then current Christian accounts.[42] However, if the Gospel accounts of Jesus are historically accurate, why is there no mention of him in earlier rabbinical accounts?[43]

Let us suppose that historical scholarship that suggests that earliest references to Jesus are found in the second-century rabbinical literature are mistaken and that this literature represents in part an independent historical source of information that is either contemporary with or earlier than the life of the Jesus of the Gospels.[44] However, on this assumption the Talmud *contradicts* the Gospel accounts. For example, the Talmud contains several references to Yeshu ben Pantera (also called Pandera and Panthera), a magician whose mother's name was Mary Magdala and who was crucified in B.C. 126, over a century before the Jesus of the Gospels.[45] Other passages in the Talmud refer to Yeshu the Nazarene who practiced magic and committed heresy in the reign of Alexander Jannaeus, the ruler of Palestine from 104 to 78 B.C.[46] But again this was long before the Jesus of the Gospels.

Thus, the evidence of the Talmud presents the following problem. On the one hand, if the references to Jesus are earlier than the second century and provide independent evidence, they tend to contradict the Gospel account. On the other hand, if the references are no earlier than the second century, they provide no independent evidence. The lack of earlier Talmudic evidence can be used as indirect evidence against the historicity of Jesus only if this lack can be plausibly explained in other terms.

In the Tol'doth Jeshu, early and late Talmudic stories about Jesus are brought together. They date mostly from the fifth century, but some date from the second century or earlier. The account they give of Jesus is rather different from that of the Gospels because these stories assume that Jesus was not born of a virgin and that he was not resurrected. Nevertheless, some scholars speculate that the stories were based on the Gospels; whether they were is not known.[47] In any case, these stories cannot be used as support for the historicity of Jesus because it is unclear that they are an independent source of information.

The Pagan Witnesses

The *Annals* of Cornelius Tacitus (A.D. 55–120), written shortly before his death, is sometimes cited as supporting the historicity of Jesus. Tacitus says that Christians "derived their name and origin from Christ, who, in the reign of Tiberius, had suffered death by the sentence of the procurator Pontius Pilate" (*Annals* 15.44).[48] This is the only known reference to the death of Jesus at the hands of Pontius Pilate in early Latin literature and it would be important for confirming the historicity of Jesus if there was good reason to suppose that this passage is not a later Christian interpolation and that Tacitus was not simply repeating information that he obtained from Christian sources but had actually obtained his information from Roman records. Some scholars have argued that this passage is a later Christian interpolation.[49] Let us assume that it is not. Still, the evidence suggests that Tacitus did not obtain his information from earlier Roman records. He refers to Pilate by the wrong title, for Pilate was a prefect, not a procurator; the term "procurator" was current in his lifetime, not in Pilate's. Furthermore, he refers to the executed man as "Christus," which is derived from the Greek word "Christos" and means the "Anointed One" or "Messiah," not as "Jesus." It is unlikely that Tacitus would have found a reference to the Messiah in Roman archives.[50] Consequently, this passage cannot serve as an independent source of information and is useless in confirming the historicity of Jesus.[51]

Thallus, another pagan writer, in a work now lost but referred to by Julius Africanus in the third century, is alleged to have said that Jesus' death was accompanied by an earthquake and an unusual darkness that Thallus, according to Africanus, wrongly attributes to an eclipse of the sun. However, we have no clear idea when Thallus wrote his history or how accurate Africanus's account is. Some scholars believe that Thallus wrote as late as the second century and consequently could have obtained his ideas from Christian opinion of his time.[52] Therefore, he cannot be used to support the historicity of Jesus.

In Celsus's anti-Christian work *The True Word*, written around A.D. 178, the historicity of Jesus is presupposed.[53] Celsus's account agrees closely with the stories of Jesus found in the Talmudic literature, which probably were its major source. But this source is thought by scholars to be a reaction to the then current Christian teaching.[54] If so, the same point obtains as was made above about the relevance of the Talmudic stories to the historicity of Jesus. They provide no independent evidence for the historicity of Jesus.

Suetonius, *The Lives of the Ceasars*, written around A.D. 120, mentions an agitator named Chrestus: "Since the Jews constantly made disturbances at the instigation of Chrestus, [Emperor Claudius in A.D. 49] expelled them from Rome" (Claudius 5.25.4). This passage has sometimes been used to confirm the historicity of Jesus, but it is unlikely that it refers to Jesus. "Chrestus" was the Latin form of a common Greek name, whereas "Christus" was the Latin form of the Greek word "Christos," which means "Anointed One." Many scholars maintain that it is likely that Suetonius is not referring to Jesus at all but to some messianic Jewish agitator named "Chrestus."[55] We know on independent grounds that there were Jewish messianic groups in Rome at this time. Other scholars have suggested that perhaps because of the sameness of the two words Suetonius wrongly was led to believe that the rioters were Christians.[56] But even if he was referring to Christian rioters, this hardly provides any evidence for the historicity of Jesus.[57] No one denies that there were Christians in the middle of the first century.

The writings of Pliny the Younger (A.D. 62–114) are sometimes used to support the historicity of Jesus. In a letter to the Emperor Trajan in A.D. 112 asking for instructions about how to deal with the Christians in the area of the Roman Empire that he governed, he describes the then current Christian ceremonies and practices. But again such evidence is useless for establishing the historicity of Jesus. No one doubts that by that time there were Christians who worshiped Christ and that Pliny's descriptions are accurate.[58] His testimony is thus irrelevant for establishing the historicity of Jesus.

The above survey of pagan witnesses indicates that there is no reliable evidence that supports the historicity of Jesus. This is surely surprising given the fact that Jesus was supposed to be a well-known person in the area of the world ruled by Rome. One would surely have supposed that there would have been *some* surviving records of Jesus if he did exist. Their absence, combined with the absence of Jewish records, suggests that NEP applies and that we are justified in disbelieving that Jesus existed.

The Mystery of Saint Paul's Ignorance

One of the great mysteries of biblical scholarship is why Paul seems to be ignorant of the details of Jesus' life and his ethical teaching. Scholars believe that Paul started preaching around A.D. 45, which is about twelve years after the traditionally stated date of Jesus' death. Consequently, one would have expected that he would have been well acquainted with the details of Jesus' life and teachings. However, in the Pauline letters now admitted to be genuine by most scholars (Romans, 1 and 2 Corinthians, and Galatians), as well as those letters that are considered probably or possibly authentic (Philippians, 1

Thessalonians, Philemon, and Colossians), Paul does not speak of the parents of Jesus, the place or manner of his birth, his trial before Pilate, the place of his crucifixion, or his ethical views. Paul does talk about the Last Supper and the Eucharist (1 Cor. 11:23–26), the Crucifixion (2 Cor. 13:4; Gal. 3:1), and the Resurrection (Rom. 4:23–24; Rom. 10:9; 1 Cor. 15:4), but he does not give a precise historical setting for these events. He maintains that Jesus, after his death, appeared to people in Paul's time—including Paul himself in a vision—but he does not say that Jesus *lived* in Paul's time (1 Cor. 15:3–8). Indeed, Paul does not describe Jesus in terms that suggest that Jesus had died recently (Col. 1:15–18).

In particular, Paul does not associate Jesus' death with the trial before Pilate. At times he attributes Jesus' death to the Jews (1 Thess. 2:14–16), but this idea, as Ronald Charles Tanguay points out, could well have been derived from the Old Testament, "which predicted that the Messiah would be killed by his own people."[59] At other times he attributes Jesus' death to "the rulers of the age" (1 Cor. 2:8). Commentators such as Wells maintain that angels and demons and not human rulers are what is meant here.

> By the beginning of our era, the Jews were so conscious of the undeniable evil in the world that they could no longer accept that God ruled it. Therefore they repudiated the view, held in the Old Testament, that Satan and other angels were obedient instruments of God's will, and supposed instead that these demonic powers had rebelled and seized control of the world.[60]

Paul's view is apparently that these demonic governors instigated men to crucify Jesus.

Paul's views concerning the relation between demons and Jesus is so different from the Gospels that one can only infer that he knew nothing of the Gospel stories. Paul implies that Jesus lived an obscure life in bondage to evil spirits (Gal. 4:3–9; Col. 2:20) who did not recognize his true identity and only in death did he gain mastery over them (Col. 2:15). This suggests that Jesus in his lifetime did not use his supernatural powers to defeat demons and indeed did not let his supernatural status be known. But this is in marked contrast to Gospel stories such as Mark 9:14–29, where demons recognize Jesus and he drives them out of the sick.

Paul gives no indication that Jesus worked any miracles in his lifetime, although it seems natural to have done so if he believed that

Jesus had. He refers to miracles that are associated with the Christian ministry as gifts by the one Spirit (1 Cor. 12:10, 28) and says that among the "signs of a true apostle" are "signs and wonders and mighty works" (2 Cor. 12:12). One would have thought that he would have cited Jesus' own "mighty works" at this point.

Although Paul believed that Jesus was raised from the dead on the third day, his belief was "in accordance with the Scripture" (1 Cor. 15:4) and did not seem to be based on eyewitness reports. He does not refer to the women going to the tomb to anoint Jesus, to the empty tomb, or to Jesus' appearances to the disciples immediately after. One can only surmise that he knew none of these stories.

As Wells makes clear, Paul does not refer to Jesus' teachings as stated in the Gospels even when it would be to his advantage to do so. For example, when Paul advocates blessing those that persecute you (Rom. 12:14), protracted celibacy (1 Cor. 7), and the doctrine that resurrected bodies will be of an imperishable form, he does not refer to Jesus' teaching (Matt. 19:12, Mark 12:25) although it would have supported him.

Indeed, sometimes he goes against this teaching.[61] For example, Jesus instructed his disciples to baptize men everywhere (Matt. 28:19), but Paul said that "Christ did not send me to baptize" (1 Cor. 1:17); Jesus warned his followers to "go nowhere among the Gentiles" (Matt. 10:5–6), whereas Paul claimed that he was called by God "to be a minister of Christ Jesus to the Gentiles" (Rom. 15:16); Jesus said to "judge not, that you be not judged" (Matt. 7:1–2), but Paul says that he has "pronounced judgment in the name of the Lord Jesus" on the sexual immorality of a man who was living with his father's wife (1 Cor. 5:1–5); Paul's advice on paying taxes (Rom. 13:6–7) conflicts with Jesus' to Peter on the same subject (Matt. 17:25–27).

One can perhaps summarize what Paul knew about Jesus from a passage from 1 Corinthians that many scholars believe was used as a credo of the early church. It is likely that it stated everything the early Christians believed about Jesus before the Gospels were written:[62]

> For I delivered to you as of first importance what I also received, that Christ died for our sins in accordance with the scriptures, that he was buried, that he was raised on the third day in accordance with the scriptures, and that he appeared to Cephas, then to the twelve. Then he appeared to more than five hundred brethren at one time, most of whom are still alive, though some have fallen asleep. Then he appeared

to James, then to all the apostles. Last of all, as to one untimely born, he appeared also to me. (1 Cor. 15:3–8)

There is one passage in Paul's letters that has been used to argue that Paul believed that Jesus was a contemporary. Paul says: "But I saw none of the other apostles except James the Lord's brother" (Gal. 1:19). One obvious interpretation of this passage is that Paul is referring to James the brother of Jesus. If so, then this would suggest that Jesus had not died very long before.

But another plausible interpretation is possible. It is important to notice that Paul does *not* say "James Jesus's brother," but rather "James the Lord's brother." Wells suggests:

> James is given this title because he belongs to a Jerusalem group which Paul calls the brethren of the Lord (1 Cor. 9:5), a term which is perfectly intelligible as the title of a religious fraternity. Paul complains (1 Cor. 1:11–13) of Christian factions which bore the titles "of Paul," "of Apollos," "of Cephas," and—most significant of all—"of Christ." If there was a group at Corinth called "those of the Christ," there may well have been one at Jerusalem called the brethren of the Lord, who would have had no more personal experience of Jesus than Paul himself. At Mt. 28:9–10 and Jn. 20:17 the risen Jesus is made, in similar circumstances in both passages, to call a group of unrelated followers his "brothers." John did not know Mt. and "brothers" is not used in this sense elsewhere in either gospel. This suggests that both drew the incident from a common source where the risen Jesus spoke of his "brothers," meaning his close followers. If so, then the term was used in this sense before the gospels, which correlates well with Paul's use of it in this sense.[63]

This explanation of the reference to "James the Lord's brother" must be understood in the entire context of the critique of Jesus' historicity. If Paul's Jesus is the Jesus of the Gospels, then it is strange and puzzling that this reference is the only clear evidence of his recently earthly existence in Paul's letters. In Wells's interpretation, "James the Lord's brother" does not refer to what it might seem to. Hence, the strangeness is eliminated. On the other hand, Wells's interpretation may seem ad hoc and arbitrary. However, he attempts to eliminate this apparent ad hocness by arguing that there is independent confirmation for his interpretation. He shows that there are independent reasons to suppose that the "Lord's brother" refers to membership in a religious group and not a blood relationship. Wells's interpretation is strengthened by these independent reasons as well as by the support that his general thesis acquires from the lack of Jewish and pagan evidence for Jesus' historicity.

Jesus in the Non-Pauline Epistles

An essential aspect of the Wellsian argument against the historicity of Jesus is that the early and later non-Pauline Epistles picture Jesus differently.[64] Wells shows that the early non-Pauline Epistles, that is, those that are likely to have been written before the end of the second century and probably before A.D. 90 (2 Thessalonians, Ephesians, Hebrews, 1 Peter, and James), refer to Jesus in basically the same way as Paul did. They stress the Resurrection and Second Coming but do not refer to his ethical teachings or the miracles he performed; they say nothing about the precise historical context of his crucifixion and death. However, two of these letters are less vague about the period during which Jesus is alleged to have lived on earth. Although they do not place Jesus in some definite period of time they refer to him as living in "the last time," a still unspecified but comparatively recent period of time. On the other hand, in some, but not all, of the later canonical and noncanonical Epistles, those written after A.D. 90 (1 and 2 Timothy, 2 Peter, Titus, 1, 2, and 3 John, Jude, the First Epistle of Clement, and the letters of Ignatius and Polycarp), Jesus begins to be portrayed as he is in the Gospels and is placed in a definite period of time.

Although two of the earliest letters (2 Thessalonians, Ephesians) purport to be written by Paul, they probably were not. In any case, they give no details of Jesus' life and teachings and consequently provide no confirmation that Jesus lived in the early part of the first century. For example, in Ephesians (4:25–32) although the author advocates speaking the truth, controlling anger, doing honest work, and being mutually forgiving and kind, he does not cite the teachings of Jesus. One can only infer that he did not know what Jesus taught. In 2 Thessalonians the author maintains that the Second Coming is not to be expected soon, thus contradicting both the view of Paul (1 Thess. 1:10) and the teachings of the Gospels (Mark 9:1, Matt. 16:28). Furthermore, the author warns in the name of Jesus (2 Thess. 3:6) against idleness. But far from forbidding idleness, the Jesus of the Gospel seems to encourage it (Matt. 6:25–26).[65]

The Epistle to the Hebrews, although sometimes attributed to Paul, is probably not written by him. It also gives no details of Jesus' life and does not place Jesus at the beginning of the first century. That the author was not acquainted with Gospel teachings is made clear in a number of ways.[66] For example, although he advocates brotherly love, hospitality to strangers, and honoring marriage (13:1–4), he does not invoke Jesus' teachings. However, there is one new development. The author of Hebrews maintains that Jesus lived and died "at the end of the age" (9:26). It might be natural to interpret this to mean that Jesus lived and died in the recent past. However, whether the author of Hebrews intended this is by no means clear.

The First Epistle of Peter does not place Jesus in some defined period of time either and also seems to be ignorant of his teachings. For example, Peter says that Jesus was manifested at "the end of the times" for our sake (1:20), but he does not say precisely when this occurred. Although he gives ethical advice ("But even if you do suffer for righteousness sake, you will be blessed" [3:14]) that is similar to Jesus' teaching ("Blessed are those who are persecuted for righteousness sake" [Matt. 5:10]), he does not invoke Jesus' name.

The author of the Epistle of James is also silent about the details of Jesus' life and teaching.[67] Indeed, in this letter nothing is said about the Resurrection. He speaks of the coming of the Lord (5:7) but not of the Second Coming. Although he tells his readers, among other things, not to judge your neighbor (4:11–12), to love your neighbor (2:8), not to use oaths (5:12), to be perfect (1:4), and to avoid anger (1:19–20), he does not seem to be aware that Jesus taught very similar precepts.[68]

Some of the later epistle writers also show ignorance of the Gospel stories and Jesus' teachings and fail to place Jesus in any definite time period. For example, the First Epistle of Clement, which was probably written about A.D. 95 and is not part of the New Testament, maintains that the apostles received the gospel from Jesus who was sent from God (chap. 24).[69] However, it is not clear from the text that they received their instruction during his life on earth. The writer of the letter does not cite written gospel material and does not even allude to it insofar as it would help his argument. He does refer to certain moral teachings of Jesus that were then available, but this was not apparently taken from the gospels. Although he says that Jesus gave his blood for us (chaps. 21, 49), he gives no indication of the circumstances of Jesus' death or resurrection.

Some of the later letters that are included in the New Testament also show ignorance of the teachings of Jesus and leave unspecified when he existed on earth. For example, the author of 2 Peter and the authors (or author) of 1, 2, and 3 John give no biographic details of

Jesus' life and make no explicit mention of his sayings or teachings. In two passages (2 Pet. 1:17 and 2:20) the author of 2 Peter alludes to two passages in Matthew (17:5 and 12:43–45), but there are no direct quotations and no knowledge of biographical details is demonstrated.

The exact dates of the letters of Ignatius, which are not part of the New Testament, are controversial. While some scholars place them after the middle of the second century others prefer the end of the first century or the beginning of the second.[70] Ignatius mentions more details of Jesus than any of the epistle writers considered so far. For example, he maintains that Jesus was born of a virgin, was a descendant of David through Mary (Trallians 9), was crucified in the days of Pontius Pilate (Magnesian 11; Trallians 9). Ignatius probably did not know Luke or John, but he may have known Matthew or some of the traditions that were utilized by him.

The letters of 1 and 2 Timothy and Titus are called the pastoral letters because they give advice on how to conduct the affairs of the church. Although they purport to be written by Paul, they very probably are not for they are composed in a different style and express different theological doctrines from those expressed in the genuine Pauline letters.[71] They are thought by scholars to have been written sometime between A.D. 100 and A.D. 140 by the same person. The author of these letters apparently does not know Jesus' ethical teachings, since he does not cite them when discussing the same topics (1 Tim. 2:8 and Mark 11:25, Matt. 5:23–24, 6:12, and 1 Tim. 2:10 and Matt. 25:31–46). The author believes that Jesus came into the world to save sinners (1 Tim. 1:15), gave himself as a ransom (1 Tim. 2:6), was raised from the dead (2 Tim. 2:8), brought life and immortality to light through the Gospels (2 Tim. 1:10), and will judge the living and the dead (2 Tim. 4:1). Like Ignatius, the author believes that Jesus was descended from David (2 Tim. 2:8) and explicitly places him in the early part of the first century by linking Jesus' death to his trial before Pilate (1 Tim. 6:13–14).

Polycarp's letters to the Philippians, which is not part of the New Testament, was probably written sometime between A.D. 120 and A.D. 135. It contains quotations from a wide range of Christian literature including Paul, 1 Clement, and Ignatius. Most scholars believe that the contents of this letter indicate that Polycarp knew Matthew and Luke. For example, he uses phrasings similar to those in the Sermon on the Mount and actually presents them as the sayings of Jesus. He advocates the doctrine that Jesus came "in the flesh" but unlike

Ignatius does not cite details of Jesus' life in its defense. This probably does not indicate that he was ignorant of these details but only that his purpose in writing the letter was to provide ethical counsel, not to controvert heretical teaching.[72]

Conclusion Concerning the Christian Epistles

Wells concludes from his analysis that there are four layers of Christian thinking.[73] The first layer consists of Paul's teaching of "Christ crucified" in which Jesus is not placed in a historical context and the biographical details of his life are left unspecified. The second layer consists of the early non-Pauline letters that also show a deep ignorance of the historical context of his life and time. However, some of these mention that Jesus lived in "the last time," that is, in an apparently recent, yet unspecified, time. The third layer consists of the letters of Ignatius and the pastoral Epistles, which place Jesus at a definite period of time and mention other doctrines that had come to be associated with him—the Virgin Birth, his descent from David, and his trial before Pilate. The final layer is the story of Jesus as told by the Gospels in which various details are filled in. Wells concludes his account by saying:

> Some overlap in date between these four strata is to be expected: for on the one hand a given tradition often arises somewhat earlier than the oldest of the extant documents in which it is recorded; and on the other it does not disappear as soon as a later tradition, which in due course is to supplant it, has arisen. But although the strata are not to be kept rigidly and completely apart, they can be clearly distinguished. The view that "Jesus Christ is the same yesterday and today and for ever" (Hebrews 13:8) is the reverse of the truth; he is an idea gradually constructed and modified over a considerable period of time.[74]

Criticisms of the Wellsian Thesis

Wells's theory that Jesus is a myth is highly controversial and not widely accepted. Because of this it is important to see what his critics say and whether their criticisms are justified. However, it should be pointed out that the correctness of his thesis should not be judged simply by whether it is widely embraced or accepted.

For example, it should not be rejected as Michael Grant does in *Jesus: An Historian's Review of the Gospels* by arguing that "in recent years 'no serious scholar has ventured to postulate the non-historicity of Jesus'—or at any rate very few, and they have not succeeded in disposing of the much stronger, indeed very abundant, evidence to the contrary."[75] Although Grant cites Wells in a footnote, he makes no effort to consider his argument and to determine if Wells has in fact disposed of what he refers to as the "abundant evidence" for the historicity of Jesus. Indeed, he does not even bother to specify what this abundant evidence is.

There are two arguments against the thesis that Jesus is a myth that can be extracted from Grant's book. First, he points out that we do not believe that pagan personages do not exist because different pagan historians describe them in different terms. To be sure, Grant says, legends have grown up around pagan figures such as Alexander the Great but "nobody regards *him* as wholly mythical or fictitious."[76] But, as should be clear from the above, Wells's argument is not simply that different Christian writers describe Jesus differently or that legends have developed about Jesus. If this were all Wells was saying, then no serious scholar should take him seriously.

Second, Grant maintains that certain stories in the Gospels are so surprisingly uncomplimentary to Jesus that one must assume that they are true. For example, he mentions Jesus' false claim that the Kingdom of God was imminent, his rejection by his family because "he was beside himself," his burial by a Jew, and the story of the Gerasene swine. But are these stories as surprising or uncomplimentary as he supposes?

Consider, for example, the story of the Gerasene swine (Mark 5:2–17). Jesus is reported to have driven "unclean spirits" from a man who was possessed into a herd of two thousand swine who rushed into the sea and drowned. When what Jesus had done became known, he was asked to depart from the neighborhood (Mark 5:17). But, as Wells points out, the writer of the story is simply "painting Jesus as a figure of great power who inspires fear. There is no suggestion that he wished to continue preaching in the area and was frustrated in his intentions."[77] From our modern perspective, one might question, as Bertrand Russell has done, whether Jesus' action is acceptable moral conduct, since he was not kind to the swine.[78] But it is doubtful that this moral attitude toward animals was shared by people of the first century.[79]

Another incident that is sometimes cited as being so uncomplimentary that it must be authentic is one related in Mark 3:20–22: "Then he went home and the crowds came together again, so that they could not even eat. And when his friends heard it, they went out to seize him, for they said, 'He is beside himself.' " However, the phrase "his friends" is probably a mistranslation, since the context makes clear that his family is being referred to. That Jesus' family would reject him, thinking that he is out of his mind, is not at all surprising in the light of biblical literary traditions. For example, Jesus Wisdom literature represents agents of God as coming to earth and being rejected.[80] Furthermore, Pauline literature represents Jesus' life on earth as one of suffering and humiliation. Mark believed that the Son of man will suffer and be treated with contempt (Mark 9:12), and passages from the Old Testament were cited by early Christians to support the view that the Messiah would be "despised and rejected by men" (Isaiah 53:3). In the light of these traditions one can give a plausible account of why stories of Jesus might contain accounts of his rejection and yet not have any historical accuracy.

According to Mark (15:42–46), Joseph of Arimathea, who was not a disciple, buried Jesus. Some have argued that this story must be authentic since "no Christian would have fabricated a tradition which made Jesus receive burial from a Jew instead of from his own support-ers."[81] However, that he was buried by a person who was not a disciple is also not surprising in light of the biblical tradition mentioned above. As we have seen, in Jewish Wisdom literature the agents of God are rejected by men and in the Pauline tradition Jesus lived a life of suffering and humiliation. The story that Jesus was not buried by his own disciples—a severe form of rejection—is surely in keeping with these traditions.

Another allegedly surprising aspect of the New Testament story if Jesus' historicity is called into question is his pronouncement about his imminent Second Coming. In Mark 13:30 Jesus says, "Truly I say to you, this generation will not pass away before all these things take place," and in Mark 9:1 he says, "Truly, I say to you there are some standing here who will not taste death before they see the Kingdom of God come with power." Since these sayings turned out to be false, why, it may be asked, would they appear as part of the Jesus myth? Since Mark was writing at least a generation after the alleged death of Jesus, the author of Mark would not have invented these sayings. He must have been dutifully recording the genuine pronouncements of Jesus that he himself believed were false.

However, there is another interpretation. In Mark 9:1 Jesus says only that *some* will not taste death before the coming of the Kingdom of God. There certainly could have been people living at the end of the first century when Mark was written, for example, around A.D. 80, who were alive when Jesus was supposed to have made this pronouncement, for example, around A.D. 30. In Mark 13:30 he speaks vaguely of "this generation." This could simply mean all the people presently living. Again this is compatible with the writer of Mark believing that Jesus' pronouncement would still come true. Some people living when this pronouncement was allegedly made could still have been living when Mark wrote. Thus, there is no reason to suppose that the author of Mark thought he was inventing a myth and as part of the myth inexplicably portrayed Jesus as being deluded.

In Matthew one see signs that doubts about Jesus' Second Coming were starting to be expressed. Matthew takes the apocalyptic discourse of Mark 13 and adds to it a number of parables and warnings. He urges his readers at great length to be watchful and ready (Matt. 24:37–25:46). As Wells notes: "Such long and detailed emphasis of this single point can only mean that the non-appearance of the end had caused the Christians to whom Matthew was appealing to waver in their expectancy."[82]

In Luke we see further signs of embarrassment. Although the writer of Luke incorporates the doctrine of Mark 13:30 that "this generation shall not pass away before all has taken place" (21:32), he attempts to portray Jesus as maintaining that the end of the world will come later than Mark specified. For example, in adapting Mark 13 he has Jesus declare not that the end of the world will follow immediately after the fall of Jerusalem but that "Jerusalem will be trodden down by the Gentiles, until the times of the Gentiles are fulfilled" (Luke 21:24). Then will follow a time of "distress of nations" and "the powers of heavens will be shaken" and people will see the Son of man come in power and glory (Luke 21:25–27).

These attempts by both Matthew and Luke are perfectly compatible with Wells's thesis. As the evidence of a false prophecy began to mount, Christian writers began to either reassure the faithful or modify the myth. One need not assume any deliberate attempt on the writers' part to deceive. Their actions could well be simply groping attempts to save the doctrine of the Second Coming in the light of evidence. Since the term "generation" is vague, they could still have had a small hope that what they thought Jesus had proclaimed would come to pass. However, in John the doctrine of the Second Coming is eliminated. By the time the author of John wrote, it was presumably no longer credible to attempt to save the doctrine of the Second Coming. Even a vague term like "generation" could only be stretched so far.

I conclude that the allegedly surprisingly uncomplimentary stories of Jesus in the Gospel are either not surprising or not uncomplimentary at least to the people of the time. Consequently, they cannot be used as evidence against Wells's thesis.

Another criticism of Wells has been given by Ian Wilson in *Jesus: The Evidence*. After admitting that sources such as Tacitus and Pliny the Younger provide "scarcely a crumb of information to compel a belief in Jesus' existence,"[83] Wilson argues that the two passages in Josephus's *Antiquities* do provide such evidence. He admits that it "has long been undeniable" that the Testimonium Flavianum has been adulterated in a clumsily pro-Christian way.[84] However, he questions whether this passage is a complete invention. His reason for doubt is that the second passage in *Antiquities* in which Josephus refers to "the brother of Jesus, who was called Christ, whose name was James" is known to have existed in very early version of the text. For example, it was referred to by Origen in the third century. Wilson argues: "This information from Origen is incontrovertible evidence that Josephus referred to Jesus before any Christian copyist would have had a chance to make alterations."[85] Taking this second passage as authentic he goes back to the first passage, the Testimonium Flavianum, and attempts to reconstruct what Josephus actually wrote by removing the Christian elements from it. Following the Jewish scholar Geza Vermes he suggests that Josephus probably wrote something approximating the following:

> At about this time lived Jesus, a wise man. . . . He performed astonishing feats (and was a teacher of such people as are eager for novelties?) He attracted many Jews and many of the Greeks. . . . Upon an indictment brought about by leading members of our society, Pilate sentenced him to the cross, but those who had loved him from the very first did not cease to be attached to him. . . . The brotherhood of the Christians named after him, is still in existence.[86]

This reconstruction plus the evidence from the first passage about James, the brother of Jesus, Wilson argues, provides positive evidence for Jesus' historicity.

There are several problems with Wilson's argument, however. First, it is unclear why he believes that Christian copyists could not have added to the second passage in the *Antiquities* before the third century, the time that Origen wrote. Surely, the evidence from Origen is not "incontrovertible," as Wilson claims, but must be judged in the light of other considerations. Wilson does not acknowledge the fact that several well-known scholars have argued that this passage should be set aside as an interpolation.[87] Second, the attempt to restore the passage known as Testimonium Flavianum to its original state before Christian additions does not explain why the text reads smoothly if the entire passage is eliminated. The most plausible explanation for this is that the passage was not just added to but was inserted at a later date. But if it was inserted, then the only evidence that remains is the second passage about James's brother in which Jesus is mentioned merely in passing. And, as I have already pointed out, even this passage has been thought by many scholars to be a later addition. Further, the term "Christ" appears *only* in the two passages already noted. As Wells says, "this hardly strengthens the case for their authenticity."[88] In addition, as we have seen, it seems very unlikely that if Jesus existed, he would be mentioned only in two passages.

Wilson also finds evidence of Jesus' historicity in the Talmud. He cites passages there that mention Yeshu the Nazarene and Yeshu ben Pantera and points out some of the similarities between the Talmudic stories and the Gospel stories. He concludes that this evidence "indicates beyond reasonable doubt that this Yeshu was one and the same as the Jesus of the Gospels."[89] However, Wilson fails to mention that most scholars believe that such literature was written no earlier than the second century and is not an independent source of information; it is simply a reaction to the then-current Christian accounts. Wilson also fails to mention that the Yeshu ben Pantera of the Talmud was supposed to have lived long before the beginning of the first century. So there *is* reasonable doubt that this Yeshu was one and the same as the Jesus of the Gospel.

Wilson also attempts to explain Paul's silence about the details of Jesus' life. He maintains:

> Paul had very good reasons for ignoring most factual details of Jesus' earthly life. Although directly contemporary with many of the apostles, he suffered from the considerable disadvantage of never having known the human Jesus, and he was not one to embark on a retrospective study of Jesus' life. . . . To have had an experience of the resurrected Jesus was everything he needed, and it is therefore scarcely surprising that *his* Jesus, as distinct from the one of the gospels, should seem ephemeral and unconvincing.[90]

There are two problems, however, with this defense. As we have seen, not only does Paul fail to mention details about Jesus' life, he does not even mention Jesus' teachings when it would be to his advantage to do so. Indeed, he sometimes makes pronouncements that are in conflict with Jesus' teachings. Further, it is not just Paul's silence that needs explaining. Other early Christian writers also fail to mention Jesus' teachings when it would be to their advantage to do so, and they also say things that are incompatible with them. Indeed, Wells stresses that Paul's silence could perhaps be explained away if he were the only early writer not to speak about the historical details of Jesus' life and if his silence about these details was the only thing that needed to be explained.[91]

Thus, Wilson's conclusion that "on the most rational grounds, therefore, we may be confident that Professor Wells is wrong, and that Jesus did indeed exist" is unwarranted.[92]

Still another criticism of Wells's thesis is offered by Gary Habermas in *Ancient Evidence for the Life of Jesus.*[93] According to Habermas the most important problem with Wells's thesis is his incorrect view concerning the early books of the New Testament. Habermas argues that despite what Wells says these books

> do exhibit much interest in the life, death, and resurrection of the historical Jesus, including the preservation of eyewitness testimony to these facts. It is no coincidence that Paul is the author who includes one of the most important indications of this interest in 1 Cor. 15:13ff., where he incorporates a very early Christian creed which is much older than the book in which it appears.[94]

Unfortunately, Habermas has completely missed the thrust of Wells's argument and consequently his response is beside the point. Wells does not deny that early Christians were interested in the bare facts of Jesus' death and resurrection. Rather he argues that they show no interest in the *details* of Jesus' life, death, and resurrection since they seem to have no *detailed knowledge* of these events. If Jesus lived in the first part of the first century, this is surprising, Wells maintains. In the very passage from 1 Corinthians cited by Habermas, Paul shows no such knowledge. The eyewitnesses cited by Paul testify to his recent alleged postresurrection appearances. They do not purport to have witnessed his recent life or death.[95] It is significant that Habermas provides no explanation of why Paul *and* other early Christian writers seem to have no detailed knowledge of the birth, death, and resurrection, do not appeal to his teachings when it would be to their advantage to do so and even preach doctrines that seem to be opposed to his teachings in the Gospels.

Given that he has misunderstood Wells so badly it is interesting to note that Habermas thinks that the above "problem" is the most important one. However, even if we accept the other problems that Habermas raises, they do not seem to affect Wells's thesis significantly. Habermas objects to Wells's dating of the Gospels, arguing that they should be dated twenty to twenty-five years earlier. Habermas does not attempt to refute Wells's argument directly but merely appeals to the authority of most biblical critics who he claims differ from Wells. However, Wells admits that his dating differs from many biblical scholars and provides detailed arguments for his divergence. Surely, if Habermas is to make his case, he must refute these arguments. In any case, it seems that Wells's thesis is not weakened considerably if an early date is accepted for it still remains to be explained why the earlier Christian writers showed ignorance of the detailed life and death of Jesus.

Habermas uses the earlier dating of the Gospels to raise still another problem with Wells's thesis. Wells cannot argue, he says, that because of the late writing of the Gospels, its authors guessed and accepted "facts" that fitted their preconceived ideas. Since they were written earlier than Wells supposes "they could be controlled by eyewitness testimony and thereby point strongly to the reliability of the material."[96] But if they were "controlled by eyewitness testimony" it is hard to understand why the early Christian writers did not show knowledge about the details of Jesus' life, death, and teaching and why there should be such great divergences in the Gospel stories themselves.

The final problem Habermas finds with Wells's thesis is "his usage of ancient mystery religions to explain the early Christian worship of Jesus."[97] Habermas argues that early Christians based their beliefs on eyewitnesses to Jesus' resurrection, that the early mystery religions had great differences from Christianity, that mystery religions with a resurrected god did not appear until the second century, and that Judaism of the first century was not congenial to such doctrines. In response it should first of all be noted that Habermas spends less than two pages attempting to refute a thesis of Wells's that is carefully developed over twenty pages. Second, Habermas does not state the thesis correctly. The most important part of Wells's thesis is that the germs of the idea of a god who lived among humans, who was crucified, suffered, and resurrected is found in *Jewish* literature and tradition.

Two aspects of Habermas's critique are answered in Wells's own writing—the claim that Christianity is unique and the claim that mystery religions with a resurrected god did not appear until after Christianity[98]—and we need not repeat them here. However, perhaps a few words are required about Habermas's argument that original Christianity was based upon the testimony of eyewitnesses. Wells need not deny that Paul and others claimed that they were eyewitnesses to Jesus' postresurrection *appearances* and that the original creed of Christianity was based on these claims. This is quite compatible with the thesis that the Jesus of the Gospels is a legend based primarily on ideas derived from Jewish tradition and literature. The legend of Jesus grew, according to Wells, when these alleged eyewitness reports were interpreted, embellished, and added to in terms of this tradition and literature.

I conclude that Habermas's criticisms have not damaged Wells's argument.

Conclusion

Wells's argument against the historicity of Jesus is sound, and recent criticisms against his argument can be met. So on the basis of Wells's argument there is good reason to reject not only Orthodox Christianity but even those versions of Liberal Christianity that assume that although Jesus was not the Son of God he was an ethical teacher who lived in the first century. However, since Wells's thesis is controversial and not widely accepted, I will not rely on it in the rest of this book. In the chapters that follow the historicity of Jesus will not be questioned.

NOTES

1. Edwin A. Burtt, *Man Seeks the Divine* (New York: Harper and Brothers, 1957), p. 435.

2. Gordon Stein, "The Historicity of Jesus," in *An Anthology of Atheism and Rationalism*, ed. Gordon Stein (Buffalo, N.Y.: Prometheus, 1980), p. 178.

3. Ibid.

4. See Bruno Bauer, *Critique of the Gospels and History of Their Origin*, 4 vols. (1850–1852).

5. See, for example, John M. Robertson, *Christianity and Mythology*, 2d ed. (London, 1910); John M. Robertson, *Pagan Christs*, 2d ed. (London, 1911).

6. Guy Fau, *Le Fable de Jésus Christ*, 3d ed. (Paris, 1967).

7. Prosper Alfaric, *Origines Sociale du Christianisme* (Paris, 1959).

8. W. B. Smith, *The Birth of the Gospels* (New York, 1957).

9. John Allegro, *The Sacred Mushroom and the Cross* (London, 1970).

10. G. A. Wells, *Did Jesus Exist?* rev. ed. (London: Pemberton, 1986); G. A. Wells, *The Historical Evidence for Jesus* (Buffalo, N.Y.: Prometheus, 1982).

11. See, for example, Robert Morgan and John Barton, *Biblical Interpretation* (Oxford: Oxford University Press, 1988).

12. W. Trilling, *Fragen zur Geschichtlichkeit Jesu*, 3d ed. (Düsseldorf, 1969). Quoted by Wells in *Did Jesus Exist?* p. 1.

13. J. Kahl, *The Misery of Christianity*, trans. N. D. Smith (New York: Penguin Books, 1971), p. 103. Quoted by Wells in *Did Jesus Exist?* p. 2.

14. Albert Schweitzer in *The Quest for the Historical Jesus: A Critical Study of Its Progress from Reimarus to Wrede*, trans. W. Montgomery (New York: Macmillan, 1968), argues that the Jesus most people associate with the Gospels is a myth. After the first appearance of Schweitzer's work in 1910 many scholars despaired of writing a historical biography of Jesus. See, for example, the surveys by F. G. Dowing, *The Church and Jesus* (London, 1968); and H. McArthur, ed., *In Search of the Historical Jesus* (London, 1970) cited by Wells in *Did Jesus Exist?* p. 1.

15. For a brief account of Wells's view see his "Historicity of Jesus," *Encyclopedia of Unbelief* (Buffalo, N.Y.: Prometheus, 1985), vol. 1, pp. 363–68. For a more extended view see Wells, *Did Jesus Exist?* and Wells, *The Historical Evidence for Jesus*.

16. Wells cites the following scholarly works as supporting his skepticism: D. E. Nineham, *The Gospel of Saint Mark*, The Pelican New Testament Commentaries (Harmondsworth, 1972); H. Conzelmann, "Historie und Theologie in den synoptischen Passionsberichten," *Zur Bedeutung des Todes Jesu*

(Gütersloh, 1967); M. Werner, *Der protestantische Weg des Glaubens*, vol. 2 (Bern and Tübingen, 1967).

17. Wells cites Albert Schweitzer and D. P. Davies.

18. Wells, "Historicity of Jesus," p. 365.

19. Ibid.

20. See for example, Wells, *The Historical Evidence for Jesus*, p. 167.

21. Wells, "Historical Evidence for Jesus," p. 366.

22. For more on Wisdom literature sources of Christianity, see Wells, *The Historical Evidence for Jesus*, pp. 37–42.

23. Wells, "Historicity of Jesus," p. 366.

24. Ibid., p. 367.

25. Ibid.

26. Ibid., p. 368.

27. Wells, *Did Jesus Exist?* p. 78.

28. Ibid., p. 84.

29. C. H. Roberts, *An Unpublished Fragment of the Fourth Gospel* (Manchester, 1935). Cited in Wells, *Did Jesus Exist?* p. 91.

30. "Then Jesus left the vicinity of Tyre and went through Sidon, down to the Sea of Galilee and into the region of the Decapoli" (Mark 7:31). It has been pointed out that given these directions Jesus would have been traveling directly away from the Sea of Galilee. See Ronald Charles Tanguay, *The Historicity of Jesus: A Survey of the Evidence for the Historical Jesus and the Mythical Nature of Christ* (Privately published, 1988), p. 117.

31. For example, popular accounts of famous disappearances of ships and planes that occurred from 1840 to 1973 in the area of the Atlantic Ocean known as the Bermuda Triangle have been shown to be myths and are completely unjustified by the historical evidence. See Larry Kusche, *The Bermuda Triangle Mystery—Solved* (New York: Harper and Row, 1975).

32. See G. A. Wells, *Religious Postures* (La Salle, Ill.: Open Court, 1988), pp. 57–63.

33. Ibid., pp. 61–62.

34. Cf. Michael Scriven, *Primary Philosophy* (New York: McGraw-Hill, 1966), p. 102. These conditions are to be understood as jointly sufficient for disbelief and not as individually necessary.

35. See, for example, F. F. Bruce, *Jesus and Christian Origins Outside the New Testament* (Grand Rapids, Mich.: Eerdmans, 1974), p. 37; Helmut Koester, *Introduction to New Testament History and Literature of Early Christianity*, vol. 2 (Philadelphia: Fortress Press, 1982), p. 14; Paul Johnson, *A History of Christianity* (New York: Atheneum, 1987), p. 21; J. W. Drane, *Introducing the New Testament* (San Francisco: Harper and Row, 1986), p. 138; Abraham Schalit, "Flavius Josephus," *Encyclopedia Judaica* (1971), vol. 10, p. 251. Cf. Gary R. Habermas, *Ancient Evidence for the Life of Jesus* (Nashville, Tenn.: Thomas Nelson Publishers, 1984), p. 91, who defends the

70   HISTORICITY OF JESUS

authenticity of the passage. However, he seems to be neglecting the opposing scholarly opinion and does not consider the argument against its authenticity presented here.

36. Tanguay, *The Historicity of Jesus*, pp. 39–42.

37. See, for example, Origen, *Contra Celsum* 1.47, and *Commentary on Matthew* 10.17. Quoted in Tanguay, *The Historicity of Jesus*, pp. 39–40.

38. See, for example, J. G. Davies, *The Early Christian Church: A History of Its First Five Centuries* (Grand Rapids, Mich.: Baker Book House, 1965), p. 7; R. Joseph Hoffman, *Jesus Outside the Gospels* (Buffalo, N.Y.: Prometheus, 1984), p. 55; Wells, *The Historical Evidence for Jesus*, p. 18.

39. Wells, *Did Jesus Exist?* p. 11.

40. J. C. O'Neill, "The Silence of Jesus," *New Testament Studies* 15 (1968–1969): 153–67.

41. J. Klausner, *Jesus of Nazareth*, trans. H. Danby (London, 1925), p. 20. Quoted in Wells, *Did Jesus Exist?* p. 12.

42. S. Sandmel, *We Jews and Jesus* (London, 1965), pp. 17, 28. Cited in Wells, *Did Jesus Exist?* p. 12.

43. Some scholars maintain that the silence of the earlier rabbinical literature concerning Jesus can be accounted for without assuming that Jesus did not exist. See R. Joseph Hoffmann, *Jesus Outside the Gospels*, p. 38.

44. See Tanguay, *The Historicity of Jesus*, p. 28. Cf. Habermas, *Ancient Evidence for the Life of Jesus*, p. 98. Habermas quotes from the Talmud to confirm Jesus' death by crucifixion but he does not note that some passages place Jesus' death over one hundred years before the Gospel account.

45. Tanguay, *The Historicity of Jesus*, p. 28. See also Hoffmann, *Jesus Outside the Gospels*, pp. 44–47.

46. Baraitha, Sanhedrin 107b, cited in Tanguay, *The Historicity of Jesus*, p. 29. See also Hoffmann, *Jesus Outside the Gospels*, p. 44.

47. Hoffmann in *Jesus Outside the Gospels* argues that "the *Tol'doth Jeshu* differs from the Gospel accounts in so many respects that the theory of literary dependence of the former on the latter must be rejected" (p. 51).

48. Quoted in Wells, *Did Jesus Exist?* p. 13.

49. Tanguay, *The Historicity of Jesus*, p. 52.

50. Wells, *Did Jesus Exist?* p. 14; Wells, *The Historical Evidence for Jesus*, p. 17.

51. Cf. Habermas, *Ancient Evidence for the Life of Jesus*, pp. 87–89. Habermas seems unaware of the problems involved in accepting Tacitus's evidence as independently confirming Jesus' death.

52. See Wells, *Did Jesus Exist?* pp. 12–13; Tanguay, *The Historicity of Jesus*, pp. 59–61. Cf. Habermas, *Ancient Evidence for the Life of Jesus*, p. 93. Habermas seems to uncritically accept the traditional date of A.D. 52 for Thallus's history.

53. Although Celsus's writing did not survive, a large part of *The True*

Word is quoted by Origen in his *Against Celsus.* See Tanguay, *The Historicity of Jesus,* p. 58.

54. See Wells, *Did Jesus Exist?* p. 15 and p. 16, n. 4.

55. Wells, *The Historical Evidence for Jesus,* p. 16; Tanguay, *The Historicity of Jesus,* pp. 54–55.

56. Stein, ed., *An Anthology of Atheism and Rationality,* pp. 180–81; F. F. Bruce, *Jesus and Christian Origins Outside the New Testament,* p. 21.

57. Cf. Habermas, *Ancient Evidence for the Life of Jesus,* p. 90.

58. Wells, *The Historical Evidence for Jesus,* p. 16.

59. Tanguay, *The Historicity of Jesus,* p. 66.

60. Wells, *The Historical Evidence for Jesus,* p. 34.

61. Tanguay, *The Historicity of Jesus,* p. 71.

62. Ibid., p. 72.

63. Wells, *Did Jesus Exist?* p. 21. See also Wells, *The Historical Evidence for Jesus,* chap. 3.

64. Wells, *Did Jesus Exist?* pp. 21–22. For further discussion of this point see Wells, *The Historical Evidence for Jesus,* p. 167ff.

65. See Wells, *The Historical Evidence for Jesus,* p. 228, n. 5.

66. Ibid., p. 61.

67. James is sometimes identified as Jesus' brother. However, there is good reason to think that he is not. First, many commentators believe that the Epistle of James was not written until the end of the first century. Moreover, he does not refer to himself in this way and calls himself "a servant of God and of the Lord Jesus Christ" (1;1). Moreover, he writes in what one commentator calls the finest Greek in the New Testament. (See Wells, *Did Jesus Exist?* p. 162.) In addition, he seems to have known nothing about Jesus' life.

68. Wells, *The Historical Evidence for Jesus,* p. 70.

69. Ibid., pp. 79–83.

70. Ibid., pp. 101–2.

71. For example, they express a different view of the Second Coming than Paul's letters. Paul seemed to believe that the Second Coming was imminent while the author of 1 Timothy does not (1 Tim. 6:14–15).

72. Wells, *The Historical Evidence for Jesus,* p. 104.

73. Wells, *Did Jesus Exist?* p. 65.

74. Ibid.

75. Michael Grant, *Jesus: An Historian's Review of the Gospels* (New York: Charles Scribner's Sons, 1977), p. 200.

76. Ibid.

77. Wells, *Did Jesus Exist?* p. 213.

78. Bertrand Russell, *Why I Am Not a Christian and Other Essays on Religion and Related Subjects* (New York: Simon and Shuster, 1957), pp. 18–19.

79. See John Passmore, *Man's Responsibility to Nature* (New York: Charles Scribner's Sons, 1974), pp. 111–12.

80. Wells, *Did Jesus Exist?* p. 149.

81. Wells, *The Historical Evidence for Jesus*, p. 190.

82. Ibid., p. 121.

83. Ian Wilson, *Jesus: The Evidence* (San Francisco: Harper and Row, 1984), p. 60.

84. Ibid.

85. Ibid., p. 61.

86. Ibid.

87. Wells mentions L. Herrmann, in *Chrestos. Témoignages païens et juifs sur le christianisme du premier siècle* in *The Historical Evidence for Jesus*, p. 18; and Schürer, Zahn, von Dobschütz, and Juster in *Did Jesus Exist?* p. 11.

88. Wells, *Did Jesus Exist?* p. 11.

89. Wilson, *Jesus: The Evidence*, p. 64.

90. Ibid., p. 65.

91. Wells, *Did Jesus Exist?* p. 207.

92. Ibid. Wilson also seriously misrepresents Wells's view concerning the date of the Resurrection. Wilson argues that even Wells admits that the belief took hold that Jesus appeared to people soon after his death. See Wilson, *Jesus: The Evidence*, p. 137. However, Wells only admits that the earliest witness, Paul maintained that Jesus' after-death appearances occurred in his own time. But what Wells stresses is that this "does not tell us anything about [Paul's] idea of the date of Jesus' death." See Wells, *Did Jesus Exist?* p. 207.

93. Habermas, *Ancient Evidence for the Life of Jesus*, pp. 31–36.

94. Ibid., pp. 32–33.

95. The only possible evidence cited by Habermas that could indicate that Jesus lived near the time of Paul is his reference to James the brother of the Lord, which Wells maintains does not refer to Jesus' brother.

96. Habermas, *Ancient Evidence for the Life of Jesus*, p. 35.

97. Ibid., p. 35.

98. See Wells, *Did Jesus Exist?* pp. 182–83, 201.

3

The Resurrection

Orthodox Christianity assumes that Jesus was crucified on the order of Pontius Pilate and was then resurrected. Thus the Apostles' Creed proclaims that Jesus "suffered under Pontius Pilate, was crucified, dead, and buried; he descended into hell; the third day he rose again from the dead." The Nicene Creed maintains that Jesus "was crucified also for us under Pontius Pilate; He suffered and was buried; and the third day he rose again according to Scriptures."[1] Furthermore, the Resurrection has been considered by Christians to be a crucial element of Christian doctrine. For example, nearly two thousand years ago Paul proclaimed: "If Christ has not been raised, then our preaching is in vain and your faith is in vain. We are even found to be misrepresenting God. . . . If Christ has not been raised, your faith is futile" (1 Cor. 15:14–17). Many contemporary Christians seem to agree. Hugh Anderson, a New Testament scholar, writes:

> With all assurance we can say that, save for Easter, there would have been no New Testament letters written, no Gospels compiled, no prayers offered in Jesus' name, no Church. The Resurrection can scarcely be put on a par with certain other clauses in the Apostles' Creed—not if the New Testament is our guide. . . . Easter, therefore, is no mere addendum to other factors in the story of Jesus Christ; it is constitutive for the community's faith and worship, its discipleship and mission to the world.[2]

Terry Miethe, a Christian philosopher at Oxford, has maintained that " 'Did Jesus rise from the dead?' is the *most important* question regarding the claims of the Christian faith."[3] Let us examine this question now.

Initial Obstacles to Belief in the Resurrection

To evaluate if Jesus was resurrected we must first specify what "resurrection" means. The New Testament seems to understand the term literally: to be resurrected entails being restored to life after physical death; furthermore, being restored to life involves having a body of some kind although not necessarily a physical body in the usual sense. Furthermore, the Scriptures assume that the Resurrection was a miracle;[4] that is, it was brought about by the exercise of a supernatural power, namely, the power of God.

However, this assumption immediately raises obstacles to its acceptance. First, the believer in Jesus' alleged resurrection must give reasons to suppose that it can probably not be explained by any unknown laws of nature. Since presumably not all laws have been discovered, this seems difficult to do. The advocates of Jesus' resurrection must argue that it is probable that Jesus being restored to life will not be explained by future science utilizing heretofore undiscovered laws of nature. Given the scientific progress of the last two centuries such a prediction seems rash.[5] People are kept alive today in ways that only a few years ago would have seemed impossible. It is not implausible that restoring life to some people will be medically possible in the future. But, it may be objected, Jesus is supposed to have been restored to life without the benefit of modern medical technology. Still, breakthroughs in medical knowledge could make it understandable how on rare occasions people can come back to life without such technology.

It could be argued that some events not only are unexplained in terms of laws of nature but are in conflict with them and Jesus' resurrection might be considered one of them. The difficulty here lies in knowing if the conflict is genuine or is merely apparent. This brings us to the second great obstacle that has to be overcome in establishing a miracle. Believers in miracles must argue that it is more probable that the conflict is genuine than apparent, but this is difficult to do for there are many ways that appearances can mislead and deceive in cases of this sort.

If one's knowledge of the laws governing nature is incomplete, an event may appear to be a miracle even when it is not. A scientific law holds only under some conditions and not under all conditions. Thus, Boyles's law holds only for gases in a certain temperature range; Newton's laws only correctly predict the mass of a body at accelerations not close to the speed of light. Often the range of application of a law becomes known with precision only years after the law itself was first formulated. Thus, although physiological and psychological laws governing life seem to conflict with the apparent miracle of restoring to life, these might only hold in a wide range of applications, and in special circumstances other laws of nature might explain the restoration of life. Both sorts of laws could be derivable from a comprehensive, but as yet unknown, theory. The advocates of the Resurrection must maintain that an explanation of the event in terms of such a theory is less likely than an explanation invoking some supernatural power.

Deception, fraud, or trickery can also make it appear as if a conflict has occurred. The difficulties of ruling them out are well known. We have excellent reason today to believe that some contemporary faith healers use fraud and deceit to make it seem that they have supernatural powers and are performing miracle cures.[6] Although they do not normally claim to be able to restore people to life there is no doubt at all that they could make such claims and by various tricks deceive a gullible public into believing them. It is unlikely that people are more gullible today than in biblical times.

Further, alleged miracles may be due not to some trick or fraud but to misperception based on religious bias. A person full of religious zeal may see what he or she wants to see, not what is really there. We know from empirical studies that people's beliefs and prejudices influence what they perceive and report.[7] The question therefore arises, was Jesus restored to life and did he appear to his disciples or was his body stolen and did his disciples "see" what they wanted to see?

In addition, religious attitudes often foster uncritical belief and acceptance. Indeed, in religious contexts uncritical belief is often thought to be a value, while doubt and skepticism are considered vices. Thus, a belief arising in a religious context and held with only modest conviction may tend to reinforce itself and develop into an unshakable conviction. It would hardly be surprising if, in this context, some ordinary natural event was seen as a miracle.

Finally, it might be the case that what we thought were strictly deterministic laws are in fact statistical laws. These are compatible with rare occurrences of uncaused events. Thus, the events designated as miracles may be wrongly designated; they may be uncaused in the sense of being neither naturally nor supernaturally determined. Advocates of the miracle hypothesis, then, must show that the existence of miracles is more probable than the existence of some uncaused events. It is not inconceivable that on very rare occasions someone being restored to life has no natural or supernatural cause.

In summary, the advocates of the view that Jesus was resurrected (H_r) must show that H_r is more probable than the following:

H_s = Jesus' being brought back to life, but this will be explained when in the course of scientific progress more laws of nature are discovered.

H_g = Jesus seemed to be resurrected but he was not.

H_u = Jesus' resurrection was uncaused.

What are the comparative probabilities of these hypotheses prior to looking at the actual historical evidence for the Resurrection? There is no easy way to assess them. However, as we have already seen, the progress of science, and the history of deception and fraud connected with miracles and the paranormal, and the history of gullibility and misperception all strongly suggest that H_s and H_g are better supported than H_r relative to our prior background knowledge. Thus, evidence for the Resurrection must be very strong to overcome the prior improbability of supposing that Jesus was resurrected.

It is less clear what one should say about the comparative prior probability of H_r and H_u. Both seem unlikely in the light of the background evidence but it is certainly not obvious that H_u is less likely than H_r. On the one hand, science already allows indeterminacy on the microlevel, for example, in quantum theory. On the other hand, macroindeterminacy, the sort that would be relevant to explaining miracles, is no less incompatible with the present scientific worldview than it is with H_r. At the very least, one can say that there is no reason to prefer H_r over H_u on probabilistic grounds relative to our background knowledge.

The Evidence for the Resurrection

Nothing I have said so far should lead one to believe that the Resurrection is impossible. I have only argued that in the light of our background knowledge other hypotheses are either more or equally probable. However, we have more than background knowledge to consider, for there is evidence from the New Testament (the testimony of eyewitnesses to Jesus' postresurrection appearances) and other historical sources (the records of Jewish and pagan historians). It is certainly possible that this evidence could outweigh the background knowledge and make the Resurrection more probable than alternative hypotheses. However, it would have to be reliable and strong in order to do this.

What factors would affect the reliability and strength of this evidence?[8] First, if various accounts of an event are consistent, this would tend to increase their evidential weight whereas inconsistencies would tend to lower it. Thus, the consistency of the Easter story and its sequel are important in evaluating its evidential worth. Second, eyewitness accounts are generally more reliable than accounts that are second or third hand. Consequently, if the accounts of the Resurrection were second or third hand, this would tend to decrease their evidential weight. Third, if the eyewitnesses to some event are known to be reliable and trustworthy, this should increase their evidential worth. When we have reason to suppose that the witnesses are not reliable, or even when we have no reason to suppose that they are, their evidential value is weakened. Fourth, independent testimony that is in agreement should tend to increase our confidence of its reliability; failure of independent confirmation should lower our confidence. Finally, if an author's purpose in writing a document leads us to believe that the document was not a reliable historical account, then this would lower the evidential weight of the document. Thus, if the Gospel writers' purpose leads us to suppose that the Gospels are not reliable historical accounts, this would lower the evidential value of the Resurrection story.

THE PURPOSES OF THE GOSPEL WRITERS

Many biblical scholars have argued that the Resurrection story was shaped by the theological aims of the evangelists. Thus, they say that the writers of the Easter stories took the information that was available to them and constructed narratives that were influenced by their own purposes. Although they acknowledge that there are significant differences in the purposes of the evangelists, New Testament scholars like Willi Marxsen argue that all of them wanted *"to show that the activity of Jesus goes on."*[9] Reginald Fuller, another New Testament scholar, maintains that Gospel narratives "can no longer be read as direct accounts of what happened, but rather as vehicles for proclamation. Such was their original intention. . . . [The Evangelists] used them not simply to relate the past events . . . but in order to assert, e.g. the identity-in-transformation between the earthly and the Risen Jesus."[10]

However, if the Gospel stories of the Resurrection were indeed shaped by the purposes of the evangelists and intended as vehicles of proclamation useful in preaching the Christian message, we should be suspicious of their reliability. Indeed, it is difficult enough to determine the reliability of documents that are intended only as accurate accounts of the past. Documents that are acknowledged to be shaped by other purposes could be historically accurate and reliable, but to overcome our initial suspicion they must meet strict historical standards. The question is whether the Gospel accounts of the Resurrection do.

THE INCONSISTENCY OF THE RESURRECTION STORY

The story of the Resurrection varies from Gospel to Gospel.[11] Let us divide the story into two parts—what happened at the tomb after Jesus' death and what happened in the days that followed—and examine each in turn.

After Jesus' death on the cross he is placed in a tomb. What happened then? This part of the story varies widely from one Gospel to another.[12] In Matthew, when Mary Magdalene and the other Mary arrived toward dawn at the tomb there is a rock in front it, there is a violent earthquake, and an angel descends and rolls back the stone: "And behold there was a great earthquake; for an angel of the Lord descended from heaven and came and rolled back the stone and sat upon it" (Matt. 28:2). In Mark, the women arrive at the tomb at sunrise and the stone had been rolled back: "And very early on the first day of the week they went to the tomb when the sun had risen and they were saying to one another, 'Who will roll away the stone for us from the door of the tomb?' And looking up they saw that the stone was rolled back, for it was very large" (Mark 16:2–4). In Luke, when the women arrive at early dawn they find the stone had already been rolled back. "But on the first day of the week, at early dawn, they went to the tomb, taking the spices which they had prepared. And they found the stone rolled away from the tomb" (Luke 24:1–2).

In Matthew, an angel is sitting on the rock outside the tomb (Matt. 28:2) and in Mark a youth is inside the tomb: "And entering the tomb, they saw a young man sitting on the right side dressed in a white robe, and they were amazed" (Mark 16:5). In Luke, two men are inside: "While they were perplexed about this, behold, two men stood by them in dazzling apparel" (Luke 24:4).

In Matthew, the women present at the tomb are Mary Magdalene and the other Mary: "Now after the sabbath, toward the dawn of the first day of the week, Mary Magdalene and the other Mary went to see the sepulchre" (Matt. 28:1). In Mark, the women present at the tomb are the two Marys and Salome: "And when the sabbath was past, Mary Magdalene, and Mary the mother of James, and Salome bought spices, so that they might to go and anoint him" (Mark 16:1). In Luke, Mary Magdalene, Mary the mother of James, Joanna, and other women are present at the tomb: "Now it was Mary Magdalene and Joanna and Mary the mother of James and the other women with them who told this to the apostles" (Luke 24:10).

In Matthew, the two Marys rush from the tomb in great fear and joy, run to tell the disciples, and meet Jesus on the way: "So they departed quickly from the tomb with fear and great joy, and ran to tell the disciples. And behold Jesus met them and said 'Hail!' " (Matt. 28:8–9). In Mark, they run out of the tomb in fear and say nothing to anyone: "And they went out and fled from the tomb; for trembling and astonishment had come upon on them; and they said nothing to any one, for they were afraid" (Mark 16:8). In Luke, the women report the story to the disciples who do not believe them and there is no suggestion that they meet Jesus: "And returning from the tomb they told all this to the eleven and to all the rest. . . . but these words seemed to [the apostles] an idle tale, and they did not believe them" (Luke 24:9–11).

Given these various accounts what should one believe? Can the Gospel according to John help decide? Unfortunately, John contradicts much of the three other Gospels (John 20:1–18). According to John, only Mary Magdalene came to the tomb when it was still dark, thus contradicting the three other Gospels. She sees that the stone has been moved and rushes to tell Simon Peter and the other disciples who apparently take her story seriously since they run to the tomb. This directly conflicts with the accounts of Mark and Luke. In John, before she runs to tell Simon Peter and the disciples she does not see any angels, or a youth, thus contradicting the other three Gospels. Moreover, since there is no report of her entering the tomb before she tells Simon Peter and the disciples, Mark and Luke are contradicted. Only after she returns to the tomb with the disciples, they inspect the tomb and find linen wrapping and a head napkin, and they leave and she is standing outside weeping does she see two angels inside the tomb. This, of course, is in conflict with the three other Gospels. At this point, according to John, she also sees Jesus who she does not at first recognize. This also contradicts the other Gospels.

The account of what happens in the days after the discovery of the empty tomb also differs from Gospel to Gospel. In Matthew, the disciples go to Galilee, to the mountain where they have been directed to go by Jesus. There they worship him but some are doubtful. He tells them to go forth into the world and spread his teachings.

> Now the eleven disciples went to Galilee, to the mountain to which Jesus had directed them. And when they saw him they worshiped him; but some doubted. And Jesus came and said to them, "All authority in heaven and on earth has been given to me. Go therefore and make disciples of all nations, baptizing them in the name of the Father, and of the Son and of the Holy Spirit, teaching them to observe all that I have commanded you; and lo, I am with you always, to the close of the age" (Matt. 28:16–20).

One version of Mark ends at 16:8. Another version includes 16:9–20. In the longer version Jesus first appears to Mary Magdalene. But when she reports his appearance she is not believed. Later he appears to two other women but they are not believed either. Jesus then appears to the disciples while they are at a table (it is unclear where they are) and rebukes them for not believing those who saw him. He tells his disciples to go into the world to preach his gospel and maintains that only those who are baptized will be saved while everyone else will be condemned. He asserts that signs will accompany those who believe: they will be able to drink poison, pick up serpents, speak in tongues, and heal the sick by laying on hands. He is then taken up into heaven and sits on the right hand of God. The disciples go forth to preach the gospel and the Lord works with them confirming their message by the signs that accompany it.

In Luke, a still different account is presented (Luke 24:13–53). Two of the women who go to the tomb are on their way to Emmanus and meet Jesus, but he is not immediately recognized. Only later, when he breaks bread with them, do they recognize him. He then vanishes and they return to Jerusalem to tell the disciples that the Lord has risen. At this very moment Jesus appears to the disciples and rebukes them for their doubt. He asks them for something to eat. He asks them to preach his gospel, leads them as far as Bethany, blesses them, and departs. In some versions of Luke it is said that Jesus is carried up into heaven. The disciples then return to Jerusalem with great joy.

In John, a still different account is given (John 20:19ff.). On the Sunday evening after the empty tomb is discovered Jesus appears to the disciples who are behind closed doors. Thomas is not with the rest of the disciples at this visit, but when he is told about their seeing Jesus he is skeptical. When Jesus appears eight days later in a room with the doors closed he invites Thomas to touch his wounds. Thomas does so and is convinced. Later Jesus reveals himself to several of his disciples by the Sea of Tiberias in Galilee. He eats breakfast with them, talks to them, and leaves with one of them.

In sum, the accounts of what happened at the tomb are either inconsistent or can only be made consistent with the aid of implausible interpretations. Without such interpretations they simply could not all be true. The accounts of what happens in the days after finding the empty tomb, although not perhaps contradictory, are certainly very different and hard to reconcile. Marxsen sums up the problem in this way: "The conclusion is inescapable: a synchronizing harmony of the different accounts [of the Resurrection] proves to be impossible. Anyone who persists in the attempt must alter the texts and declare the differences to be trivialities."[13]

THE LACK OF EYEWITNESSES

According to the Gospel story there were no eyewitnesses to Jesus' actual resurrection. Belief in it must therefore be based on inferences. What are these inferences based on? First, there are the appearances of the resurrected Jesus. Second, there is the empty tomb. Given these two alleged facts one infers that the miraculous event occurred sometime before the discovery of the empty tomb and the postresurrection appearances of Jesus. According to the Gospels, there were indeed eyewitnesses to the resurrected Jesus. However, we have only one contemporary eyewitness account of a postresurrection appearance of Jesus, namely Paul's. In all the other cases we have at best second- or thirdhand reports of what eyewitnesses claimed to see that were recorded several decades after the Crucifixion.

What about Paul's own account of the appearance of Jesus? Written many years after the event, it gives no description of the resurrected Jesus. After mentioning other alleged appearances of Jesus, Paul says: "Last of all, as to one untimely born, he appeared to me" (1 Cor. 15:8). It is unclear from this if Paul's experience was that of an embodied Jesus and, if it was an experience of a body, if other people would have had a similar experience if they had been similarly situated. (It is worth noting that the description of Paul's experience of the risen Jesus in Acts 22:6–8 is merely of a light and a voice, not of a body.) Thus, we have no good reason to suppose that Paul's experience was not a hallucination.

What about the empty tomb? As we have seen, although there were supposed to be cyewitnesses to the empty tomb, just who exactly these were differs from one Gospel account to another. In any case, there were no contemporary eyewitness accounts.

Furthermore, New Testament scholars even differ on when the stories of the empty tomb entered the Christian tradition. Yet this is surely relevant to their evidential value, for the later they entered the tradition the less value they have. Werner Kümmel[14] and Hugh Anderson[15] maintain that these stories entered late in the tradition; Reginald Fuller[16] maintains that the stories entered early; and Willi Marxsen[17] believes that the evidence does not enable us to determine when the stories entered it. One excellent reason for supposing they entered the tradition late is that these stories were not mentioned by Paul and other early Christian letter writers even when it would have been to their advantage to do so. This strongly suggests that they did not know the stories.[18]

THE RELIABILITY OF THE EYEWITNESSES, THE REPORTERS, AND THE SCRIBES

Do we have any good reason to suppose that the alleged eyewitnesses to the postresurrection appearances of Jesus or to the empty tomb were reliable and trustworthy? Do we have any reason to suppose that the people who reported the eyewitnesses' accounts were? That those who wrote the stories down were?

As far as the Gospel eyewitnesses to postresurrection appearances are concerned, they are Jesus' friends and disciples who by their relation to him one would not expect to be objective observers. Without independent reason to believe their reliability one must therefore be suspicious. Further, we do not know who reported these stories or how many times they were told and retold before they were finally written down. They were presumably passed down by word of mouth and not recorded until several decades after the event.

But who were these reporters? What were their motives? Were

they reliable and trustworthy? Did they have reason to embellish the stories? Did they have reason perhaps to make up stories that suited their purposes? We do not know the answers to these questions with any certainty and until we do we have little reason to suppose that there were eyewitnesses or, if there were, that their accounts were being transmitted accurately. In fact, there is some reason to distrust the accuracy of these reporters. In the first place, the great differences among postresurrection appearance stories and the difficulty of reconciling them certainly suggests that oral transmission has generated inaccuracies. Moreover, as has already been noted, many biblical scholars maintain that the evangelists who wrote the Gospels constructed narratives that were influenced by their own purposes. If this is so, there is just as much reason for this construction to affect the oral transmission of the stories as the ones that were finally compiled by the Gospel writers.

Paul reports many eyewitnesses to Jesus' postresurrection appearances: Cephas, the twelve, more than five hundred brethren, James, the disciples, himself (1 Cor. 15:5–8). How seriously should we take these reports? First, we have no reason to suppose that these eyewitnesses, including Paul himself, are reliable or trustworthy. Moreover, we have no information about how Paul got his information about the eyewitness reports of others. Were they reported to him directly? Were they passed on by third parties to Paul? If they were, were the intermediate sources reliable? Unlike the Gospel stories we have no details of Jesus' appearances to the eyewitnesses. For example, did Jesus appear in bodily form or were the appearances like the one described in Acts 22:6–8? The reliability of Paul's sources would certainly be impugned if these stories were not confirmed by independent sources. As I shall show in a moment, they are not.

It is sometimes argued that Paul's own experience of the risen Jesus should be given special evidential significance because he was a skeptic who was converted by it. However, we do not know if Paul's account of his experience and conversion is accurate. Paul, no less than other early Christians, could have constructed stories that furthered his own purpose of spreading Christianity. We know that certain aspects of Paul's account of the first three years of his life as a Christian are contradicted by the account in Acts.[19] Further, there are no contemporary eyewitness accounts that independently support Paul's story of his conversion.

However, suppose that Paul's report of his experience is accurate.

Why should the fact that Paul persecuted Christians and was subsequently converted to Christianity by his religious experience be given special existential significance? Whatever his past record, at the time of his report he was a zealous, religious believer and not a religious skeptic. (See Gal. 1:14.) Down through the ages many people have been converted to one set of religious beliefs from other. For example, Muhammad was converted to monotheism from his former polytheistic beliefs by a religious experience. However, it was also revealed to Muhammad that Jesus was not God Incarnate. Defenders of the Resurrection would hardly allow that Muhammad's experience be given special evidential significance.

The reliability of the eyewitnesses to the empty tomb is completely unknown. Indeed, because the account of who discovered the empty tomb varies from Gospel to Gospel, it is not even clear who the witnesses were. However, whoever they are—the two Marys, Salome, Joanna—they seem to have been friends of Jesus, people who were probably not objective observers. Moreover, there were no known contemporary eyewitnesses. What these witnesses reported was related by others to the Gospel writers. We have no reason to suppose that these reporters were reliable. Indeed, for the reasons already given, we have grounds for supposing that they were not. The contradictions between different Gospel stories of the empty tomb suggests that oral transmission generates inaccuracies. There is reason to suppose that the reporters of empty tomb stories, like the Gospel writers themselves, constructed them to further their own purposes.

LACK OF INDEPENDENT CONFIRMATION

So far I have argued that the Gospel accounts of the Resurrection are difficult to harmonize, that the actual resurrection was based on inferences from two dubious sources of evidence: the postresurrection appearances of Jesus and the empty tomb. Given these problems and the fact that the Resurrection is understood as a miracle and, thus, although not impossible, has high prior improbability, it is extremely important that there be some independent confirmation before the Resurrection story is accepted.

Can other parts of the New Testament provide such confirmation? In the Acts of the Apostles (1:1–11), it is reported that Jesus appeared to the disciples for forty days in Jerusalem. After speaking to them about the power of the Holy Spirit and about their being his witnesses "he was lifted up, and a cloud took him out of their sight"

(Acts 1:9). Two angels then appeared and said that Jesus, who was taken up in heaven, "will come in the same way as you saw him go into heaven" (Acts 1:11). But far from confirming the accounts given in the Gospels, this account gives a still different report of what happened in the days after the discovery of the empty tomb. Furthermore, the idea that Jesus was taken to heaven in a cloud is incredible since it is based on the primitive assumption that heaven is somewhere up in the sky.

As we saw in Chapter 2, the genuine Pauline epistles and the earlier non-Pauline letters provide no independent support for the thesis that Jesus lived at the time of Pontius Pilate. Consequently, they cannot provide support for his crucifixion and resurrection at that time. To be sure, Paul and other earlier epistle writers thought Jesus was crucified and was resurrected. But there is no good evidence that they believed that these events occurred at the beginning of the first century. They give no details of Jesus' life or death. Indeed, as we have already noted, they provide no independent support for the empty tomb stories.

Moreover, the Resurrection is not confirmed by Jewish or pagan sources. Josephus, in the passage known as the Testimonium Flavianum, reports that Jesus was resurrected from the dead. However, as we have seen, this passage is almost universally acknowledged by scholars to be a later Christian interpolation. Significantly, in no other place in the *Antiquities* is Jesus' resurrection mentioned. This is surprising given the centrality of this idea to Christianity.

In the Talmud and other Jewish sources there are discussions of the Resurrection but they are always skeptical. For example, in the *Tol'doth Jeshu* the death of Jeshu or Yeshu ben Pantera is reported as follows:

> The body was taken down while it was still the eve of the Sabbath . . . and immediately buried. A gardener, Yehuda, removed the body from the tomb and cast it into a ditch and let the water flow over it. . . . The disciples discovered that the body was not in the tomb and announced to the Queen that Yeshu had been restored to life.[20]

As was mentioned in Chapter 2, many scholars believe that such literature was merely a second-century Jewish reaction to current Christian doctrines and can neither support or disconfirm them. On the other hand, if the Resurrection was a historical event of the early part of the first century, it is surprising that Jewish reaction is not found until the second century. Moreover, if despite what many scholars suggest, this Jewish literature is in fact based on an older tradition, it would tend to disconfirm the Christian story of the Resurrection. Recall from our earlier discussion that Talmudic literature places Yeshu ben Pantera's death much earlier than the earlier part of the first century. If these stories are taken seriously, they would tend to refute the Christian belief that Jesus died and was resurrected at the time of Pontius Pilate. The earlier date of Yeshu ben Pantera's death also seems to count against the view that these stories are simply reactions to second-century Christian doctrine. If the second-century rabbis were reacting to the Christian doctrine of the Resurrection, it is likely they would have placed their skeptical stories of Jeshu in the first century, the time that Christians maintained that Jesus lived and died.

Furthermore, pagan sources do not confirm the Resurrection. As has already been noted, Tacitus, in one well-known passage in his *Annals* (15.44), reported that Pontius Pilate ordered the execution of Jesus. However, there is good reason to suppose that this passage, if not a later Christian interpolation, was written nearly ninety years after the alleged death of Jesus and was based not on independent historical research but on information provided by Christians of the second century. In any case, even if one takes this passage as providing independent historical evidence, it would only provide evidence of Jesus' death, not his resurrection.

Other pagan writers such as Suetonius and Pliny the Younger provide no support of the Resurrection of Jesus since they make no mention of it. However, Thallus, in a work now lost but referred to by Africanus in the third century, is alleged to have said that Jesus' death was accompanied by an earthquake and an unusual darkness that he Thallus, according to Africanus, wrongly attributed to an eclipse of the sun. However, as was argued earlier, it is unclear when Thallus wrote his history or how reliable Africanus's account of Thallus is. Some scholars believe that Thallus wrote as late as the second century and consequently could have obtained his ideas from Christian opinion of his time.[21] Clearly then, Thallus cannot be used to support the Christian account of the Resurrection.

The Shroud of Turin has sometimes been used as evidence for the Resurrection. First surfacing in the Middle Ages, this strip of cloth has an impression of the back and the front of a naked man on it and has been claimed by its advocates to be Jesus' burial shroud. The face, hands, side, and feet of the impression supposedly shows evidence of blood stains that advocates claim are consistent with the story of the Crucifixion. Advocates of the shroud's authenticity have argued that the shroud supports the Resurrection since if Jesus had not been resurrected, his decaying body would have destroyed the impression and finally the cloth.[22]

However, recent radiocarbon dating of the shroud indicates that it does not date from the first century but from the Middle Ages.[23] This evidence should not come as a surprise to those who have studied its history and the arguments against its authenticity, because there was excellent reason to suppose that the shroud was a forgery prior to its radiocarbon dating.[24] Beside the finding of Walter McCrone, an analytic chemist, that the "blood" was made of artist's pigments, the different accounts of Jesus' burial in the Gospels (for example, the account of John (19:40) suggesting that Jesus was washed and anointed as was the burial custom of the Jews) are difficult to reconcile with the claim that the shroud showed blood stains.

Habermas's Defense of the Resurrection

Perhaps the most sophisticated defense of the Resurrection to date has been produced by Gary Habermas.[25] Since there is good reason to suppose that if this defense fails, then other less sophisticated defenses not examined here will also, let us see examine Habermas's defense of the Resurrection in his debate with Antony Flew.

Habermas first attacks the view that miracles are a priori impossible, a view that he seems to attribute to both David Hume and Antony Flew.[26] It is doubtful that either Hume[27] or Flew[28] maintained this but, in any case, this is not the position taken here. I have argued that in terms of our background evidence miracles are unlikely and that in order to overcome the prior improbability of a miracle occurring the evidence must be very strong. Habermas fails to present any argument to show that there is no prior improbability.

Habermas also maintains that philosophical objections against miracles wrongly suppose that the laws of nature are all deterministic. Maintaining that many of the laws of modern science are statistical, he argues that modern science does not exclude miracles.[29] However, no such assumption about the laws of nature is made here. I admit that some events could occur without any cause. However, the implications of indeterminism for the Resurrection debate seem to have escaped

Habermas's notice. If the laws of nature are statistical, then Jesus' being restored to life could have no cause at all, that is, neither a natural nor supernatural one. The hypothesis that Jesus' being restored to life is uncaused in fact *competes* with the hypothesis that Jesus' being restored to life is a miracle. This hypothesis can hardly used to support the case for the miraculous nature of the Resurrection.[30]

Finally, Habermas maintains that the critic "ignores the strong historical evidence for the Resurrection of Jesus."[31] Let us examine what Habermas takes this to be, keeping in mind the factors considered above that would tend to undermine the claim that the historical evidence is strong.

Habermas argues that "practically all critical scholars who deal with this topic today" agree that certain facts are known. Indeed, he lists eleven "events . . . considered to be knowable history by virtually all scholars" and "a twelfth event . . . considered to be knowable history by many scholars."[32] Among the events that are listed as agreed to by virtually all critical scholars are Jesus' death by crucifixion, his burial, and the disciples' experiences of what they believed were literal appearances of the risen Jesus. The event that Habermas claims is considered knowable by many scholars is the discovery of the empty tomb.

But is there the degree of agreement among scholars that Habermas claims? That he has at least exaggerated this agreement can be inferred from the following. W. Trilling argues that "not a single date of [Jesus'] life" can be established with certainty,[33] and J. Kahl maintains that the only thing that is known about him is that he "existed at a date and place which can be established approximately."[34] Other scholars argue that the quest for the historical Jesus is hopeless.[35] Ian Wilson argues that, concerning the Resurrection, "Ultimately, we must concede that on the basis of the available evidence, knowledge of exactly what happened is beyond us."[36] H. Conzelman finds that the Passion narratives are shaped by the evangelists' own theological convictions, that they are the results of "intensive theological interpretation,"[37] and that they establish only the bare fact that Jesus was crucified: "Everything else about the sequence of events is contestable." C. F. Evans argues that "almost all the main factors" in the Passion story "have become problematic."[38] Dieter Georgi maintains that since Paul's writing omits any mention of an empty tomb this raises the possibility that Jesus' body was still inside. He also suggests that the empty tomb stories may have been added to the Gospels after the sack of Jerusalem in A.D. 70 at which time the tomb may have been empty.[39] We have already seen that scholars such as Marxsen, Fuller, Kümmel, and Anderson disagree over whether the empty tomb stories entered the Christian tradition early or late.

However, even if Habermas were correct about the agreement of scholars this would hardly be conclusive. One would have to examine the reasons for their agreement. Habermas suggests ten items of evidence that he maintains support the truth of the Resurrection, among them:

1. the empty tomb
2. the eyewitness experiences of the disciples of the postresurrection appearances of Jesus
3. the early proclamation of the Resurrection by the eyewitnesses
4. the transformation of eyewitnesses into people who were willing to die for their conviction
5. the Jewish leaders could not disprove the disciples' message even though they had the power and motivation to do so
6. the conversion of two skeptics, Paul and James, by the appearances of Jesus

Let us consider these items of evidence.

1. It is difficult to take seriously the alleged fact of the empty tomb given: the inconsistencies in the stories, the lack of contemporary eyewitnesses, the unclarity of who exactly the eyewitnesses were, the lack of knowledge of the reliability of the eyewitnesses, the failure of early Christian writers to mention the empty tomb, the failure of the empty tomb story to be confirmed in Jewish or pagan sources. It is significant that Habermas does not even consider the problem of the failure to confirm the empty tomb story by independent sources.

2. As we have seen, the so-called eyewitness reports of the disciples were not, with the exception of Paul's, *contemporary* but were at least second or third hand. The nature of Paul's experience is unclear; it may not even have been of an embodied Jesus. Further, we have no evidence to suppose that the eyewitnesses, including Paul, were reliable or that the people that reported them were. We know from contemporary psychological studies of eyewitnesses that they are often unreliable and see what they want to see. Surely, eyewitnesses of nearly two thousand years ago would be no different.

Furthermore, the account of the appearances differ from Gospel to Gospel and some of the appearances reported by Paul are not confirmed by the Gospel stories. Moreover, none of these stories is confirmed by Jewish and pagan sources. For example, Paul reports that after his resurrection Jesus appeared "to more than five hundred brethren at one time" (1 Cor. 15:6). If such an event really happened, it would have been the strongest evidence that Christians had for their belief in the Resurrection. Surely they would have used it whenever they could. Furthermore, the fact that five hundred people reported seeing a resurrected man would surely have attracted wide attention in the region and would have come to the notice of the authorities and historians who were writing at the time. Yet this most remarkable phenomenon is neither mentioned in any other part of the New Testament nor confirmed by either Jewish or pagan sources. One must conclude that it is extremely unlikely that this incident really occurred, yet Paul mentions it in the same breath and with the same confidence that he mentions Jesus' postresurrection appearances to Cephas, to the twelve, and to himself. Surely this does not inspire confidence in Paul as a reliable source.

When the failure to confirm the story of the five hundred is brought up by Flew in the Habermas–Flew debate Habermas responds in the following way:

> The Gospel of Matthew does say that Jesus appeared on a hillside. More may have been there than just the eleven disciples. Besides, I never mentioned the five hundred. I don't think I brought them up once. I still want to base the case on the eleven disciples who claimed they saw the risen Jesus.[40]

Surely if Matthew believed that Jesus appeared on the hillside to over five hundred people, he would have said so. Such evidence would have been much more impressive than Jesus appearing to his own disciples. Furthermore, it is likely that if this amazing incident was true, news of it would have spread far and wide. One can understand, of course, why Habermas does not want to bring up the story of the five hundred. Failure to independently confirm Paul's most easily confirmable claim concerning Jesus' postresurrection appearances indirectly casts doubt on Paul as a reliable source. Yet Habermas relies on Paul.

3. Habermas is correct that the Resurrection was proclaimed by the early Christians. But what he fails to note is that the trial before Pilate, Jesus' agony on the cross, the empty tomb, and all of the other details of the Passion story were not proclaimed by early Christians

and only came to be so around end of the first century. This should count against the accuracy of the story.

4. It is difficult to understand why Habermas thinks that the fact that eyewitnesses to Jesus' postresurrection appearances were transformed into people who were willing to die for their conviction should be given special evidential weight. People who have *not* claimed to be eyewitnesses to Jesus' appearances have also been transformed into people who were willing to die for their Christian beliefs. In addition, Christian heretics have been willing to die for their beliefs. Let us not forget either that Muslims, Mormons, followers of James Jones, kamikaze pilots, and many others have been willing to die for what they believed. Surely many of these people were transformed by previous experiences and became martyrs because of their experiences. The fact that people are willing to die for their beliefs can show many things: strength of character, extreme devotion, and even fanaticism. But it is hard to see that it indicates that what is believed is true or even that the evidential bases of the beliefs should be taken seriously.

5. Habermas maintains that the fact that the Jewish leaders could not disprove the disciples' message even though they had the power and motivation to do so should be evidence for the truth of the Resurrection. Now Jewish historians of the time, such as Josephus, do not even mention the Resurrection except in the clearly forged passage known as the Testimonium Flavianum. This hardly suggests that Jewish leaders were actively engaged in attempting to refute the Resurrection story but failing in their efforts. Moreover, as we have seen, many scholars believe that Talmudic discussion of the Resurrection was a second century reaction to the then current Christian doctrine. By that time—over seventy years after the Crucifixion—it is difficult to see how Jewish leaders could have had the power to disprove the Resurrection stories. Eyewitnesses were presumably unavailable. In what exactly would a disproof consist? The *Tol'doth Jeshu* does raise skeptical questions and proposes an alternative account. It is unclear what else Jewish critics could have done at that moment.

6. Habermas argues that the conversion of two skeptics, Paul and James, by the postresurrection appearances of Jesus should be given special evidential significance. However, the New Testament does not say directly that James was a skeptic. In John 7:5 we are told that even Jesus' brothers did not believe in him. In Galatians 1:19 James is spoken of as "the Lord's Brother." However, Paul tells us (1 Cor. 15:7) that James was an eyewitness to a postresurrection appear-

ance of Jesus. Finally, in Acts James is identified as the leader of the Christian community in Jerusalem. Putting these passages together some scholars have assumed that Jesus' brother, James, who did not believe in him in his life, was converted by experiencing a postresurrection appearance of Jesus. Whether all of these Jameses are identical is not completely clear but even if they are, it is dubious that "James the Lord's Brother" means "James, Jesus' brother."[41] So perhaps we should set aside James's testimony as evidence of the conversion of a skeptic.

This leaves Paul's testimony. However, not only do we not know if his own account of his conversion is accurate, the failure to confirm Paul's claims about Jesus' appearance to the five hundred makes one suspicious of his other claims where confirmation is not so likely. Further, even if we had good reason to suppose that Paul's conversion happened as he described it, it is unclear that his former opposition to Christianity should be given much weight. If we count Paul's conversion as being evidence for the truth of the Resurrection, should we not count Muhammad's conversion to Islam from polytheism as being evidence for the truth of the claim that Jesus was not resurrected? (Muslims reject Jesus' resurrection.) But then, conversions can hardly be as important as evidence as Habermas supposes. The evidential value of Paul's conversion and Muhammad's conversion for the truth of the Resurrection tend to cancel each other out.

Habermas maintains that the evidence he cites makes what he calls naturalistic theories extremely unlikely. For example, he maintains that the disciples' experiences of the postresurrection appearances of Jesus disprove the "hallucination theory" since "such phenomena are not collective or contagious, being observed by one person alone and taking place at a wide variety of times and places."[42] Furthermore, Habermas argues that since the original teaching concerning the Resurrection is based on real eyewitnesses, the Resurrection is not based on legend. The Resurrection cannot be based on fraud, according to Habermas, since the disciples' transformation shows that they really believed that Jesus rose from the dead, and it would be unlikely that people who were liars would become martyrs.

Habermas's dismissal of naturalistic theories seems too quick. Is it really true that there is no such thing as mass hallucination? In fact, psychologists have studied a closely related phenomenon known as collective delusion or mass hysteria. In this phenomenon "a significant part of the population of an area, which can be as small as a single building or as large as a nation, becomes convinced that some strange event is taking place for which there is no immediately obvious explanation. . . . Sometimes paranormal . . . causes are proposed and accepted."[43]

There have been many collective delusions down through history.[44] For example, starting in 1969 and lasting for about ten years there were many reports of the death and mutilation of cattle in the western part of the United States. It was thought that these events could not be due to natural causes since there were alleged to be surgically sharp incisions in strange parts of the bodies of the cattle, for example, their eyes, testicles, and tongues. Various hypotheses were suggested to explain the cattle mutilations including UFOs and satanic cults. However, in 1979 the Justice Department funded an investigation by the former FBI agent K. Rommel. His report[45] and a book by D. Kagan and I. Summer[46] showed that the cattle were dying from natural causes and that their bodies were being attacked by scavengers who found it difficult to chew through the tough hides and consequently attacked the soft parts of the body. In fact, the incisions made by the scavengers were not sharp when compared to actual cuts made by a knife. They simply looked sharper than they were when the wounds were stretched as the body decomposed and gas built up.

In this case the media played an important role in fostering the hysteria promoted by sensational speculations. A natural phenomenon was misinterpreted by many people and occult causes were postulated to account for the "evidence." The scope of this misinterpretation spread as the wild speculation about the explanation of the "evidence" became known. Surely, it is not beyond the realm of possibility that a natural phenomenon, for example, a person who looked like Jesus, could have triggered a collective delusion among Jesus' followers that was fed by wild rumors and speculation. It should be noted that in some of the postresurrection stories Jesus is not immediately recognized by his disciples and those who knew him well. For example, in John 20:15 Mary Magdalene mistakes Jesus for the gardener.

Furthermore, we know from psychiatric literature that there is an unusual type of psychosis called *folie à deux*. It is a "communicated form of mental disorder" in which "one of two intimately associated people develops certain mental symptoms, particularly delusions, which are communicated to and accepted by the second person."[47] There seems to be no a priori reason why a similar phenomenon could not happen among a group of people. It might well have been the case that Jesus' disciples were so intimately related that the hallucinations and delusions of one could have been communicated to the others. There is reason to suppose that Mary Magdalene had mental problems.[48] It could be significant that she was the first person after Jesus' Resurrection to claim to see him.

We also know from the history of witchcraft that people who are thought to be bewitched had hallucinations that caused those around them to have hallucinations also. For example, Cotton Mather told the story of Mercy Short, a seventeen-year-old Boston servant girl who, in 1692, was cursed by Sarah Good, "a hag."[49] Thinking herself bewitched Mercy started to exhibit various symptoms, including hallucinations of groups of specters. Mather, who treated her with prayers, described in detail not only Mercy's symptoms but the experiences of those near her. In one incident she had an experience of a group of specters dancing on Christmas Day (which was considered by the Puritans to be a pagan festival). Those "attending her most plainly heard and felt a dance, as of bare footed people upon the floor, whereof they are ready to make oath before any lawful authority."[50] Moreover, sometimes people observing Mercy's bewitchment not only heard the spectral dance but "had their arms cruelly scratched and pins thrust into their flesh by. . . . Fiends while they were molesting Mercy Short."[51] Several persons claimed that they actually laid "their hands upon these Fiends."[52] Furthermore, when on another occasion Mercy had a hallucination of spectral fire Mather reported that "we saw not the flames, but once the room smelled of brimstone."[53]

Another case treated and described by Mather was that of Margaret Rule. Margaret, like Mercy, had hallucinations of specters as well as other symptoms of the bewitched. Mather reported that people who observed her having an experience of specters forcing scalding brimstone down her throat thought that they smelled brimstone. "Scores of witnesses" were prepared to testify that the whole house smelled "so hot of brimstone we were scarce able to endure it." On one occasion "the standers by plainly saw something of that odd liquor itself on the outside of her neck." The witnesses also claimed to see spectral powder thrown into Margaret's eyes and "one time some of this powder was fallen actually visible upon her cheek, from whence the people in the room wiped it with their handkerchiefs."[54]

It seems clear that in the context of seventeenth-century New England, where witches and demons were taken for granted, one person's hallucination somehow triggered visual, auditory, tactile, and olfactory hallucinations in those nearby. Surely, it is not beyond the realm of psychological possibility, as Habermas seems to assume it is, that in first-century Palestine, among the unsophisticated people who believed in the divinity of Jesus, one disciple's hallucination of Jesus could have triggered corresponding hallucinations in the others. The context, background, and psychological state of the disciples were no less congenial to this sort of collective hallucination than those of the people in Salem or in Boston about three hundred years ago.

What about the fraud theory? Habermas seems to suppose that if there was a fraud it was perpetrated by means of a conspiracy of Jesus' disciples. He argues that since the disciples were willing to become martyrs it is highly unlikely that they were involved in one. But a fraud could have been perpetrated by a group or a person who was not identical with the disciples or by some person who was not a disciple. We know from UFO research and from investigation of the paranormal that people who perpetrate a fraud are not always the ones who report it. Could not some group or person have perpetrated a fraud *on* the disciples making them suppose that they had seen Jesus after his death? In this case the martyrdom of the disciples would not have been unexpected.

Of course, this theory does not answer all the remaining questions. How did the people involved in the fraud perpetrate it? By using a person who looked and acted like Jesus? By hypnosis? Why was the fraud perpetrated? Just for the fun of it? For some political motive? To show how gullible the disciples were? However, that one cannot answer these questions does not make the fraud theory less likely than the Resurrection story. It is well to remember that the traditional Resurrection story raises questions that it does not answer.

Even if Habermas's dismissal of naturalistic theories is accepted, his refutation of them presumes that we know certain facts that we do not. As Flew reiterates in his debate with Habermas, the evidence for the postresurrection appearances of Jesus is simply not good enough to know which theory one should believe.[55] For example, Habermas's attempted refutation of the hallucination theory assumes that there were many postresurrection appearances of Jesus. However, the evidence for this is not as good as Habermas supposes. His criticism of the legend theory seems to assume that early Christians believed that Jesus was recently crucified and that other details of the traditional Passion story were true. However, there is reason to suppose that the dating of Jesus' Resurrection in the reign of Pilate and the other details of the story came to be accepted by the Christian community only at the end of the first century and that early Christians did not accept these doctrines. However, this is precisely what one would expect if the Passion story was a legend that grew and developed over time. Habermas's rejection of the fraud theory assumes that all of the *original* disciples were martyrs and were willing to die for their beliefs. There is little independent confirmation of this. To be sure, there is independent reason to suppose that *later* Christians were willing to die for their faith. But these are not the Christians that Habermas is talking about.

The last piece of evidence for the Resurrection cited by Habermas is the Shroud of Turin. Although he argues that scientific evidence can change and "nothing in the Christian faith depends on the shroud"[56] he maintains that the evidence at the time of his writing (around 1985) indicates that the shroud is authentic. Recent radiocarbon dating makes it clear that the shroud provides *no* support for the Resurrection. But Habermas was not justified in any case in supposing that in 1985 the evidence supported the shroud's authenticity. Quoting with approval "an agnostic scientific critic of the shroud"[57] who maintained in *The Skeptical Inquirer*, "I agree . . . on all of this. If the shroud is authentic, the image is that of Jesus,"[58] Habermas fails to mention that this agnostic scientific critic brought up many objections to the authenticity of the shroud, including objections to the arguments found in Habermas and Stevenson's book on the subject.[59] Habermas also fails to note that other authors in the same issue of *The Skeptical Inquirer* did so as well. Thus, Walter McCrone adduces evidence indicating that the "blood stains" on the shroud were made of artists' paint pigments.[60] Habermas confidently endorses a report that stated that no paint pigment, paint, dye, or stain had been found on the shroud. Indeed, Habermas leads us to believe that the consensus of scientific opinion at the time was that the shroud was authentic. This was simply not so. His failure to acknowledge negative evidence hardly adds to the credibility of his other arguments for the truth of the Resurrection.

Conclusion

I conclude that the available evidence should lead a rational person to disbelieve the claim that Jesus was resurrected from the dead around A.D. 30. Consequently, there are good reasons to reject one of fundamental doctrines of Orthodox Christianity. I further conclude that the recent attempt by Habermas to defend the Resurrection is unsuccessful.

Even if there were good grounds to suppose that the Resurrection occurred, would this establish that the Christian God exists? Would it show that Jesus was the Son of God? In order to answer these questions we must consider the more general question of what is the relation between belief in miracles and belief in God. Could one consistently believe that the Resurrection occurred and was a miracle and advocate atheism? This all depends on what one means by "atheism." Let us understand atheism in a narrow sense to be the belief that there is no theistic God, that there is no being that is all-knowing, all-powerful, and all-good; and atheism in the broad sense to be the belief that there is no god or gods. [61] Certainly it would be logically possible for miracles to occur if atheism in the narrow sense was true. They could be brought about by a supernatural being who was not God. Thus, it would be perfectly consistent for an atheist in the narrow sense to believe that Jesus was restored to life.

But could miracles occur if atheism in the broad sense is true? They could so long as "god" is not coextensive with "supernatural being." Recall that atheism in the broad sense is the disbelief in a god or gods. But could there be supernatural beings that were not gods? It is unclear what "god" means and I will make no attempt to explicate this notion here. However, it is not implausible to suppose that although having supernatural powers is a necessary condition for being a god it is not a sufficient condition. If this is correct, then disbelief in a god or gods is compatible with belief in supernatural beings. If there could be such nongod-like supernatural beings, then these beings by definition would have supernatural powers and could work miracles. So it is not completely clear that even atheism in the broad sense is incompatible with miracles. Thus, it does not seem completely out of the question for an atheist in the broad sense to believe that Jesus was resurrected. He or she could believe that Jesus was restored to life by the exercise of the powers of some supernatural being who was not a god.

It should also be clear from the above considerations that if miracles occurred, this would not entail that the Christian God exists. The miracles could be the result of another god or perhaps of a supernatural being that is not a god. Thus, if the resurrection of Jesus did occur and was a miracle, this would not establish the existence of a theistic God or that Jesus was his Son. Moreover, the existence of a miracle such as the Resurrection would not make the existence of the theistic God more likely than not. This is because there is no good reason to suppose that miracles would be less likely on some rival hypotheses than on Christian theism.

What sort of evidence would make it probable that God, rather than some other supernatural being, was the cause of the Resurrection? It has been argued that at the very least one would have to show that the Resurrection fitted into a larger pattern of events that revealed God's purposes.[62] This pattern would perhaps give us reason to suppose that God was the cause of the Resurrection. But what sort of pattern would this be? Presumably it would involve *other* miraculous events that God brought about. If one had evidence of $Miracle_1$, $Miracle_2$, $Miracle_3$, and so on, *and* evidence of the Resurrection, one might then be able to discern a pattern and infer from it a divine purpose that would indicate that God was behind the Resurrection.

However, the implication of this is damaging to Christianity. The historical reliability of reports of the other miraculous events reported in the Scriptures is no better and is often worse than the evidence for the Resurrection. In these accounts, as in the account of the Resurrection, there are inconsistencies, lack of eyewitness testimony, second- and thirdhand reporting, failure of independent confirmation, and questions about the reliability of the witnesses. For example, as we shall see in Chapter 4, the evidence for the Virgin Birth is just as problematic as that for the Resurrection. There is then a serious obstacle in concluding that God was the cause of the Resurrection even if one could establish that Jesus was restored to life and that this was a miracle.

Let us suppose that theism is true. Could we expect miracles to occur? We could not. If theism is true, then miracles would be *possible* since there would be a supernatural being who *could* bring them about. But it does not follow that miracles would be more likely than not. Indeed, God might have good reason never to use miracles to achieve his purposes. On the other hand, if certain other rival hypotheses were true, then the existence of miracles would be certain. For example, consider a class of very powerful but finite miracle-working supernatural beings whom we will call Finite Miracle Workers, or the FMW for short. If any member of FMW exists, then the existence of miracles would be certain. Thus, if a theistic God exists, then it does not follow that we should expect the Resurrection. God may have good reasons not to work miracles including the Resurrection. However, one or more members of FMW could have overriding reasons for resurrecting Jesus. Let us call this subset of beings the Resurrecting Finite Miracle Workers, or the RFMW for short. If any member of the RFMW exists, then the Resurrection of Jesus would be certain.

However, let us suppose that the theistic God exists and he has as part of his purpose the salvation of the world by means of his Incarnation, that is by becoming a human being named Jesus who lived at the beginning of the first century, and that he planned to carry out his purpose by the use of miracles. Would the Resurrection be likely then? It is unclear that it would. Today one is so used to the dramatic story of Jesus' birth, ministry, betrayal, trial, crucifixion, and resurrection that no alternative stories seem possible given God's purpose of salvation. But surely this is an illusion. Since God is all-powerful there are an indefinite number of ways that he could have carried out his purpose. For example, instead of dying on the cross, Jesus could have become transformed into an obviously heavenly being. Instead of Matthew 27:49 reading "And Jesus cried again with a loud voice and yielded up his spirit," it could read "And the earth shook and lighting flashed and angels appeared proclaiming his glory and Jesus descended from the cross with his wounds healed and arrayed in a shining garment and his head bathed in a heavenly light."

In Mithraism, a religion of the ancient world, the god Mithras is born in human form and ascends to Heaven. Scholars have noted many remarkable similarities between Mithraism and Christianity besides this but it is important to note that Mithras is *not* killed before he ascends. Nevertheless, the historical evidence indicates that this religion was quite as capable of gaining converts as Christianity. Indeed, for several centuries it seemed as likely as Christianity to gain supremacy in the Roman world.[63] The Christian God could have chosen to save the world in a way similar to that portrayed in Mithraism, that is, in a way that did not involve the death of Jesus. Although this change in the Gospel story would have brought further changes in the story of the Resurrection, it is not clear that this scenario and these further changes would have been any less effective in fulfilling God's purpose.

But even if God elected to have Jesus die on the cross, it is unclear why it was necessary for him to resurrect Jesus from the dead. As I suggested above, to be resurrected entails being restored to life after physical death and this involves some form of a body. But could not Jesus have been restored to life in some nonbodily form? And if so, why would this have been less effective in fulfilling God's purpose? That Jesus was the Son of God surely could have been known without the Resurrection, and Jesus' followers would not necessarily have been more skeptical or less devoted without it. It is well to remember that any objection to alternative scenarios must take into account that God is all-powerful and could have operated in alternative and equally effective ways.

Thus, even if the resurrection of Jesus was justified by the evidence, it would not support the belief that the Christian God exists and that Jesus is the Son of God.

NOTES

1. The Athanasian Creed does not say that Jesus was crucified under Pilate but only that he "suffered for our salvation, descended into Hades, rose again of the third day."

2. Hugh Anderson, *Jesus and Christian Origins* (New York: Oxford University Press, 1964), pp. 186–87.

3. Terry Miethe in *Did Jesus Rise from the Dead? The Resurrection Debate, Gary Habermas, and Antony G. N. Flew*, ed. Terry Miethe (San Francisco: Harper and Row, 1987), p. xi.

4. Elsewhere I have argued that a miracle is an event brought about by the exercise of a supernatural power and have characterized a supernatural power as one that is markedly superior to those powers possessed by mere human beings and is possessed by supernatural beings, for example, gods, angels, Superman, and devils. It should be noted that in this conception of miracle, a miracle need not be an unrepeatable event. There in fact could be many miracles of the same type, for example, many cases of people being restored to life by the exercise of supernatural power. Furthermore, it need not be in violation of a law of nature: A supernatural being's powers may be governed by laws of nature in a broad sense of "nature" that includes all entities (supernatural and natural) and their activities (determined by natural and supernatural powers). The only things not included in nature in this sense are entities that are incapable of any casual interaction, for example, numbers or sets. So a miracle, on this view, is not an event that cannot be explained by laws of nature but one that cannot be explained by laws of nature that govern mere human beings and other nonsupernatural entities. Thus, when I speak of laws of nature in what follows I should be understood to be speaking of laws

of nature in the narrow sense, that is, laws that govern nonsupernatural entities. See Michael Martin, *Atheism: A Philosophical Justification* (Philadelphia: Temple University Press, 1990), chap. 7.

5. John B. Gill, "Miracles with Method," *Sophia* 16 (1977): 19–26, has argued that miracle claims are compatible with scientific progress since such claims may be only tentatively held and are compatible with reconsidering the claim in the light of new evidence. Although it may well be true that such open-mindedness is logically compatible with miracle claims, one wonders if it in fact works this way. Historically it seems clear that belief in miracles has been detrimental to scientific progress and given the psychology of the many typical believers it is likely to remain so. Moreover, even if such claims are put forth tentatively, the question is whether they are justified in the light of the rapid increases in knowledge in certain fields, for example, medical science.

6. See James Randi, " 'Be Healed in the Name of God!' An Exposé of the Reverend W. V. Grant," *Free Inquiry* 6 (Spring 1986): 8–19. See also James Randi, *The Faith Healers* (Buffalo, N.Y.: Prometheus, 1987).

7. See, for example, A. Daniel Yarmey, *The Psychology of Eyewitness Testimony* (New York: Free Press, 1979).

8. Cf. James A. Keller, "Contemporary Christian Doubts About the Resurrection," *Faith and Philosophy* 5 (1988): 41.

9. Willi Marxsen, *The Resurrection of Jesus of Nazareth* (Philadelphia: Fortress Press, 1970), p. 77.

10. Reginald Horace Fuller, *The Formation of the Resurrection Narratives* (New York: Macmillan, 1971), pp. 172–73.

11. I am indebted here to the analysis of the Resurrection given by Paul Kurtz, *The Transcendental Temptation* (Buffalo, N.Y.: Prometheus, 1986), pp. 153–60.

12. I will not consider here the question whether the evidence from the Gospel supports the view that Jesus rose on the *third* day. For an argument that it does not, see W. S. Ross ["Saladin"], "Did Jesus Christ Rise from the Dead?" reprinted in Gordon Stein, *An Anthology of Atheism and Rationalism* (Buffalo, N.Y.: Prometheus, 1980), pp. 205–11. If Ross is correct, then this would call into question even further the reliability of the account.

13. Marxsen, *The Resurrection of Jesus of Nazareth*, p. 74.

14. Werner Georg Kümmel, *The Theology of the New Testament* (Nashville: Abingdon Press, 1973), pp. 98–99.

15. Anderson, *Jesus and Christian Origins*, pp. 192–95.

16. Fuller, *The Formation of the Resurrection Narrative*, pp. 52–57.

17. Marxsen, *The Resurrection of Jesus of Nazareth*, p. 161.

18. See Keller, "Contemporary Christian Doubts About the Resurrection," p. 58, n. 17.

19. G. A. Wells, *The Historical Evidence for Jesus* (Buffalo, N.Y.: Prometheus, 1982), chap. 7.

20. Quoted in Ronald Charles Tanguay, *The Historicity of Jesus: A Survey of the Evidence for the Historical Jesus and the Mythical Nature of Christ* (Privately published, 1988), p. 32.

21. See Wells, *Did Jesus Exist?* pp. 12–13; Tanguay, *The Historicity of Jesus*, pp. 59–61.

22. See, for example, D. E. Nineham, *Explorations in Theology*, vol. I (London, 1970), p. 76. Cited by Wells in *The Historical Evidence for Jesus*, p. 186.

23. Joe Nickell, "Unshrouding the Shroud," *Free Inquiry* 9 (Winter 1988/89): 51–52.

24. See, for example, Wells, *The Historical Evidence for Jesus*, chap. 9; Joe Nickell, "The Shroud of Turin—Solved," *Humanist* 38 (1978): 30–32; Marvin M. Mueller, "The Shroud of Turin: A Critical Appraisal," *The Skeptical Inquirer* 6 (Spring 1982): 15–34; Walter McCrone, "The Shroud Image Is the Work of an Artist," *The Skeptical Inquirer* 6 (Spring 1982): 35–36; Steven D. Schafersman, "Science, the Public and the Shroud of Turin," *The Skeptical Inquirer* 6 (Spring 1982): 37–56; Joe Nickell, "Update on the Shroud of Turin," *Free Inquiry* 5 (Spring 1985): 10–11.

25. See Gary Habermas and Antony G. N. Flew, *Did Jesus Rise from the Dead?* Gary Habermas, *The Resurrection of Jesus: An Apologetic* (Grand Rapids, Mich.: Baker Book House, 1980).

26. Habermas, "Affirmative Statement," *Did Jesus Rise from the Dead?* pp. 16–17.

27. See Martin, *Atheism: A Philosophical Justification*, chap. 7.

28. See Flew, "Rebuttal," *Did Jesus Rise from the Dead?* p. 34.

29. Habermas, "Affirmative Statement," *Did Jesus Rise from the Dead?* p. 18.

30. Habermas also objects to the assumption made by skeptics such as Flew that miracles are nonrepeatable (ibid). However, no such assumption is made here.

31. Ibid., p. 19.

32. Ibid.

33. W. Trilling, *Fragen zur Geschichtlichkeit Jesu*, 3d ed. (Düsseldorf, 1969), p. 64. Cited by Wells in *Did Jesus Exist?* p. 1.

34. J. Kahl, *The Misery of Christianity*, trans. N. D. Smith (New York: Penguin Books, 1971), p. 103. Cited by Wells in *Did Jesus Exist?* p. 2.

35. See, for example, the surveys by F. G. Dowing, *The Church and Jesus* (London: 1968); and H. McArthur, ed., *In Search of the Historical Jesus* (London: 1970). Cited by Wells in *Did Jesus Exist?* p. 1.

36. Ian Wilson, *Jesus: The Evidence* (San Francisco: Harper and Row, 1984), p. 142.

37. H. Conzelmann, "Historie und Theologie in den synoptischen

Passionsberichten," in *Zur Bedeutung Todes Jesu* (Gütersloh, 1967), pp. 37–38. Cited in Wells, *The Historical Evidence for Jesus*, p. 15.

38. C. F. Evans, *Explorations in Theology* (London, 1977), vol. 2, p. 28. Cited in Wells, *The Historical Evidence for Jesus*, p. 15.

39. Cited in Wilson, *Jesus: The Evidence*, p. 142.

40. Habermas, "Head to Head: Habermas–Flew," *Did Jesus Rise from the Dead?* p. 53.

41. Wells, *Did Jesus Exist?* pp. 21–22; Wells, *The Historical Evidence for Jesus*, pp. 167–74.

42. Habermas, "Affirmative Statement," *Did Jesus Rise from the Dead?* pp. 25–26.

43. Terrance Hines, *Pseudoscience and the Paranormal* (Buffalo, N.Y.: Prometheus, 1988), pp. 278–79.

44. See Charles Mackay, *Extraordinary Popular Delusions and the Madness of Crowds* (New York: Bonanza Books, 1980).

45. K. Rommel, *Operation Cattle Mutilation* (Albuquerque, N.M.: District Attorney, First Judicial District, State of New Mexico, 1980).

46. D. Kagan and I. Summer, *Mute Evidence* (New York: Bantam Books, 1983).

47. Lester Grinspoon and Alan D. Persky, "Psychiatry and UFO Reports," *UFO—A Scientific Debate*, ed. Carl Sagan and Thornton Page (Ithaca, N.Y.: Cornell University Press, 1972), p. 238.

48. See Luke 8:2. Since mental disorders in biblical times were identified with demon possession, the fact that Mary Magdalene was possessed by demons suggests that she had some form of mental illness.

49. See Cotton Mather, *Another Brand Plucked Out of the Burning* in George Lincoln Burr, *Narratives of the Witchcraft Cases, 1648–1706* (New York: Charles Scribner's Sons, 1914), pp. 259–87. Mather's reports of Mary Short and Margaret Rule are quoted at length in Chadwick Hansen, *Witchcraft at Salem* (New York: George Braziller, 1969), pp. 172–83.

50. Hansen, *Witchcraft at Salem*, p. 173.

51. Ibid., p. 177.

52. Ibid.

53. Ibid., p. 176.

54. Ibid., p. 183.

55. See Flew, "Rebuttal" and "Head to Head: Habermas–Flew," *Did Jesus Rise from the Dead?*

56. Habermas, "Affirmative Statement," *Did Jesus Rise from the Dead?* p. 28.

57. Ibid., p. 27.

58. Schafersman, "Science, the Public and the Shroud of Turin," p. 27.

59. See Kenneth E. Stevenson and Gary R. Habermas, *Verdict on the*

Shroud: Evidence for the Death and Resurrection of Jesus (Ann Arbor, Mich.: Servant Books, 1981).

60. McCrone, "The Shroud Image Is the Work of an Artist," pp. 35–36.

61. In *Atheism: A Philosophical Justification*, I also distinguish between positive atheism, which is the disbelief in God or gods, and negative atheism, which is having no belief in God or gods. This further refinement does not seem relevant to the present discussion.

62. See Keller, "Contemporary Christian Doubts About the Resurrection," p. 51.

63. Royston Pike, *Encyclopaedia of Religion and Religions* (New York: Meridian Books, 1958), p. 258.

4

The Virgin Birth and the Second Coming

Being an Orthodox Christian involves much more than believing in the Resurrection. One of the basic assumptions of Orthodox Christianity is that Jesus was born of a virgin around the beginning of the first century. Thus, according to the Apostles' Creed, Jesus "was conceived by the Holy Ghost, born of the Virgin Mary," and, according to the Nicene Creed, he "was incarnate by the Holy Ghost of the Virgin Mary." The Second Coming is also an essential part of Orthodox Christian doctrine. All three creeds of Christendom say that Jesus ascended into Heaven and sat on the right hand of God and that he shall "come to judge the quick and the dead."

Are these two doctrines justified by the evidence? Let us begin with the Virgin Birth.

The Virgin Birth

THE STORY

According to Matthew, the news of the coming birth of Jesus is conveyed to Joseph in a dream:

> Now the birth of Jesus Christ took place in this way. When his mother Mary had been betrothed to Joseph, before they came together she was found to be with child of the Holy Spirit, and her husband Joseph, being a just man and unwilling to put her to shame, resolved to divorce her quietly. But as he considered this, behold, an angel of the Lord appeared to him in a dream, saying "Joseph, son of David, do not fear to take Mary your wife, for that which is conceived in her is of the Holy Spirit, she will bear a son, and you shall call his name Jesus, for he will save his people from their sins. All this took place to fulfil what the Lord had spoken by the prophet: "Behold, a virgin shall conceive and bear a

son, and his name shall be called Emmanuel" (which means, God with us). When Joseph woke from sleep, he did as the angel of the Lord commanded him; he took his wife, but knew her not until she had borne a son, and he called his name Jesus. (Matt. 1:18–25)[1]

According to Luke, Mary is told directly by the Angel Gabriel:

In the sixth month [of the pregnancy of Elizabeth] the angel Gabriel was sent from God to a city of Galilee named Nazareth, to a virgin betrothed to a man whose name was Joseph, of the house of David; and the virgin's name was Mary. And he came to her and said, "Hail, O favored one, the Lord is with you!" But she was greatly troubled at the saying and considered in her mind what sort of greeting this might be. And the angel said to her, "Do not be afraid, Mary, for you have found favor with God. And behold, you will conceive in your womb and bear a son, and you shall call his name Jesus.

He will be great, and will be called the Son of God of the Most High; and the Lord God will give to him the throne of his father David, and he will reign over the house of Jacob forever; and of his kingdom there will be no end."

And Mary said to the angel, "How can this be, since I have no husband?"

And the angel said to her, "The Holy Spirit will come upon you, and the power of the Most High will overshadow you; therefore, the child to be born will be called holy, the Son of God. And behold, your kins-women Elizabeth in her old age has also conceived a son; and this is the sixth month with her who was called barren. For with God nothing will be impossible."

And Mary said, "Behold I am the handmaid of the Lord; let it be to me according to your word." And the angel departed from her. (Luke 1:26–38)

What are we to make of these stories? Is there any good reason to take them as factual accounts of what happened? If these stories are true, do they supply strong evidence for other claims of Christianity, for example, that Jesus was the Son of God? We will approach these questions by first considering whether the biblical story of Jesus' birth is historically accurate. Then we will consider whether, if the historical evidence for the biblical story of Jesus' birth is weak, one should still believe in the Virgin Birth on faith. Finally, we consider what one can infer about other important Christian doctrines if this story is accepted as true.

THE EVIDENCE

What historical evidence is there for the Virgin Birth of Jesus? The claim of the Virgin Birth is only made in two of the four Gospels and these accounts differ.[2] As I have already noted, in Matthew the news of the coming birth of Jesus is conveyed to Joseph in a dream; in Luke, Mary is told directly by the Angel Gabriel. Furthermore, Matthew implies that when Jesus was born his parents lived in Bethlehem and they left when King Herod began a search to find and kill Jesus:

> Now when [the wise men] had departed, behold, an angel of the Lord appeared to Joseph in a dream and said, "Rise, take the child and his mother, and flee to Egypt and remain there till I tell you; for Herod is about to search for the child, to destroy him." And he rose and took the child and his mother by night, and departed to Egypt, and remained there until the death of Herod. This was to fulfil what the Lord had spoken by the prophet, "Out of Egypt have I called my son."
>
> Then Herod, when he saw that he had been tricked by the wise men, was in a furious rage, and he sent and killed all the male children in Bethlehem and in all that region who were two years old or under, according to the time which he had ascertained from the wise men. (Matt. 2:13–16)

However, in Luke Jesus' parents traveled from their home in Nazareth to Bethlehem for a Roman census:

> In those days a decree went out from Caesar Augustus that all the world should be enrolled. This was the first enrollment, when Quirinius was governor of Syria. And all went to be enrolled, each to his own city. And Joseph also went up from Galilee, from the city of Nazareth, to Judea, to the city of David, which is called Bethlehem, because he was of the house and lineage of David, to be enrolled with Mary, his betrothed, who was with child. And while they were there, the time came for her to be delivered. And she gave birth to her first-born son and wrapped him in swaddling cloths, laid him in a manger, because there was no place for them in the inn. (Luke 2:1–7)

It is perhaps possible to reconcile the two accounts of the announcement of the Virgin Birth by saying that Mary and Joseph were notified in different ways.[3] However, there is certainly no suggestion of this in the two Gospels; they lead one to believe that *only* one notification was made. Indeed, it seems likely that if there were two independent notifications of the Virgin Birth, this would have been mentioned in at least one of the two Gospels. In addition, because of the ways in which Mary and Joseph were notified—by an angel and through a dream—the announcements of the Virgin Birth are unsubstantiated by anyone other than Mary and Joseph. In the case of the story of Mary's visitation by the Angel Gabriel there could have been other witnesses but there were not; Mary was alone. In the case of Joseph's dream there could not have been other witnesses since only the dreamer is a "witness" to his or her own dream. Consequently, we have no independent confirmation of the witnesses to the two supernatural notifications.

Furthermore, there are serious historical problems involved in Luke's story of the circumstances surrounding the birth of Jesus even if we do not suppose it was a Virgin Birth.[4] We know from Josephus' *Antiquities* (18.1) that Quirinius held a census shortly after Judea had been annexed by Rome in either the year A.D. 6 or 7. But by this time Jesus had lived at least a decade. We know from Luke (1:5) and Matthew (2:1) that Jesus was born during the time of Herod. But since Herod died in 4 B.C. Jesus would have been at least ten years old by the time of the census. Apologists have attempted to argue that Quirinius could have held an earlier unrecorded census. But at the time of Jesus' birth Rome had no jurisdiction in this area and thus there could not have been a Roman census.

In addition to this problem Luke's story is implausible. Since Joseph's hometown was Bethlehem one would have expected that he would have stayed with friends or relatives. Why then was he forced to seek accommodations at an inn? Moreover, given what we know, it is surprising that Mary should travel with Joseph to Bethlehem for the census. There is no reason to suppose that she was from Bethlehem and she would not have been required by law to go there for the census. Furthermore, since she was not yet married to Joseph she would not be accompanying him as his wife. In addition, the journey was long and difficult and she was near term. Given these circumstances it seems unlikely that Mary would accompany Joseph to Bethlehem.

Matthew seems to contradict Luke about the circumstances surrounding the birth of Jesus and there seems to be no remotely plausible way of reconciling the two accounts. There is no mention of a census, inn, or manger in Matthew. Indeed, in Matthew it is implausible to suppose that Jesus was born in a manger since the wise men visited him in a "house" (2:11). This is hardly surprising since Matthew leads us to believe that Bethlehem was the permanent residence of Joseph and Mary.[5] Furthermore, like Matthew's story, Luke's account has its own historical improbabilities. The account of Herod's order to kill children under two years old is not supported by any independent historical source although far less important facts were dutifully recorded by historians of the day.[6]

In addition to all the apparent contradictions, historical inaccuracies, and implausibilities of Matthew and Luke, neither Mark nor John give *any* account of Jesus' birth.[7] On the supposition that the doctrine of the Virgin Birth was a widely held belief among the earlier Christians this is remarkable. In particular, why would Mark, the earliest written Gospel, fail to mention this doctrine if it was widely believed in the last part of the first century?[8] Indeed, why would John, according to many accounts the last Gospel, fail to mention it if it was widely held? Surely, the most likely explanation is that Mark and John did not consider the Virgin Birth to belong to a correct account of Jesus' life. This surely detracts from the plausibility of the Virgin Birth story.

The Virgin Birth of Jesus is not mentioned by Christian epistle writers such as Paul who wrote before Mark.[9] This again is extremely difficult to understand if such a view was embraced by the early Christian communities[10] and it further detracts from the plausibility of the Virgin Birth story. Nor is the Virgin Birth of Jesus mentioned by early Jewish or pagan sources. For example, Flavius Josephus fails to say anything about his Virgin Birth.[11] This is also surprising given the importance of this event to Christians and the miraculous nature of the event.

As we have seen, some biblical scholars argue that the earliest references to Jesus in rabbinical literature such as the Talmud occur no earlier than the second century. According to them, the rabbis of the second century had no independent knowledge of the historical assumptions of Christianity but were simply reacting to the then current Christian accounts.[12] However, if the Gospel account of the Virgin Birth is historically accurate, it is surprising that there is no mention of this in earlier rabbinical accounts.

Let us suppose, however, that historical scholarship suggesting that the earliest references to the Virgin Birth are found in the second-century rabbinical literature are mistaken and that this literature represents an independent historical source of information that is either contemporary with or earlier than the life of the Jesus of the Gospels.[13] On this assumption the Talmud tends to disconfirm the Gospel account of the Virgin Birth. Some passages in it maintain that

Jesus was born to an adulteress, a woman who turned away from her husband.[14] In the Tol'doth Jeshu, which collected early and late Talmudic stories about Jesus, one finds passages such as the following: "Miriam, however, was seduced by a handsome fellow named Joseph ben Pondera, who tricked her on a Sabbath eve."[15] Indeed, some scholars maintain that the Talmudic references to Jesus as Jeshu ben Pandira, Pandera, Pantira, or Panthera are intended as puns since the Greek word for panther is similar to the Greek word for virgin and this was the Jew's way of making fun of the Christian belief in the Virgin Birth.[16]

Pagan sources do not support the idea of the Virgin Birth or even in most cases the idea that early Christians believed in a Virgin Birth. Although Tacitus,[17] Suetonius,[18] and Pliny the Younger[19] have sometimes been cited as supporting the existence of the historicity of Jesus, they can provide no support for the Virgin Birth of Jesus. This is because, even when they mention Christ or Christians, they supply no details about the birth of Christ. Tacitus, for example, although he refers to Christ as being brought to punishment by Pilate gives no details about Christian beliefs about Christ's birth.[20] But even if Tacitus, Suetonius, and Pliny had supplied such details, this would hardly provide support for the truth of the belief.

With Celsus we have a different situation. In his anti-Christian work *The True Word*, written around A.D. 178, he argues that the Virgin Birth was fraudulent. According to this account Jesus was the son of a soldier, named Panthera, who learned magic in Egypt and invented the story of being born of a virgin.[21] Celsus' account agrees closely with stories of Jesus' birth found in the Talmudic literature which may have been its major source. If so, the same point can be made here as was earlier about the relevance of Talmudic stories to the historicity of Jesus. If they are simply reactions to current Christian views, they supply no independent confirmation of the Virgin Birth. But if they are based on older independent sources, they tend to disconfirm the Christian view.

THE COHERENCE OF THE VIRGIN BIRTH
WITH JESUS' GENEALOGY

So far we have argued that the stories of the Virgin Birth of Jesus in Matthew and Luke are unsupported by other Gospels, early Christian epistle writing, and Jewish and pagan sources. Further, the circumstances surrounding the birth as related by Matthew and Luke seem to contradict one another and are based on historical inaccuracies and implausibilities. In addition, the stories of the announcement of the Virgin Birth as told by Matthew and Luke not only differ in fundamental ways but report experiences of people that are not substantiated by independent witnesses.

Additionally, the Virgin Birth is inconsistent with another doctrine of the Gospels: that Jesus is the Messiah. According to Jewish tradition the Messiah was to be born in Bethlehem and had to be a descendent of King David. (Indeed, the whole point of supposing that Jesus was born in Bethlehem is that this was the city of David.) In Luke it is made clear that Joseph is of the house of David and Jesus is a descendent.

It is hardly surprising, then, that both Matthew and Luke attempt to trace the genealogy of Jesus back to David. What is surprising is that their genealogies are very different and cannot both be correct. For example, Matthew says that there are twenty-eight generations between Jesus and David (Matt. 1:17) while Luke lists no fewer than forty-one for the same period that is represented by Matthew's twenty-eight (Lk. 3:23–32).[22] Luke says that the father of Joseph is Heli (Luke 3:23) but Matthew maintains that his father is Jacob (Matt. 1:16).

Although various attempts[23] have been made to reconcile the contradiction between the two genealogies, they seem implausible.[24] The main contradiction has yet to be noted however. If Jesus is born of a virgin, then his biological father cannot be Joseph and he cannot be descended from the house of David. Thus, Jesus cannot be the Messiah according to Jewish tradition. Yet, according to the Gospels, he is the Messiah.

It is likely that this obvious contradiction disturbed later copyists who made alternations in the text. Thus, Charles Guignebert argues:

> The original reading of the genealogy of Matthew undoubtedly concluded with the attribution to Joseph of the *procreation* of Jesus. Our certainty of this is confirmed by a text of Epiphanius, which informs us that the heretics of the second century, such as Cerinthus and Carpocrates, made the genealogy of Matthew the basis of their claim that Jesus was in reality the son of Joseph and Mary. Eusebius attributes the same opinion and the same defense, and the same defense of it, to the Ebionite Symmachus. Our accepted text of Matthew 1:16, however, employs the following form of expression: "And Jacob begat Joseph, the husband of Mary and of *her* was born Jesus called the Christ." In other words, the editor means to imply that Joseph was only the *apparent*

father of the child of his wife Mary, and he has, in fact, wiped out with one word all the work of the genealogist. In all probability this obvious emendation was not the first. Two manuscripts read: "And Jacob begat Joseph; and Joseph, to whom was married the Virgin Mary, begat Jesus," which is probably an earlier form than our own, in which the editor has simply interpolated, as a kind of supplement, the assertion of the Virgin Birth. This peculiar combination is even more naively and awkwardly exhibited in the following reading: "Jacob begat Joseph, the husband of Mary, of whom was born Jesus called the Christ, and Joseph begat Jesus called the Christ."

In the case of the text of Luke, we have been less fortunate, and the manuscripts do not permit us to trace the manner in which it has been altered. But that it has been, is self-evident, and sufficiently proved by the reading of 3:23: "Jesus . . . being the son, *as was supposed* of Joseph." The words "as was supposed" betray an alteration designed, as Alfred Loisy justly observes, "to abrogate the idea of natural sonship which the text of this passage originally suggested." The belief in the Virgin Birth is thus unquestionably later than the desire to establish the Davidic descent of Jesus, the Messiah.[25]

Further confirmation for the hypothesis that the Virgin Birth is a later addition to Christianity is found in Paul's letters. For example, Paul maintains that Jesus was descended from David "according to the flesh" (Rom. 1:3), which certainly suggests that Jesus was procreated by a human.

In conclusion, Christianity can only maintain the consistency of the doctrines of the Virgin Birth and the Messiah by modifying one or the other. They have apparently chosen to modify the latter. For example, Luke's words suggest that Jesus was apparently the son of Joseph but in fact was not. Consequently, one must infer that Jesus apparently descended from David but in fact did not. But, according to Jewish tradition, the Messiah would *in fact* descend from David. His descent would not be just apparent. Jesus then can be only the apparent Messiah. Unfortunately, some Christians seem to ignore this and want to have it both ways: they assert that Jesus was born of a virgin *and* that he is the Messiah. But it is clear that they cannot. It is perhaps significant that none of the three creeds of Christendom proclaim the doctrine of the Messiah. According to them, the belief that Jesus is the Messiah is not required.

BELIEF IN THE VIRGIN BIRTH AND IMPROBABILITIES

Given the problems with the hypothesis of Jesus' Virgin Birth and the problems with the account of his birth even if we do not suppose it was a Virgin Birth is it still possible to have faith that Jesus was born of a virgin? In Chapter 1 I argued against believing Christian doctrines on the basis of faith and this argument certainly applies in this case. Moreover, there are independent reasons for rejecting an appeal to faith in the case of the Virgin Birth.

In the first place, Jesus' Virgin Birth is supposed to be a miracle. Although a claim that a miracle has occurred could be true, as we saw in Chapter 3, in terms of our background knowledge miracle claims are initially improbable. So there is a defeasible presumption against miracles: unless the evidence is excellent we should disbelieve claims of miracles. But the evidence in the case of the Virgin Birth is not excellent.

Miracles by their very nature are improbable and they require extraordinarily strong evidence for us to believe in their existence. Now given the definition of miracle introduced earlier, a virgin birth need not be a miracle. It could be explained by some law of nature that science has not yet discovered. For instance, parthenogenesis occurs in some animals and it is conceivable that future genetic engineering will make it possible for it to occur in human beings.

However, as *the* Virgin Birth is usually understood it is a miracle in the sense I am using. As Christians usually understand Jesus' birth it is not an event that will someday be explained by medical science utilizing some hitherto undiscovered law of nature. Orthodox Christians believe that Jesus' birth was the result of the exercise of God's powers. Consequently, Christian apologists have the difficult task of showing not only that Jesus was born of a virgin but that his birth could not be explained in naturalistic terms.

But independent of this point, a strong case can be made that the negative evidence principle (NEP) applies to the Virgin Birth. Recall that according to this principle one ought to disbelieve a claim if all evidence for its being true is shown to be inadequate, and it is the sort of claim that, if it were true, there would be available evidence that would be adequate to support it.

Could not a Christian easily argue that the Virgin Birth is not the sort of belief in support of which there could be available evidence? It could be pointed out that in Luke only Mary witnessed the announcement of the Virgin Birth and in Matthew only Joseph witnessed the announcement. According to these two Gospels, it might thus be argued, there is no other evidence hence our failure to find any is hardly surprising or damaging.

But this contention surely construes the relevance of the historical evidence too narrowly. One would plausibly assume that if the doctrine of the Virgin Birth was true, it would be widely believed by the various Christian communities of the first century. Of course, it is *possible* that the doctrine is true and was not widely believed. But this seems unlikely. Indeed, it is very hard to understand how, if the Virgin Birth really happened, it would not have soon become an important element of Christian doctrine and why it would not have been widely preached and promulgated.[26] Mary's and Joseph's testimonies concerning the supernatural announcements of Jesus' birth would surely have been taken seriously by Jesus' followers. Yet it was apparently not by Mark, John, or Paul. Nor was this doctrine apparently associated with Christianity in early Jewish and pagan sources. It would seem, therefore, that NEP would apply. Thus, faith in the Virgin Birth is faith in an event that is improbable; it is not merely faith in an event for which there is no evidence.

Furthermore, the stories of the Virgin Birth as told by Luke and Matthew seem to contradict one another and can only be made consistent by rather implausible interpretations. If one's faith in the Virgin Birth is based on these two Gospels, it is based on arbitrary interpretations of otherwise inconsistent passages. If, on the other hand, one's faith in the Virgin Birth is based on something beside these two Gospels, in what sense is it Christian? In addition, faith in the Virgin Birth contradicts belief in Jesus being the Messiah. Yet the latter doctrine is an important part of the Gospels. According to the Apostles' Creed and the Nicene Creed the Virgin Birth must be believed. Thus, in order not to have faith in impossibilities it would be necessary to give up the belief that Jesus is literally the Messiah—a doctrine that is found widely throughout the Gospels and the epistles and that many believe is basic to Christianity.

THE RELEVANCE OF VIRGIN BIRTH TO THE TRUTH OF THEISM AND THE INCARNATION

Can it be shown that Jesus was born of a virgin and that this cannot be explained by a law of nature? Would this be strong evidence of a theistic God? It should be clear from the considerations raised in Chapter 3 that if Jesus was born of a virgin and this was a miracle, this would not show that the existence of the theistic God was more likely than rival hypotheses. This is because there is no good reason to suppose that a miracle such as the Virgin Birth would be less likely on some rival hypotheses than on theism. Moreover, it is even unclear that evidence of the Virgin Birth would make the probability of Christianity more likely than without this evidence. This would be true only if one could infer that the Virgin Birth would be more probable on the assumption of the existence of the theistic God than its nonexistence on the same assumption. But there is no good reason to make this inference.

However, let us suppose that a theistic God exists and that he has as part of his purpose the salvation of the world by means of his Incarnation—that is by becoming a human being named Jesus who lived at the beginning of the first century—and that he plans to carry out his purpose by the use of miracles. Would the existence of the Virgin Birth be more likely than its nonexistence? It is unclear that it would. Today one is so used to the dramatic story of Jesus' life in which the Virgin Birth figures significantly that no alternative stories seem possible given God's purpose of salvation. But surely this is an illusion. God is all-powerful. There are an indefinite number of ways that he could have carried out his purpose. For example, instead of Jesus being born of virgin he could have simply appeared on earth. Or if he was born, he could have had a human father who miraculously sired a divine son. In Mithraism the god Mithras is born in human form but not to a virgin. It might be objected that if Jesus was born of a human father, he would have been born in sin. However, there seems to be no reason why an all-powerful God could not have miraculously made Jesus free from sin and yet born of a human father.

The Second Coming

The Second Coming, or the Parousia, is usually interpreted as the descent of Jesus from Heaven in glory, and so understood it is embedded in a larger eschatology. Thus, the Apostles' Creed says that after Jesus ascended into Heaven and sat on the right hand of God he shall "come to judge the quick and the dead." The Nicene Creed adds to this that he will come "in glory" and that his "kingdom shall have no end." The Athanasian Creed repeats the ideas of the Apostles' Creed that he ascended to Heaven and sat on the right hand of God and reiterates the prediction that he will come "to judge the quick and the dead." It does not say either that he will come in glory or that his kingdom shall have no end, but it adds: "At whose coming all men shall rise again with their bodies: and shall give account of their own works. And they that have done good shall go into life everlasting; and they that have done evil into everlasting fire." Combining the statements of the three creeds of Christendom we obtain the following: Jesus ascended to Heaven; he sat on the right hand of God; he will come in glory to Earth; he will raise the dead; he will judge both those who are alive and those he has raised from the dead; he will reign forever.

THE EVIDENCE: WHAT DID JESUS TEACH?

Were all these aspects of Christian eschatology in fact taught by Jesus? In particular, was the Second Coming—his coming in glory to the Earth—taught? Not all biblical scholars agree on the answer to these questions. For example, John A. T. Robinson in *Jesus and His Coming* and Michael Grant in *Jesus: An Historian's Review of the Gospel* maintain that a careful examination of the texts raises serious doubts that Jesus actually taught the doctrine of the Second Coming;[27] that is, that he would come "from heaven to earth in manifest and final glory."[28]

Robinson, for example, admits that some early Christians such as Paul preached the Parousia. But he points out that Paul does not attribute this doctrine explicitly to Jesus.[29] Indeed, he argues that the evidence indicates that not until the second century was the view widely held that Christ would come for a *second time* "in glory and judgment."[30] According to Robinson, primitive Christianity "remained content to express its certainty about the future as part of its conviction of the present and continuing sovereignty of Christ, already enthroned as history's Lord and history's Judge."[31] Grant maintains: "According to later Christian doctrine this ultimate consummation would take the form of Jesus' own Second Coming (Parousia). But there is no reliable evidence that Jesus ever believed that it would be himself who would come again. For his *apparent* references in the Gospels to such an event are posthumous and inauthentic."[32]

But what did Jesus teach? Robinson holds that Jesus taught that despite his humiliation and death he would be *immediately* vindicated[33] and with his vindication there would be an impending and overwhelming crisis. Jesus' "generation was about to be overtaken by events that must finally decide their destiny as the People of God."[34] Grant argues that Jesus preached that the Kingdom of God had already begun to arrive and that the final realization was very near. Indeed, on occasion he was extremely precise and specific about when the great day would come. Thus, in Mark Jesus maintains, "Truly I say you, there are some standing here who will not taste death before they see the kingdom of God come with power" (Mark 9:1). In Matthew he says, "Truly, I say to you, there are some standing here who will not taste death before they see the Son of man coming in his kingdom" (Matt. 16:28). In Luke he asserts: "Truly, I say to you, this generation will not pass away till all has taken place" (Luke 21:32). Thus, Grant concludes: "Jesus fomented a constant excited expectation of its coming: the imminence of the Kingdom was the very heart of his message. All therefore who wanted to enter it must make every possible preparation for its arrival. They must be ready for action, their belts fastened, their lamps lit. 'What I say to you I say to everyone: keep awake.' "[35]

However, even if scholars such as Robinson and Grant are mistaken and Jesus did believe that he would come from Heaven in glory, the New Testament makes clear that he thought this event would take place very soon. For example, chapter 13 of Mark, which contains allusions to the Parousia and which is considered by Grant to be inauthentic, says that "this generation will not pass away before all these things take place" (Mark 13:30).

THE EVIDENCE: WAS JESUS CORRECT AND WHAT DIFFERENCE WOULD IT MAKE?

Whether one interprets Jesus as advocating his descent from Heaven in glory or merely the coming of his Kingdom it is clear that the Scriptures teach that this event would happen very soon. But on either interpretation Jesus was mistaken. As Grant sums up the problem, "His ministry was based on an error."[36]

But why not admit that Jesus was mistaken and change Christian doctrine? After all, Christians believe that Jesus was a man and could make errors. T. W. Manson, for example, has argued that Jesus made mistakes in medical diagnosis and in literary criticism, and he says that "the unfulfilled prediction of the early Parousia may well be a similar case."[37] But this view has problems.[38] Mistakes concerning medical diagnosis and literary criticism are hardly in the same category as a mistake about the nearness of the Parousia or the Kingdom of God. The former, one might say, are about unimportant technical matters but the latter concerns a theological doctrine that is central to Jesus' mission. Furthermore, if Jesus was wrong about the nearness of Parousia or the Kingdom of God, he could have been mistaken that the Parousia or the Kingdom of God was coming at all. In addition, he might have been mistaken that one should turn the other cheek and love one's neighbor.

There is, of course, another alternative. One could argue that the Kingdom of God has come but that it is not noticeable. A. L. Moore, for example, maintains:

> The End has—*in a hidden manner*—come; that its coming in manifest form cannot therefore be far off, though for the moment it is held back in the interests of grace, allowing an opportunity to be given to men to repent and believe. There is, therefore, no question of abandoning an *outmoded* hope; no necessity to re-interpret (or demythologize) an expression of the early church's expectation which is now no longer tenable.[39]

Unfortunately, this interpretation has at least two serious problems. There is little scriptural justification for the idea that the Kingdom of God will come in two stages—the first, which is hidden, and lasting nearly two thousand years and the second, which is manifest and "cannot be far off." Indeed, it seems clear that Jesus believed that the *manifest* Kingdom of God was near to his time. For example, Mark says, "Truly, I say to you, there are some standing here who will not taste death before they *see* the Kingdom of God come with power" (Mark 9:1; emphasis added). Furthermore, the same argument used by Moore could have been used by apologists each year for the last two thousand years. But their predictions would have been wrong each time; the manifest Kingdom of God was not near. Indeed, Moore's statement was made over two decades ago and the manifest Kingdom of God has not appeared, although Moore maintained at that time that it could not be far off.

In fact, there have been many Christian Adventist sects throughout history who have made incorrect predictions about the manifest coming of the Kingdom of God. The only difference between their predictions and Moore's is that these sects have been much more specific than he. H. P. Smith, an Old Testament scholar, referred in 1921 to twenty-seven different dates that had been stated between 557 and 1734 as the time of the end of the world and of the Second Coming, and noted that incorrect predictions have been made up to our time.[40] William Miller, a nineteenth-century Adventist organizer, predicted that the world would end in either 1843 or 1844.[41] The Jehovah's Witnesses have looked to specific dates—1874, 1878, 1881,

1910, 1914, 1918, 1920, 1925, and others—as having eschatological importance.[42]

However, even if such predictions had had the unspecificity of Moore's claim that the manifest Kingdom of God "cannot be far off," they would still be wrong. After all, as we usually understand the expression "cannot be far off," if someone says that X cannot be far off and X has not occurred after twenty years, we assume the person is mistaken. It seems clear, then, that the interpretation proposed by Moore is simply a desperate and rather implausible attempt to save the doctrine of the nearness of the coming of the Kingdom of God.[43]

It is, of course, important not to evaluate Jesus' error in isolation. We have seen that there are good reasons why other doctrines that define Orthodox Christianity—the Virgin Birth and the Resurrection— should not be believed. Perhaps it would be possible to maintain the Second Coming or the Kingdom of God if they were firmly established. One might argue, for instance, that since we can be assured that Jesus was born of a virgin and was resurrected from the dead, there must be some unknown explanation for his apparent error concerning the Parousia or the coming of the Kingdom of God. But, far from these other doctrines being firmly established, the weight of the evidence is against them. Indeed, the improbability of the Resurrection indirectly casts doubt on the Second Coming because if there is good reason to disbelieve that Jesus was resurrected, there could be no Parousia or Kingdom of God at all, let alone in the generation of people hearing his words. If Jesus was not resurrected, his error concerning his Second Coming or the Kingdom of God is *precisely* what one should expect. Thus, Jesus' error indirectly confirms the hypothesis that Jesus was not resurrected and, thus, makes it even more probable than it was before that the Resurrection did not occur. Conversely, the evidence cited above against the Resurrection makes it likely that Jesus would not return.

One must conclude that the Second Coming doctrine of Orthodox Christianity is mistaken and that the only reason it continues to be maintained today is that apologists have reinterpreted Scripture in an implausible way in order to save Christianity from refutation.

THE SECOND COMING AND FAITH
But could one still believe in the Parousia or the coming Kingdom of God on faith? I argued in Chapter 1 that there is a presumption that we only believe something that is supported by the evidence and that

there must be excellent grounds to defeat this. Belief in the Second Coming would involve going against the evidence and not simply in going beyond it. Belief in the Parousia involves belief in a miracle, namely, that Jesus was resurrected. Consequently, there is an initial assumption that it will not occur. To believe that this assumption is mistaken one needs very good evidence and there is none. Indeed, there is good reason to disbelieve that he was resurrected. Moreover, the traditional account explicitly expounded in the Athanasian Creed, and hinted at in the other creeds, is that when Jesus returns he will raise the dead from their graves. Thus, to believe in what follows *after* the Parousia involves belief in an *indefinite* number of miracles. Surely, without strong evidence to the contrary one is justified in disbelieving that millions of bodies will be raised.

Further, the various failed attempts to predict the Second Coming also give us some grounds to believe that other attempts will fail too. After all, the fact that interpreters of Scripture down through the centuries have made so many false predictions concerning the Second Coming surely constitutes inductive grounds for thinking that future interpreters will fail even if they couch their predictions in the vague language of Moore. Now, of course it is possible to couch one's prediction so vaguely that no specific temporal referent is even hinted at. For example, if one predicts simply that Jesus will come at sometime in the future, no direct evidence will disconfirm this. But then the prediction will have lost all of its contents and become so far removed from the original Christian hope that it is unrecognizable.

Could there be beneficial reasons for believing in the Second Coming despite the evidence against it? It is very difficult to see what reasons there could be that would overcome the initial strong presumption that one should not believe in something against the evidence. It might be argued that belief in the Second Coming gives Christians hope and comfort in times of trouble. Perhaps so but belief in Santa Claus does the same for children. We normally believe that grown-ups should be realistic and face life without false hopes.

Furthermore, unless the expectation of the Second Coming is projected into the indefinite future inductive evidence indicates that Christians who believe in the Second Coming will be constantly disappointed. Their disappointment will surely have adverse effects on their faith and will induce them to construct still more implausible interpretations and self-deceptive strategies to avoid refutation. This in turn will have a further degenerate effect on the religious intellectual community.

Further, if faith in the Second Coming is permissible because it provides hope and comfort despite negative evidence against it, this would justify faith in practically any prophecy despite the evidence so long as it provides hope and comfort. For example, old Nazis would be encouraged to believe in Hitler's triumphant return from the dead, evil worshipers would be justified in believing in the Devil's ultimate victory over the forces of good, members of flying saucer cults would be justified in believing that they would be saved by beings from outer space.[44] This would indeed be conducive to intellectual bankruptcy and social disaster.

Conclusion

I conclude that the available evidence should lead a rational person to disbelieve the claims that Jesus was born of a virgin and will come again in glory and judge the quick and the dead. Consequently, there are good reasons to reject these two fundamental doctrines of Orthodox Christianity.

NOTES

1. Matthew's account of the Virgin Birth story is clearly an attempt to show that Jesus' Virgin Birth was foretold in the Old Testament. He quotes Isaiah 7:14, "Behold, a virgin shall conceive and bear a son, and his name shall be called Emmanuel." However, there is some doubt that this is a proper translation of this passage. The Hebrew term used in Isaiah 7:14 is "almah." This means "a young, unmarried female." Isaiah does not use "bethulah," which literally means "virgin." Many versions of the Bible, sensitive to the linguistic difference, use the term "young woman" instead of "virgin" in translating this passage. See Wilson, *Jesus: The Evidence* (San Francisco: Harper and Row, 1984), p. 55.

2. See Wilson, *Jesus: The Evidence*, pp. 54–55; Marina Warner, *Alone of All Her Sex: The Myth and Cult of the Virgin Mary* (London: Weidenfeld and Nicolson, 1976).

3. See J. Gresham Machen, *The Virgin Birth of Christ* (Grand Rapids, Mich.: Baker Book House, 1971), p. 194, for such an attempt.

4. I am indebted to Michael Arnheim, *Is Christianity True?* (Buffalo, N.Y.: Prometheus, 1984), pp. 9–13, for much of the following historical critique of the Virgin Birth story.

5. Apologists have desperately attempted to reconcile the apparent contradictions between Luke and Matthew. For example, Machen argues that since Matthew does not explicitly deny that Joseph lived in Nazareth and went to Bethlehem for the census that Matthew and Luke are consistent. See Machen, *The Virgin Birth of Christ*, pp. 192–93. Machen does not attempt to explain why, if Jesus was born in a manger, the wise men visited him in a house.

6. Wilson, *Jesus: The Evidence*, p. 55.

7. For a refutation of the claim that the notion of the Virgin Birth appears in the other Gospels and in Paul's letters see Charles Guignebert, "The Birth of Jesus," in *The Origins of Christianity* ed. R. Joseph Hoffman (Buffalo, N.Y.: Prometheus, 1985), pp. 240–48.

8. As Vincent Taylor has argued: "Having regard to all the facts of the case, the probability is that St. Mark's silence must be explained on the ground that the Evangelist had no knowledge of the Virgin Birth tradition." See Vincent Taylor, *The Virgin Birth* (Oxford: Clarendon Press, 1920), p. 12.

9. In Galatians 4:4, for example, Paul says: "But when the time has fully come, God sent forth his Son, born of woman, born under the law." There is no suggestion that Jesus was born of a virgin.

10. Taylor, *The Virgin Birth*, p. 6.

11. See Josephus, *Antiquities* 18.63–64, 20.9.1.

12. S. Sandmel, *We Jews and Jesus* (London, 1965), pp. 17, 28. Cited in Wells, *Did Jesus Exist?* p. 12.

13. See Ronald Charles Tanguay, *The Historicity of Jesus: A Survey of the Evidence for the Historical Jesus and the Mythical Nature of Christ* (Privately published, 1988), p. 28.

14. Sanhedrin 67a. Quoted in Tanguay, *The Historicity of Jesus*, p. 29.

15. Quoted in Tanguay, *The Historicity of Jesus*, p. 31.

16. Ibid., p. 30.

17. Tacitus, *Annals* 15.44.

18. Suetonius, Claudius, *The Lives of the Caesars* 5.25.4.

19. See, for example, Pliny, *Letters* 96 and 97, Book 10.

20. See Tacitus, *Annals* 15.44.

21. Although Celsus's writing did not survive, a large part of *The True Word* is quoted by Origen in his *Against Celsus*. See Tanguay, *The Historicity of Jesus*, pp. 58–59.

22. See Arnheim, *Is Christianity True?* p. 14.

23. See, for example, Machen, *The Virgin Birth of Christ*, pp. 202–9.

24. Guignebert, "The Birth of Jesus," pp. 240–41.

25. Ibid.

26. Taylor suggests the theory that there was a private tradition of the Virgin Birth that only become public around the time of the writing of Matthew and Luke. He admits that the plausibility of this theory depends on the dates of these Gospels. For example, if Matthew and Luke are dated in the closing years of the first century, the theory becomes implausible. We would be compelled to suppose that for nearly ninety years the story was "jealously guarded, first by Mary herself and then by a chosen few to whom it was revealed. But who will believe this?" However, even if we date these Gospels earlier, say, around A.D. 60, the theory is still rather implausible. Why would the story be kept private for sixty years? See Taylor, *The Virgin Birth*, p. 121.

27. The concept of the Parousia has not always been used in this strict sense. See G. C. Berkouwer, *The Return of Christ* (Grand Rapids, Mich.: Eerdmans, 1972), p. 140ff.

28. John A. T. Robinson, *Jesus and His Coming* (New York: Abingdon Press, 1957), p. 18.

29. Ibid., p. 25.

30. Ibid., p. 33. Oscar Cullmann in his study of early Christian confessions supports this thesis. He concludes his study by saying: "It is, then, the *present* Lordship of Christ, inaugurated by his resurrection and exaltation to the right hand of God, that is the centre of the faith of primitive Christianity." Oscar Cullmann, *The Earliest Christian Confessions*, p. 58, quoted in Robinson, *Jesus and His Coming*, p. 32.

31. Ibid., p. 34.

32. Michael Grant, *Jesus: An Historian's Review of the Gospels* (New York: Charles Scribner's Sons, 1977), p. 23.

33. Robinson, *Jesus and His Coming*, p. 50.

34. Ibid., p. 69.

35. Grant, *Jesus: An Historian's Review of the Gospel*, p. 19. For further arguments that Jesus believed that the end was near see A. L. Moore, *The Parousia in the New Testament* (Leiden, Netherlands: E. J. Brill, 1966), chap. 11.

36. Grant, *Jesus: An Historian's Review of the Gospel*, p. 20.

37. T. W. Manson, *The Teaching of Jesus* (Cambridge, 1931), p. 283. Quoted in Moore, *The Parousia in the New Testament*, p. 94.

38. See Moore, *The Parousia in the New Testament*, p. 94.

39. Ibid., p. 207.

40. Henry Preserved Smith, *Essays in Biblical Interpretation* (London: Allen and Unwin, 1921), p. 180. Cited in G. A. Wells, *Religious Postures* (La Salle, Ill.: Open Court, 1988), p. 12. See also Leon Festinger, Henry W. Riecken, Stanley Schachter, *When Prophecy Fails* (Minneapolis: University of Minnesota Press, 1955), chap. 1.

41. See Grant, *Jesus: An Historian's Review of the Gospel*, p. 20.

42. See M. J. Penton, *Apocalypse Delayed: The Story of the Jehovah's*

Witnesses (Toronto: University of Toronto Press, 1985), p. 3. Cited in Wells, *Religious Postures*, p. 12.

43. For a psychological explanation of why religious believers maintain their belief in the light of discomfirming evidence see Festinger, Riecken, and Schachter, *When Prophecy Fails*.

44. See ibid. for an interesting account of a failed prophecy concerning flying saucers.

5

The Incarnation

We have not yet critically considered one of the major doctrines of Christianity: the Incarnation. As we have seen, all three creeds assume that Jesus is the Son of God. Stressing that Jesus is *both* human and divine, the second part of the Athanasian Creed is the most explicit and detailed on this point. Even the Apostles' Creed, which is the least explicit, affirms that Christ is the Son of God. The Nicene and Athanasian Creeds can be interpreted as giving definite content to this assumption. In the Nicene Creed Jesus was assumed to be "the only-begotten Son of God," "being of one substance with the Father," and "was incarnate by the Holy Ghost of the Virgin Mary and was made man." In the Athanasian Creed it is affirmed: "So the Father is God, the Son is God: and the Holy Ghost is God. And yet there are not three Gods: but one God" and "our Lord Jesus Christ, is Son of God, is God and Man."

The doctrine of the Incarnation presents both conceptual and factual problems. One can raise questions about the consistency of holding both the view that Jesus is the Son of God and the portrayal of Jesus in the Scriptures. If Jesus is the Son of God, then presumably he has the traditional attributes of God. However, if Jesus is a human being, then he seems to have attributes that are in conflict with divine ones. But given the principle of the indiscernibility of identicals—if two things are identical, then they have all of their properties in common—an obvious logical absurdity can be generated: Jesus, the Son of God, both has and does not have certain attributes. Even if this problem can be solved, other questions arise. If Jesus was omniscient, why does he act as if he is not in the Scriptures? How can Jesus be the Son of God and, hence, morally perfect and, as he is portrayed in the Scriptures, be tempted to sin?

If these conceptual questions are answered, one can also raise factual questions pertaining to the truth of the Incarnation. For example, what reasons do we have for supposing that Jesus is the Son of God? Can the truth of the Incarnation be supported by deductive or inductive arguments? What evidence would be relevant in evaluating its truth? Is Jesus' alleged ability to work miracles evidence for his being the Son of God? Is his alleged moral perfection? Is there good reason to suppose that Jesus did work miracles? Is there good reason to suppose that he was morally perfect? Until these and other matters are considered, the doctrine of the Incarnation is dubious and pronouncements about it in the creeds of Christianity remain unproven.

Can these problems be solved? The history of attempted solutions does not inspire confidence. The apparent incoherence of Jesus being at the same time the Son of God and a human being has always been a problem of the Christian faith. Since the time of the early church fathers, various christological heresies, schools of thought, and bitter debates have been generated in attempting to save Christianity from seeming logical inconsistency.[1] But even if these conceptual problems had been solved, the rationale for belief in the Incarnation remains to be well articulated and defended. Christian theologians have suggested everything from faith to deductive logic as the foundation of the belief in the Incarnation, yet none of the proposed foundations seem satisfactory. Basing belief in the Incarnation on faith is completely arbitrary whereas inferring it on the basis of a deductive inference assumes the truth of questionable premises.

In his book *The Logic of God Incarnate*, Thomas V. Morris suggests solutions to both the conceptual and factual problems connected with the Incarnation. With respect to the conceptual problem, Morris attempts to show in a logically rigorous way that the coherence of the Incarnation can be maintained without sacrifices being made either to widely accepted logical principles such as the indiscernibility of identicals or to Christian orthodox positions such as the doctrine that Jesus is literally both a human and the Son of God.[2] Morris is very much aware of the long history of the difficulties of reconciling belief in Jesus' humanity and divinity. He notes:

> Throughout the history of the church, this has been the common assumption of all the christological heresies: humanity and divinity are not compossibly exemplifiable by one and the same bearer of properties. The Psilanthropists concluded that Jesus was a mere man, the Docetists

that he was only God appearing to be man, the Arians that he was neither true God nor true man. The Nestorians attempted to affirm both divinity and humanity, but under the pressure of this common assumption ended up with the quite unusual heresy of apparently postulating in the case of Christ two distinct bearers of properties, one of the divine attributes, one of the human, in the most intimate dyadic relation possible, one to the other.[3]

Morris is also aware of the need for a new approach to the problem. He quotes with approval one contemporary commentator who has remarked that the traditional debate "badly needs, as one of its components, a fresh look at the logical problems to which classical formulations in christology give rise"[4] and another who has gone so far as to claim that "all the hard logical work yet remains to be done."[5]

However, even if Morris is correct that the Incarnation can be understood in a way that is free from conceptual problems, this does not provide grounds for belief because belief in the Incarnation may be irrational on purely factual grounds. There may be no evidence for the Incarnation or, what is worse, there may be evidence against it. In addition to attempting to defend the Incarnation against the charge of incoherence, Morris also attempts to provide a defense of the possibility of rational belief in it. Thus, he argues that although deductive and inductive arguments are not relevant to support belief in the Incarnation, Christians are epistemologically justified in believing that Jesus is the Son of God.

Although Morris is not the first Christian apologist to defend the rationality of belief in the Incarnation, his attempt is one of most sophisticated and novel. One can reasonably claim that if there are problems with it, it is likely that there will be problems with others. In this chapter I argue that Morris's solution to the problem of the prima facie incoherence of the Incarnation itself has serious conceptual problems and that his defense of the rationality of belief in the Incarnation is in error. I am concerned here only with his own solution, not with his criticisms of alternative ones.

The Conceptual Problems of the Incarnation

FOUR CONCEPTUAL PROBLEMS

Morris considers four problems generated by supposing that Jesus is both the Son of God and a human being.

1. God is uncreated and necessarily so. Since he could not come

into existence, he is essentially uncreated. But human beings are created entities. Indeed, they seem to be essentially created entities. Let us assume a widely accepted logical principle that has great intuitive plausibility: If x = y, then for any property P, x has P if and only if y has P. Presumably the Son of God as part of the Trinity is also essentially uncreated. However, if Jesus is identical with Son of God, then he is essentially uncreated. But since Jesus is also human he is created and presumably essentially so. Thus, the principle of the indiscernibility of identicals combined with conflicting accounts of Jesus' being created enables us to deduce a contradiction: Jesus is both uncreated and created. But this is impossible.

   2. God is an omniscient being and necessarily so. Since he could not give up his omniscience, he is essentially omniscient. Presumably the Son of God as part of the Trinity is also essentially omniscient. But Jesus is identical with the Son of God. It follows that Jesus is essentially omniscient. However, Jesus is also human. This poses a conceptual problem. Humans are certainly not omniscient; indeed, one is inclined to suppose that their nonomniscience is part of their essence. If so, it follows by the principle of indiscernibility of identicals that Jesus is and is not omniscient. But this is impossible.

   3. Even if one could show that it was coherent to suppose that Jesus was omniscient, there is a scriptural problem. Jesus of the Gospels was portrayed as an omniscient being. He certainly did not act as if he was omniscient and this fact cries out for some explanation.

   4. God is morally perfect and necessarily so. Thus, it is part of God's essence that he could do nothing that is morally wrong. Presumably since the Son of God is part of the Trinity, God the Son could do nothing that is morally wrong. However, given the indiscernibility of identicals and the supposition that Jesus is identical with God the Son, Jesus could do nothing that is morally wrong. It seems to be an analytic truth that if a person could do nothing that is morally wrong, this person could not be tempted. So Jesus could not be tempted. However, since Jesus is a human being he could be tempted and, indeed, Scripture teaches that Jesus was tempted. But it is logically impossible that Jesus was tempted and could not be tempted.

   Can these problems be solved? If not, Christians will either have to accept that logical contradictions are contained in the concept of the Incarnation or else give up the idea that Jesus and the Son of God are literally identical. Needless to say, neither of these options is welcome. The first would mean that there are irrationalities at the heart of

Christian doctrine. The second would be tantamount to giving up Christianity as it is usually understood. Furthermore, even if the concept of the Incarnation is shown not to be logically inconsistent, there is still the scriptural problem. How can one explain Jesus' less than omniscient behavior? Why did Jesus seem less than morally perfect by being tempted to sin?

MORRIS'S SOLUTION

Morris attempts to explain away these prima facie contradictions and to give explanations of the scriptural problem outlined above by providing a plausible metaphysics of the Incarnation that is based on simple conceptual distinctions and on what he calls the two minds theory. Together, Morris says, these enable us to avoid both the pitfalls of traditional solutions to the prima facie contradictions and various Christian heresies.

Three Distinctions

Morris draws a distinction between properties that are essential and ones that are common to human beings. A common property is one "which many or most human beings have. A limiting case of commonality would be a property which was universally shared by all humans alike."[6] He argues that just because a property is universally shared by human beings it does not mean that it is essential. For example, living on the surface of the Earth is now a universal property of human beings but it is not essential because some day humans might live on space stations or on other planets.

Once we draw a clear distinction between commonality and essence, Morris asks, "What forces the Christian to count as essential any common human properties which would preclude a literal divine incarnation? I can think of nothing which would do this."[7] Indeed, he argues that Christian philosophers and theologians should develop their philosophical anthropology in the light of their doctrine of God. Developed in this way our view about what is essential to human beings presumably could not be in conflict with our views about God and the Incarnation. Thus, although being created, nonomniscient, and morally temptable are common properties of human beings, Morris maintains that they are not essential. Consequently, there is no inconsistency in supposing that Jesus is a human being who is not created, omniscient, and not morally temptable.

A second distinction Morris introduces is that between being merely human and being fully human. He argues that although Jesus was fully human he was not merely human. Because he was not merely human he could be uncreated, omniscient, and morally perfect since being fully human does not entail being created, nonomniscient and morally imperfect. According to Morris, a person is merely human if he or she has "all the properties requisite for being fully human (the component properties of human nature) and also some limitation properties as well."[8] He does not say precisely what he means by "limitation properties," but they seem to be those properties the lack of which prevents some entity from being divine. Thus, he counts as a limitation property that of being created. Morris argues: "These limitation properties will not be understood as elements of human nature at all, but as universal accompaniments of humanity in the case of any created human being."[9] On the other hand, a person is fully human when he or she has all the properties essential for being human.

But what properties are these? Morris maintains that it is "exceedingly difficult" to say exactly which ones are essential for being human.[10] Indeed, he says we can know a priori very few properties that are essential to human beings and that most of the nontrivial essential properties can only be known a posteriori. One essential human property that we can know a priori is the modal one of possibly being conscious at one time.[11] Of course this property is also essential to many animals. What essential properties distinguishes humans from nonhuman animals? According to Morris, humans have rational, moral, aesthetic, and spiritual qualities that nonhuman animals lack.[12]

However, although these properties may distinguish humans from nonhuman animals they do not distinguish humans from divine beings. Morris suggests two properties—presumably known a posteriori—that do this: "the property of having a body at some past or present time during one's existence of the genetic type or basic structure of present human bodies" and "the property of having at some time in one's career a certain sort of consciousness, a certain sort of experiential field and mental structure such as the sort we find ourselves to have."[13] He maintains that if God the Son had never taken on these properties, he would not have "exemplified human nature."[14] Thus, it is part of the essence of human beings to have these properties and it is *not* part of the essence of divine beings to have them.

In sum, Morris maintains that Jesus can be fully human by taking on the properties that are essential for being human and yet be God the Son by having the properties that are essential for God the Son;

for example, the properties of not being created, omniscient, and not being temptable.

Another distinction that is crucial to Morris's argument is that between individual-essence and kind-essence. An individual-essence is the individual nature of a particular entity. On this conception of essence no individual can have more than one essence: "We can consider any individual and the whole set of properties individually necessary and jointly sufficient for being numerically identical with *that individual*."[15]

In contrast to an individual essence, a kind-essence is "a shareable set of properties individually necessary and jointly sufficient for membership in that kind."[16] Not every shareable set of properties is a kind-essence however. A description of a kind-essence provides us with information about the fundamental structure of a thing; in particular, it provides us "with sorts of properties relevant to the information concerning the causal powers or dispositions the thing has or is capable of having."[17] Consequently, knowledge of a kind-essence is important in "our scientific as well as our purely metaphysical endeavors."[18]

On this account of essence one and the same individual can exemplify more than one kind-essence; that is, one individual can be a member of more than one kind. According to Morris, Jesus was both human and divine; that is, he exemplified both the kind-essence of being human and the kind-essence of being divine. Morris argues, however, that "the orthodox theologian must be metaphysically circumspect at a number of points if he wants to display a traditional doctrine free of any hint of incoherence."[19] In particular, the orthodox theologian must reject the view that every kind-nature is essential to all members of that kind. Thus, the Son of God exemplified humanity, and part of the kind-essence of humanity is the property of having a body at some past or present time during one's existence of the genetic type or basic structure of present human bodies. However, this property is not part of the Son of God's individual-essence; it is a property that the Son of God exemplified contingently and not essentially.

The Two Minds Theory of Christ

There is another problem that Morris must deal with, one that cannot be handled by the distinction just summarized. The Son of God is omniscient. Since Jesus is identical with the Son of God, Jesus must be omniscient. The distinction between being merely human and being fully human would, according to Morris, allow us to say that a fully human but not a mere human being such as Jesus is omniscient. However, the implausibility of supposing that Jesus, a human, had this attribute remains. As portrayed by the Gospels, Jesus hardly acted as one would expect an omniscient being to act.

In order to account for Jesus' apparently limited human characteristics Morris introduces the two minds theory of Christ. Although this theory was not originated by Morris, his defense of it is perhaps the most extensive yet produced.[20] In this view Jesus had two distinct ranges of consciousness:

> There is first what we can call the eternal mind of God the Son with its distinctively divine consciousness, whatever that might be like, encompassing the full scope of omniscience. And in addition there is a distinctly earthly consciousness that came into existence and grew and developed as the boy Jesus grew and developed. It drew its visual imagery from what the eyes of Jesus saw, and its concepts from the languages he learned. The earthly range of consciousness, and self-consciousness, was thoroughly human, Jewish, and first-century Palestinian in nature.[21]

The divine mind of God the Son "contained, but was not contained by, his earthly mind, or range of consciousness."[22] Thus, there is an asymmetrical accessing relation between the two minds:

> The divine mind had full and direct access to the earthly, human experience resulting from the Incarnation, but the earthly consciousness did not have such full and direct access to the content of the overarching omniscience proper to the Logos, but only such access, on occasions, as the divine mind allowed it to have. There thus was a metaphysical and personal depth to the man Jesus lacking in the case of every individual who is merely human.[23]

Morris claims many advantages for this theory. For example, he argues that it accounts for the apparent intellectual and spiritual growth of Jesus "in his humanity" and his cry of dereliction in Mark 15:34 ("My God, my God, why hast thou forsaken me?"). Moreover, he maintains that the theory, combined with his distinctions, gives "a full and adequate account of the basic features of the metaphysics of the Incarnation." Jesus is not "merely dressed up as man." He is an individual who is fully human and who "shares in the human condition, experiencing the world in a human perspective."[24]

Suggesting that we can understand the two minds theory on the basis of certain analogies, Morris says that, in the twentieth century, depth psychology has postulated various strata to the ordinary human mind. "If modern psychology is even possibly right in this postulation, one person can have different levels or ranges of mentality. In the case of Jesus, there would then be a very important extra depth had in virtue of his being divine."[25] Moreover, in cases of brain hemisphere commisurotomy and multiple personality one individual has distinct ranges of consciousness. However, he argues that although his theory has interesting similarities to cases in abnormal psychology, the analogy is not perfect. In typical cases of split personalities a person's dual mental state is not an arrangement that is voluntarily entered into and it is not conducive to the attainment of goals valuable to that person. In the case of God the Son's Incarnation, in contrast, both these features are absent. God the Son's taking on a human mind was a completely voluntary act and it was at least conducive to, and perhaps even necessary for, achieving God's purposes.

Logical and Epistemic Possibility

In order to show that there is no inconsistency between Jesus the Son of God being morally perfect and Jesus the human being tempted to sin, Morris introduces one further distinction, that between logical and epistemic possibility. It is logically impossible for Jesus to do anything morally wrong because Jesus is identical with God the Son and God the Son is morally perfect. By the principle of the indiscernibility of identicals Jesus must be morally perfect. How, then, could Jesus be tempted to sin? According to Morris he could be only if it was epistemically possible for him to sin.

Morris argues that epistemic possibility is relative to belief sets. Roughly speaking, a proposition P is epistemically possible relative to a subject S's accessible belief set B when B "neither contains nor self-evidently entails the denial of P, nor does B contain or self-evidently entail propositions which seem to S to show P to be either false or impossible."[26] At the time of Jesus' temptation, his earthly mind "could not partake of the riches of omniscience."[27] In particular, he did not have access to one crucial truth: it is logically impossible for him to sin. Recall that according to the two minds theory, Jesus had two ranges of consciousness: the earthly and the divine. Thus, relative to the accessible belief set of Jesus' earthly mind, the proposition that he could sin was not impossible. His earthly consciousness was not aware of his inability to sin; consequently, he could be tempted to sin. But the outcome of his choice to not sin could not have been otherwise than it was. According to Morris, this does not mean that Jesus' decision not to sin was "causally imposed on him by his divine nature."[28] The divine nature of being necessarily good played no causal role in Jesus' decisions.

An example should make the distinction between the two kinds of possibilities clear. Presumably it was logically impossible for Jesus to commit adultery. However, in terms of his human consciousness he did not know that this was logically impossible for him. Hence, he could have been tempted to commit adultery. According to Morris, to commit adultery means "to have certain sorts of intentions toward, or to engage in certain forms of sexual behavior with, a person to whom one does not stand in the proper relation of personal commitment which alone would render such behavior morally permissible and appropriate."[29] This definition is, of course, much broader than the standard dictionary one since it makes someone who never engaged in *any* sexual behavior an adulterer if the person has the requisite intention.[30]

Although we are clear on what Morris means by committing adultery it is unclear what he means by being tempted to commit adultery or in general what he means by being tempted to sin. Let us assume that he means what is normally meant. The dictionary gives as the primary meaning of "tempt" to be enticed or to be allured to do something unwise or immoral[31] and it defines "entice" as leading on by an exciting desire and "allure" as attracting by the offer of something desirable. Combining these ideas one can say that Jesus was tempted to sin means that he was attracted to or led on by his desire to do something immoral, that is to sin. Given Morris's account of committing adultery, one could say that Jesus could have been attracted to or led on by his desire to engage in sexual forms of behavior that are morally proscribed but because he is God the Son and morally perfect it would have been logically impossible for him to engage in such forms of behavior or even to form an intention to be so engaged. I assume, of course, that one could have been attracted to do x or led on by one's desire to do x and yet not have had an intention to do x. But this assumption seems plausible. Having an intention to do x involves having x as an object of one's plan whereas being attracted to x or led on by one's desire to do x does not.

However, this idea does not seem to capture Morris's meaning completely. In particular, it does not seem to capture the epistemological restriction that he places on temptation: one cannot be tempted to do x if one knows that it is impossible to do x. Taking this idea into account, one might suggest that to say that person P is tempted to do sinful act A is to say that P was attracted to or led on by P's desire to do act A and the proposition "P will do A" is epistemically possible relative to P's belief set.

One important question is whether a person P_1 or a thing T can tempt person P_2 without P_2 being tempted. For example, could Jesus have been tempted by the Devil to do sinful act A if it was the case that Jesus was not attracted to or led on by his desire to do A? Although ordinary usage is not completely clear on this point I am inclined to say that the answer is no. For example, a gangster does not tempt a judge by offering her a bribe to rule in favor of some criminal unless she is attracted by the offer or led on by her desire to accept the bribe. Suppose the judge is not attracted by the offer. If one is speaking carefully, one should say the gangster tried to tempt the judge but was unsuccessful. Strictly speaking then, the Devil was unsuccessful in tempting Jesus if the latter was not attracted to or led on by his desire to do what the Devil offered. One should say in this case that the Devil *tried* to tempt Jesus but he failed.

The Gospels do not say that the Devil tried to tempt Jesus but failed. They say that Jesus was tempted (Mark 1:13). Furthermore, the New Testament teaches that Jesus was not "a high priest who unable to sympathize with our weaknesses, but one who in every respect has been tempted as we are, yet without sinning" (Heb. 4:15). This suggests that, according to Scripture, Jesus was induced by the Devil to be attracted to do some immoral act that he thought it was possible for him to do.

In any case, if the latter analysis of temptation is adopted, Morris's requirement—in order for P to be tempted to do sinful act A, the proposition "P will do A" is epistemologically possible relative to P's belief set—may be unnecessary. After all, if one's being tempted to sin could simply involve another person making one some immoral offer, the rationale for Morris's epistemological restriction becomes unclear. Jesus could know that it was impossible for him to sin and yet be tempted by the Devil to sin; that is, the Devil could make him some immoral offer that he would know was impossible for him to accept. There might be independent reason, of course, to keep this restriction even if being tempted to sin does not entail having an attraction or a desire to perform an immoral act. However, Morris provides none.

EVALUATION OF MORRIS'S SOLUTION

Has Morris's theory solved the problem of the prima facie incoherence of the Incarnation? Even if he has, does his theory have other conceptual problems?

Incoherence and the Two Minds Theory

As we have seen, Morris's two minds theory is explicitly intended to explain why Jesus does not seem like an omniscient being. However, this theory also seems to serve a purpose that is not explicitly acknowledged: it attempts to prevent an inconsistency. One might argue that Jesus is both omniscient and not omniscient: Jesus, the Son of God, is obviously omniscient; but Jesus, the human being, is clearly not. According to Scripture he lacks certain knowledge; for example, Jesus says that he does not know the date of the last judgment. Morris's two minds theory can be understood as a way of attempting to avoid this inconsistency for it allows one to say that Jesus' divine mind is omniscient but that his earthly mind is not. Thus, although one seems to be simultaneously attributing contradictory properties to a single entity, one really is not. In fact, one is simultaneously attributing contradictory properties to different entities; that is, to different minds. In this way the inconsistency seems to be avoided.

However, the traditional account that Morris defends assumes that God the Son is *one* person.[32] But if God the Son is one person in any ordinary sense of the term "person," then, even if he has two minds, any predications of knowledge will have the *person* of God the Son as their subject. If one said that God the Son's divine mind knows that same proposition p, this is a misleading way of saying that God the Son knows that p and p is known by God the Son via his divine mind. But if this is so, then Morris's solution entails that the *person* Jesus, the Son of God, is omniscient and is not. Jesus is omniscient because all true propositions are known via his divine mind. He is nonomniscient because some propositions are not known via his human mind. Indeed, Jesus is omniscient and is not on Morris's theory precisely because he has two minds. Morris's use of the two mind theory obscures this obvious point.

Now it may be argued that in ordinary life one sometimes does attribute knowledge and lack of knowledge to the same person at the same time. For example, one might say of the absentminded Mr. Jones that he knows his phone number but cannot remember it[33] and that to say he cannot remember it entails that he does not know it. It might be argued that in this case one is attributing knowledge and lack of knowledge to the same person at the same time and there is no contradiction. However, the term "knowledge" is used ambiguously here. When one says that Jones knows his phone number one means roughly that his phone number is stored in his memory. But when one says that he cannot remember and, consequently, does not know it, one means that he does not have this information at the forefront of his consciousness.

If we limit our discussion to knowledge that is in the forefront of consciousness, that is, to so-called occurrent knowledge, then it is impossible to see how one person can know and not know the same information under the same description at the same time. Yet this is precisely what Morris's theory predicates of Jesus. An omniscient being knows everything in the sense of occurrent knowledge; so Jesus knows everything in this sense because of his divine mind. But there are things Jesus does not know in this sense because of his finite mind. In the case of Jesus there is no ambiguity in the term "know." Jesus simultaneously knows and does not know some piece of information in the same sense under the same description, for example, the time of the last judgment. But this is impossible.

Two Minds and One Person

Although I have criticized Morris's attempt to answer one charge of incoherence by using the two minds theory I have not yet questioned whether one person could have two minds.[34] If one supposes that $Mind_1$ of Body B has different thoughts, different moods, and comes to different decisions than $Mind_2$ also of Body B—all of which seems possible on the two minds theory—it is plausible to suppose that $Mind_1$ and $Mind_2$ are being treated as different agents. But then we should say that there are two persons, P_1 and P_2, that are sharing B. However, this two persons theory conflicts with Christian orthodoxy.

Morris attempts to deal with this problem by saying that "ordinarily, minds and persons are individuated in a one–one correlation" and that "the existence of a human mind in a merely human person may preclude the exemplification by that person of any other mind, or range of consciousness of the appropriate sort at the same time. So among mere humans the individuation of two minds at any one time will suffice for the identification of two persons." However, he argues that it is possible that "outside that context, there is no such one–one correlation." In particular, he maintains that when a mind and body are part of a larger whole "which on the two-minds view they are in the case of Jesus—they alone do not suffice to individuate a person not possibly having as well some other distinct sort of mind at the same time."[35]

However, Morris gives no good reason for supposing that a one–one correlation between a mind and a person fails to hold outside of the contexts with which we are acquainted and only says that it is possible that it fails to hold in one such context. Let us grant that such a failure is possible. The crucial question is whether there are any grounds for disbelieving that such a failure has occurred. There seem to be. If a correlation holds in every case in contexts with which we are acquainted, we have excellent prima facie grounds for supposing that it will hold in contexts that we not acquainted with unless we have independent evidence to suppose these latter contexts to be relevantly different. The mere fact that in order for the theory to work, a one–one correlation must fail in one such context surely cannot constitute such independent evidence. But Morris supplies no other reason.

One might take a different tack. Instead of saying, as Morris does, that one body has two minds one could say that one body has one fragmented mind or two fragments of a mind. In the case of Jesus one could maintain that he had one mind that consisted of a divine fragment and human fragment where the human fragment was the fragment of a human mind. But the fragmented mind theory must also be rejected as conflicting with Christian orthodoxy. A person could not be fully human with only a fragment of a human mind. Consequently, Jesus could not be fully human. However on the orthodox view he must be.

Morris is left then with the following problems. It is at least dubious whether one person could have two minds. But if Jesus is one person with two minds, then the doctrine of the Incarnation is incoherent. However, if Jesus is two persons, then Morris's theory conflicts with Christian orthodoxy. The two persons theory and the fragmented mind theory are unacceptable since they conflict with Christian doctrine.

The Explanatory Value of the Two Minds Theory

Let us suppose that somehow the above problems can be overcome. There is another serious problem. The two minds theory is meant to explain why Jesus as portrayed in the Gospels does not seem to be omniscient. On this theory Jesus seems to have limited knowledge because his human consciousness does not have access to his divine omniscient consciousness. If the two minds theory does explain why Jesus' knowledge seems limited, more needs to be explained. If Jesus is identical with the God the Son, he is also omnipotent. However, Morris admits that as portrayed in the Gospels Jesus does not seem omnipotent. Indeed, Morris admits that the supposition that Jesus, the itinerant preacher, was omniscient and omnipotent is "outlandish to the greatest possible degree." He says: "Did the bouncing baby boy of Mary and Joseph direct the workings of the cosmos from his crib? . . . Such implications of orthodoxy can sound just too bizarre for even a moment's serious reflection. How could such a view possibly be squared with the biblical portrait of Jesus as a limited man among men?"[36]

It may be maintained that as Jesus is portrayed in the Gospels he appears just as one would expect an omnipotent being to appear. However, we need not decide this here. The crucial point is that, claiming that the Jesus of the Gospels seems neither omniscient nor omnipotent, Morris only attempts to explain the apparent nonomniscience. Can the apparent nonomnipotency be explained by the two minds theory? It appears to explain why Jesus does not *seem* to be omnipotent: he does not believe that he is omnipotent because his human consciousness does not have access to his divine consciousness; as a result, he does not act like a being with infinite power.

But how would a human being with infinite power act? Although Morris does not say, it is clear that he believes that Jesus does not display the requisite behavior. If Jesus thought he was omnipotent would he have claimed to have infinite power? Would Jesus have performed more amazing miracles than he was supposed to have performed? For example, would he have changed the course of the stars and not merely stilled the storm? Would he have cured all the sick people of Judea and not just some of those he came in contact with? Would he have made wine from nothing and not just changed water into wine? Would he have floated through the air and not just walked on the water? We need not decide these questions here. Let us merely stipulate that although Jesus displayed action A_1 in the Gospels, in order to be thought to be omnipotent he would have had to display action A_2. The two minds theory provides an explanation of why he did not display A_2. Since in terms of his earthly consciousness he did not know he was omnipotent, he did not know he could perform A_2. Consequently, he did not attempt to perform A_2.

But does the two minds theory explain why he did not perform A_2? Not without making other assumptions that seem far from obvious. It should be noted first of all that if one is ignorant of one's omnipotence it seems unlikely that one would stay ignorant of this fact for very long. If one is omnipotent and wills something to happen, it instantly happens. It is implausible to suppose that an omnipotent human being who was ignorant of his or her omnipotence would not accidentally discover in the daily course of living that he or she had powers normal people lacked by simply willing certain things to occur and finding out that they did occur. If such a person had any curiosity, he or she would go on to test the limits of that power and would soon begin to suspect that there were none.

It is important to see that in order to try to will something to happen, one does not have to believe that one is likely to be successful if one tries. Indeed, it is not even necessary that one not believe that it is impossible to will something to happen. Of course, in order to try to will something to happen one must act as if it is not impossible. However, this is compatible with disbelief.

Thus, there is a plausible case to be made that even if Jesus was completely ignorant of his omnipotence, he would have accidently discovered it. However, according to the Gospels, Jesus was not completely ignorant of the fact that he had powers far beyond those of mere humans. After all, according to the Gospels he walked on water, turned water into wine, cured the sick, and worked other wonders. One would suppose that his knowledge that he had these powers would have made him curious to test their scope and limits. With a little testing his action would have been A_2; that is, he would have displayed the action—whatever it might be—that a omnipotent human would have displayed.

Further, Jesus' dawning realization of his unlimited powers would have had to have affected his limited human consciousness. As he began to realize that he could bring about anything by an act of will, he would have begun to realize that he could acquire knowledge of anything in the same way. Morris is not clear on how Jesus would have had to have acted according to the Gospels in order for us to suppose that he was omniscient. However, he believes that Jesus did not display the requisite knowledge. Would he have had to have displayed detailed knowledge of future scientific discoveries? Would he have had to have answered instantly and correctly extremely difficult mathematical problems that were put to him? Again we need not answer these questions. Let us simply stipulate that K_1 is the knowledge that Jesus in fact displayed in his human consciousness according to the Gospels and that K_2 is the knowledge that he would have had to have displayed if he was to have acted as if he was omniscient.

However, a being who is omnipotent can acquire knowledge it does not have by an act of will. Hence, one would suppose that, whatever else A_2 would include, it would include acquiring certain knowledge by an act of will. In particular, it would seem plausible to suppose that A_2 would include acquiring K_2 by an act of will. Thus, it seems likely that either accidentally or driven by natural curiosity Jesus would have performed A_2 and, thus, have acquired K_2. But then, the distinction between human and divine consciousness postulated by the two minds theory would be threatened. Jesus would realize that he was at least potentially omniscient and, indeed, could become omniscient by an act of will; that is, he could replace his limited human consciousness by an unlimited divine consciousness.

Two basic objections can be raised to this argument. First, it might be said that although Jesus was omnipotent it is not the case that he could have performed all the actions an omnipotent being could have performed by an act of will. However, it is unclear why Jesus would be limited. One would have thought that by definition an omnipotent being could bring about anything such a being could bring about by an act of will. One might argue that just as Jesus had two minds—a human and a divine—he also had two wills—a human will and a divine will. His human will, with all its limitations, was manifest in his daily life as a human being but his divine will was hidden and did not surface except in rare circumstances. In terms of his human will he could not have brought about wondrous events. But in terms of his divine will he could have and sometimes did.

There are some problems with this suggestion. First of all, in using the two wills theory one is abandoning the two minds theory as a way of explaining Jesus' apparent lack of omnipotency. Yet this theory combined with the simple distinctions Morris introduced was supposed to give "a full and adequate account of the basic features of the metaphysics of the Incarnation." Second, it is unclear that a two wills theory can be successfully articulated. Morris relies on analogies from depth psychology and abnormal psychology to make his two minds theory plausible. But are there analogies that could be drawn on to make the two wills theory plausible? This remains to be shown.

Further, it might be argued that it is possible that Jesus could have discovered accidently that he is omnipotent, despite my claim to the contrary this is very unlikely. Thus it might be argued that it is improbable that Jesus would have willed anything that he believed was inconsistent with his human limitations. However, there is good reason to suppose that Jesus would have tried to will something to happen that we today consider beyond normal human capacity. If he had, then he would have been successful and would have been on his way to discovering the truth of his omnipotence. First, biblical scholarship suggests that the worldview of people of Jesus' times was much more congenial to the magical arts, exorcism, and so on than the worldview of people today.[37] Thus, the ordinary person of Jesus' time would be much more willing to accept that some human beings had wondrous powers that most human beings did not and to engage in practices in which they might be utilized. Consequently, Jesus as a human being living in the early part of the first century would have been much more willing to believe this too and much more willing than people in our time to experiment in practices in which one willed some extraordinary event to take place. However, as I have already suggested, Jesus realized that he was not an ordinary human. He knew he could do some wondrous things. It would be remarkable if he had not attempted to determine what his limitations were. Thus, without making implausible ad hoc assumptions about Jesus' particular beliefs and attitudes— for example, that he had no curiosity about the limitations of his powers—there would be good reason to suppose that he would have attempted to test his limitations.

Consequently, not only does the two minds theory have difficulty explaining Jesus' apparent nonomnipotence, it ultimately fails to explain his apparent nonomniscience. Given Jesus' omnipotence and his human knowledge of his ability to work wonders combined with plausible assumptions about his natural curiosity concerning the limits of his abilities, one would have expected him to perform action A_2 and to acquire knowledge K_2; that is, to manifest omnipotence and omniscience. The Gospel accounts where Jesus manifests neither pose a mystery that Morris's theory does not begin to explain.

Problems of Tempting Jesus to Sin

Morris argues that it was epistemologically possible for Jesus to have been tempted to sin since in terms of his human consciousness he did not know that it was logically impossible for him to do so. But if the previous argument is correct, Jesus would have been able to acquire such knowledge, and given certain plausible assumptions, he would have done so. Consequently, it is likely that he would have come to know that he could not sin and this would have made it impossible for him to be tempted to sin.

There is a further problem with Morris's analysis. He argues that Jesus' decision not to sin was not the causal result of his divine nature. Consequently, although Jesus' sinless actions were inevitable, they were not made inevitable by his being necessarily morally perfect. Morris illustrates his thesis by the following story. Suppose that Jones is in a room in which, unknown to him, the door is locked. He decides to stay there and consequently does not leave. Of course, had he tried to leave he would have been unsuccessful. Morris argues that although Jones's not leaving the room was predestined, his decision not to leave the room was not influenced by what prevented him from leaving the room, namely the locked door. Similarly although Jesus' sinless actions could not have been otherwise, his actions were not influenced by what prevented him from sinning, namely, his moral perfection.

The problem with Morris's theory is that it makes it a mystery why Jesus decided not to sin. After all the Gospels teach that he was tempted to sin. In terms of our previous analysis of temptation to sin this would mean in part that he was attracted to or led on by his desire to do something immoral. According to Morris, although his actions were not influenced by his morally perfect nature, he *always* decided not to sin. From what we know of human beings this seems extremely unlikely at the very least. It is important to see that Morris cannot argue here that although Jesus is fully human he is not merely human. Jesus' earthly consciousness was merely human and, according to Morris, his moral actions were not influenced by his divine nature. Why then did Jesus' *always* decide not to sin?

To return to Morris's example, it would be a bit curious if Jones, not knowing the door was locked and led on by his strong desire to get out of the room, decided to stay in the room. However, his behavior would become very puzzling if this happened consistently. Suppose that he was in one thousand rooms in which the doors were locked, he did not know this in each case, he had a strong desire to get out of all the rooms, and yet he never decided to leave any of them. His consistent decisions not to leave the rooms would certainly call for some special contextual explanation. In the same way, if Jesus was tempted to sin, his decision not to sin calls for some special contextual explanations. Morris provides no such explanation and therefore leaves us with a puzzle.

There is a final problem with Morris's theory. He seems to assume that a person's being morally perfect is logically compatible with this person's being tempted to commit sins insofar as such a person lacks knowledge of his or her moral perfection. So far we have uncritically accepted this assumption. But should we? To see that we should not we need only draw out the implications of being tempted to sin. As we have seen, although Morris does not define what he means by being tempted to sin it is plausible to suppose that this entails being attracted to or led on by one's desire to do something immoral. However, it is absurd to suppose that a morally perfect being could be attracted to or led on by his desire to, for example, torture or murder. Insofar as Jesus had an attraction or desire of this sort, he could not be morally perfect. Since the Gospels teach that he was tempted, he could not be morally perfect and, consequently, he could not be God the Son. This argument does not, of course, show that Jesus could not be morally perfect and be fully human. However, it does show that Jesus could not be morally perfect *and* be tempted to sin. Morris attempts to show that both theses are true and he is not completely successful.

Earlier we considered and rejected the idea that a person or thing could tempt another person to sin without the person who was tempted being attracted to do something sinful. However, the problems with Morris's theory suggest that we should briefly reconsider this idea. If one adopted the rejected analysis, some problems of his theory would be solved. Although Jesus was tempted to sin by the Devil and others he was *never* attracted to do anything immoral. Consequently, it would be easy to explain why Jesus never decided to sin. He never decided to sin because he had no attraction to do immoral acts. Further, on the rejected theory there would be no problem in saying that a morally perfect being such as Jesus could have immoral attractions. On the rejected analysis Jesus, a morally perfect being, could be tempted to sin and yet have no immoral desires.

However, on the rejected analysis we have an explanatory problem of at least as great magnitude as on Morris's theory. Although presumably Jesus was made many immoral offers by the Devil and others and was presented with situations that would have attracted all other humans to do immoral acts, he was *never* attracted to do any immoral act. This would be easy to explain if his actions were influenced by his morally perfect nature. But, according to Morris, they were not. Why then was Jesus never attracted to do any immoral actions? It is difficult to see how this could be explained on the assumption that Jesus is fully human. Although *being fully human* may not entail *being attracted to do some immoral act at some time or other* it verges on the miraculous that anyone who is fully human would not be attracted to do some immoral act at some time or other. Was Jesus' divine mind causing him never to be attracted to sin? But then, contrary to Morris's supposition, would not this mean that Jesus' lack of attraction was caused by his morally perfect nature? Perhaps his lack of attraction to sin was caused by his strict religious training as a human being. But strict religious training does not seem to stamp out *all* such attraction in humans.

Furthermore, the rejected analysis has another problem. If Jesus was never even attracted to perform sinful acts it is difficult to see how he could be a human model for resisting sin. A person who never has sinful attractions and desires is so removed from the human situation that he would be difficult, if not impossible, to relate to when one is attracted to sin, trying to resist it and looking for an ideal to follow. Indeed, it is difficult to see why Jesus would be praiseworthy for not sinning if he was never even attracted to sin. One praises someone for resisting the attraction of sinning. Jesus, on the rejected analysis, would have had no attractions to resist. Could he perhaps be praised for not having sinful attractions? This all depends on the explanation of the remarkable absence of such attractions in Jesus which has yet to be supplied.

It is surely the case that sometimes the absence of an attraction to a sinful action is not something to be praised. A man who does not have pedophilia is hardly to be praised for not having a sexual attraction for young children. On the other hand, the absence of attraction for strong drink in a former alcoholic is ordinarily something to be praised since one assumes that the alcoholic through rigorous training and discipline has somehow eliminated the attraction. What makes Jesus' lack of attraction to sin something that one suspects is not appropriate for praise is that on the rejected analysis he *never* had the attraction.

It was not something that he had to eliminate by training and effort. How then could he be praiseworthy?

Thus, although the rejected analysis of temptation may solve some of the problems of Morris's analysis it has others that are equally as serious.

CONCLUSION ON CONCEPTUAL PROBLEMS

Morris's attempt to show the plausibility of the concept of God incarnate is unsuccessful. Despite the conceptual distinctions he introduces and his sophisticated logical apparatus the Incarnation is still an incoherent notion. Furthermore, the two mind theory does not have the explanatory value claimed for it and it is questionable whether one person could have two minds. Moreover, on Morris's theory the Gospel account of Jesus' temptation is conceptually problematic.

Given the sophistication of Morris's attempt, his great effort to take into account the problems of past attempted solutions, and the problems of the alternatives,[38] it is plausible to consider Morris's failure as still further grounds for the rejection of Christianity. Previous chapters have shown that the historicity of Jesus is doubtful, and that, even if Jesus did exist, it is unlikely that the doctrines of the Virgin Birth, the Resurrection, and the Second Coming are true. The apparent incoherence of the Incarnation and the failure of the most sophisticated attempt made thus far to reconcile it strongly suggests that one of the major doctrines of Christianity is incoherent and conceptually problematic.

However, it should be stressed that even if my criticism of Morris is mistaken or if a coherent account of the Incarnation is produced, this would hardly establish the truth of the Incarnation. Even if it were demonstrated that the Incarnation was a coherent doctrine, this would only show that it is logically possible that God *could* become incarnate in human form. It would *not* show that God did become incanate. To this problem we now turn.

The Truth of the Incarnation

Let us suppose for the sake of argument that the Incarnation is a coherent doctrine and the claim that Jesus is the Son of God does not have conceptual problems. Is there any good reason to suppose that he was in fact the Son of God? Is there any reason to suppose that he was not? Is belief in the Incarnation reasonable?

MORRIS'S DEFENSE

In addition to attempting to defend the Incarnation against the charge of incoherence Morris also tries to provide a defense of the possibility of rational belief in it. Maintaining that in deductive arguments there will be at least one premise whose positive epistemic status is not greater than the doctrine of the Incarnation itself, he rejects any attempt to base belief in the Incarnation on them. What about nondeductive arguments? He maintains that "it seems not to be the case that there is any single, isolable form of nondeductive argument typically relied upon"[39] by Christians to infer from certain facts, for example, the portrayal of Jesus in the New Testament, that Jesus is God Incarnate. Could the reasonableness of belief in the Incarnation be based, then, on direct experience and not on inference? Morris is sympathetic with this suggestion but he realizes that the objection might be raised that observational reports about physical objects and behavior undermine statements about persons and mental states and that the same thing would be true about observational reports about Jesus. No matter what we observe that Jesus did, this is compatible with his not being omniscient, omnipotent, and so on. So Morris concludes that "if seeing that an individual is God requires seeing that he is omnipotent, necessarily good, omnipresent, omniscient, ontologically independent, and the like, then the prospects for just directly seeing that Jesus is God look pretty dim, to say the least."[40]

However, Morris rejects the idea that seeing Jesus as divine requires this "seeing that" relation. In certain situations we can reasonably believe that we are observing the mental qualities of other persons and not just observing people behaving in certain ways, he says. Furthermore, he holds that it is possible that there is "an innate human capacity which, when properly functioning, allows us to see God, or, to put it another way, to recognize God when we see him."[41] For example, many people see Jesus as divine upon seeing the portrait of him in the Gospels. They do not base their belief on any argument or inference. Someone who believes that Jesus is divine on the basis of this direct seeing can as he or she matures reasonably take what he or she learns of the Christian story to be corroboration of that belief:

> Instances in the life of Jesus, for example, as recounted in the Gospels, can reasonably be thought by a responsible reader to attest to his divinity. . . . And, despite what some critics seem to imply, one need

not be exceedingly naive concerning the vicissitudes of New Testament criticism in order to be reasonable in so reading the Gospels as to find corroboration in them for a belief in the Incarnation.[42]

Morris admits that if there is an innate human capacity which when properly functioning allows us to recognize God when we see him, then if Jesus is God Incarnate, "it is clear that there are widespread and deeply rooted impediments to this capacity's functioning."[43] Morris suggests that this human capacity will only function properly with the removal of some of these impediments. But how are they to be removed? Quoting passages from the New Testament Morris implies that these can be removed only by the Holy Spirit. Thus, he admits in the end that a full account of the epistemic status of Christian belief "would require, at its core, what we might called a Spirit Epistemology."[44]

This account of the possibility of the reasonableness of the belief that Jesus is God Incarnate has serious problems. First, it relies on the idea that if human capacity is functioning properly, one will be able to see Jesus as God Incarnate. But what reason is there to suppose this is true? It seems strange that so many people who have studied the New Testament, for example, Jews, Muslims, and atheists, and who have not seen Jesus as God Incarnate have impediments to their innate human capacity. In any case, why has the Holy Spirit not removed these people's impediments? As we shall see in Chapter 7, this is especially puzzling given that Christian salvation is dependent on accepting Jesus as God Incarnate.

Furthermore, if Morris can rely on Spirit Epistemology to show that Jesus is the Son of God, other religions can use similar epistemologies to justify their doctrines. Muslims might argue that when impediments have been removed by Allah one can see Muhammad as the prophet of Allah and see Jesus as not God Incarnate. Allah has removed such impediments in the case of devout Muslims and has not done so in the case of devout Christians. Mormons might claim that one can only see Joseph Smith as seer, translator, prophet, and apostle of Jesus Christ when impediments have been removed by God. Such impediments have been removed by the Holy Spirit in the case of devout Mormons, but not in the case of non-Mormons. Indeed, if one allows Spirit Epistemology, why not allow followers of some pagan wonder workers, for example, Apollonius, to argue that he was God Incarnate since he was seen as God. The contrary opinion of their opponents can be answered by arguing that their opponent's innate capacity to see this wonder worker as God is impeded and God has chosen not to remove the impediment.

The second problem with Morris's defense is that he does not consider any of the inductive arguments used to support belief in the Incarnation. Just because there is no *single* isolable form of nondeductive argument typically relied upon to support belief does not mean that inductive arguments are not relevant and one can rely on direct observation. It may well be true, as Morris says, that many people do not base their belief in the Incarnation on inference. But this hardly shows that their belief is justified. If, as he claims, Christians typically base their belief in the Incarnation on the portrait of Jesus in the Gospels, in order to be rational they must suppose that the Gospels are so reliable and trustworthy that there is good reason to suppose that Jesus did many of the things that are claimed of him there. Surely they have no reason to believe these things without examining the historical evidence, considering the reliability of the witnesses, and so on. Until this is done, Morris's statement that one can find corroboration in the Gospels for belief in the Incarnation is unwarranted. Corroboration is possible only when what the Gospels teach is supported by the evidence.

THE EVIDENCE NEEDED

Let us consider what this evidence could be. The evaluation of the truth of the Incarnation is closely connected with the evaluation of other assumptions of Christianity. Thus, if the historicity of Jesus is dubious, then it is irrational to hold that Jesus was God the Son. The existence of Jesus is surely a necessary condition for his being the Son of God. What about the other basic doctrines of Christianity? Unlike the historicity of Jesus, the doctrines of the Virgin Birth, the Resurrection, and the Second Coming are not necessary conditions of the Incarnation. One can in all consistency reject them yet accept the Incarnation. Thus, it is logically possible that Jesus was not born of a virgin, was not resurrected, and will not return in glory and yet was the Son of God.

However, although it is logically possible to hold the doctrine of the Incarnation and reject the other doctrines, their rejection does pose a serious problem for believers in the Incarnation. The Incarnation has a central importance in Christianity since it purports to explain them.[45] Jesus' Virgin Birth is explained by supposing that he was the

Son of God: Mary was made pregnant by the Holy Spirit and gave birth to the Son of God. Jesus' Resurrection is explained by supposing that Jesus was God the Son who came to Earth, was rejected and crucified, and was brought back to life in order to fulfill his divine mission of saving the world. Jesus' Second Coming is explained by supposing that as the Son of God he will return in glory in order to complete his task.

Normally, the evidence that a theory explains provides support for it. The Incarnation as an explanatory theory is no exception. Thus, if the doctrines of the Virgin Birth, Resurrection, and Second Coming are rejected, as I have argued they should be, a large part of the evidence for supposing that Jesus is the Son of God must be set aside. With this evidence gone, there must be other evidence for the Incarnation to explain, hence, other evidence to support it. What could this be?

There seem to be two basic types of evidence that the Incarnation might still explain which in turn would support its truth. The first type consists of the miracles of Jesus, the various wondrous deeds that he is alleged to have performed. Thus, Jesus' ability to perform miracles could be explained by supposing that he is all-powerful. Since he is all-powerful, he could cure the sick, give sight to the blind, turn water into wine, and walk on water. However, he is all-powerful because he is the Son of God. The second type of evidence consists of Jesus' moral teachings and moral example. These are to be followed because he is morally perfect. He is morally perfect because he is the Son of God and the Son of God by definition must be morally perfect.

The Evidence of Miracles

Several important questions must be considered concerning the evidential value of miracles in relation to the claim that Jesus is the Son of God. If Jesus performed miracles, would this affect the probability that he was the Son of God? Are there serious obstacles to supposing that Jesus did perform miracles? Have these obstacles been overcome? Are there good historical grounds for even claiming that Jesus seemed to perform what his contemporaries considered to be wondrous feats?

Let us consider these questions.

The Probability That Jesus Is the Son of God,
Given the Existence of His Miracles

In Chapter 3 I defined a miracle as an event brought about by the exercise of a supernatural power. If it could be shown that Jesus performed miracles, would this show that he was the Son of God? It would not for the simple reason that if Jesus could work miracles in the sense defined, this would only entail that he had supernatural power *or* that some supernatural power worked through him. This is compatible with Jesus not being the Son of God.

Throughout history there have been many people who were considered to be miracle workers but few were considered to be the Son of God. Even today followers of religious healers such as Oral Roberts believe that individuals perform miracles. But they are not considered to be the Son of God and in many cases are not even considered to have supernatural powers. What is often claimed is that God is working through the healers to bring about cures.

But even if Jesus did have supernatural powers in his own right, it would not follow that he was the Son of God; that is, the Son of an all-powerful, all-knowing, all-good being and, consequently, that he had the properties that such a being would have. Why? One alternative explanation of Jesus' ability to work miracles is that he was simply a messenger of God who was endowed with very great but still limited powers. Another is that Jesus was the son of a powerful but finite god. Both of these hypotheses seem to be compatible with the evidence of the Gospels for as we have seen in our discussion of Morris's two mind theory, the Gospels do not seem to portray Jesus as an all-powerful and all-knowing being.

One might grant that Jesus' ability to work miracles does not entail that he is the Son of God yet argue that Jesus' miracles affect the probability of the hypothesis that he is the Son of God. Let us call this hypothesis H. There are two different ways that miracles could effect the probability of H. First, one might argue that if Jesus performed miracles, then this would make H more probable than ~H. However, it is difficult to see why it would. After all, ~H would include hypotheses such as that Jesus was a messenger of God with great finite powers which seem to explain the evidence just as well as H. Furthermore, these other hypotheses do not seem to have any less initial credibility than H.

Second, one might maintain that if Jesus had performed miracles, then this would make it more probable that he was the Son of God than if he had not performed miracles. But why should this be so? After all, a person could be the Son of God and want to remain anonymous and obscure. Consequently, he would not call attention to himself by performing wondrous acts. Whether the Son of God would be likely to perform miracles would be determined by his motives and purposes. Indeed, as we saw in Chapter 2, Paul's letters do not portray Jesus as a miracle worker. Paul indicates that Jesus lived an obscure life in bondage to evil spirits (Gal. 4:3–9, Col. 2:20) who did not recognize his true identity and that only in death did he gain mastery over them (Col. 2:15). His letters suggest that in Jesus' lifetime he did not use his supernatural powers to defeat demons and indeed did not let his supernatural status be known. In addition, some of the miracles allegedly performed by Christ, for example, driving the demons into the Garasene swine and cursing the fig tree, seem difficult to reconcile with belief in a kind and merciful God.[46] They seem to make it *less* likely that Jesus is the Son of God than if he had not performed them.

I conclude that even if it could be established that Jesus did work miracles, this would not mean that it was more probable than not that he was the Son of God or more probable with this evidence than without it.

Three Difficulties in Showing That Jesus
Performed Miracles

I argued in Chapter 3 that there are difficulties to overcome in order to show that Jesus was resurrected. Similar ones must be overcome in order to establish that Jesus did work miracles. First, the believer in Jesus' alleged miracles must give reasons to suppose that they will probably not be explained by any unknown scientific laws. Since presumably not all the laws that govern nature have been discovered, this seems difficult to do. The advocates of the hypothesis that Jesus performed miracles must argue that it is probable that the alleged miracles will not be explained by future science utilizing heretofore undiscovered laws. Given the scientific progress of the last two centuries such a prediction seems rash and unjustified. In medicine, for example, diseases that were considered mysterious are now understood without appeal to supernatural powers. Further progress seems extremely likely; indeed, it seems plausible to suppose that many so-called miracle cures of the past will one day be understood, as some have already been, in terms of psychosomatic medicine.

Believers in Jesus' miracles may argue that some events not only are unexplained in terms of laws governing nature but are in conflict with them. Jesus is alleged to have walked on water and it might be argued that this is something that is not only not explained by scientific laws but is in conflict with these laws. The ability to walk on water indicates the causal influences of a supernatural power that goes beyond the working of nature, it will be said.

The difficulty here is to know whether the conflict is genuine or merely apparent. This is the second great obstacle that believers in Jesus' miracles must overcome. They must argue that it is more probable that the conflict is genuine than apparent. This is difficult to do because there are many ways that appearances can mislead and deceive in cases of this sort. One way in which an apparent conflict can arise is by means of deception, fraud, or trickery. However, there are great difficulties in ruling these out. We have excellent reason today to believe that some contemporary faith healers use fraud and deceit to make it seem that they have paranormal powers and are achieving miracle cures.[47] These people have little trouble in duping a public that is surely no less sophisticated than that of biblical times.

Even in modern parapsychology where laboratory controls are used, there is great difficulty in ruling out explanations of the results in terms of fraud. By various tricks trained experimenters in ESP research have been deceived into thinking that genuine paranormal events have occurred.[48] If it takes these kind of controls and precautions today in scientific laboratories in order to eliminate fraud and deceit, what credence should we give to reports of miracles made in biblical times by less educated and less sophisticated people and where no systematic controls against fraud were used?[49] The most plausible reply is "very little." One surely must ask: Did Jesus really walk on water or only appear to because he was walking on rocks below the surface?[50] Did Jesus turn the water into wine or did he only appear to because he substituted wine for water using a magician's ploy? The hypothesis that Jesus was a magician has been seriously considered by some biblical scholars.[51] The success of some contemporary "faith healers" and "psychic wonders" in convincing the public by the use of deception and fraud indicates that if Jesus was a magician, it was possible for him to do the same.

Further, alleged miracles may not be due to trickery or fraud but to misperceptions based on religious bias. We know from empirical studies that people's beliefs and prejudices influence what they see and report.[52] Thus a person full of religious zeal may see what he or she wants to see, not what is really there. Did Jesus still the storm (Matt. 8:23–27), or did the storm by coincidence happen to stop when "he rose and rebuked the wind and the sea"? Did witnesses in their religious zeal "see" him stilling it?

In addition, religious attitudes often foster uncritical belief and acceptance. Indeed, in a religious context, uncritical belief is often thought to be a value and doubt and skepticism are considered vices. As we shall see in Chapter 6, Jesus' own teaching reinforced this value. He advocated blind obedience. Even in our day we see religious fundamentalists pride themselves on their rejection of the findings of science concerning, for example, the age of earth, and maintaining an unwavering commitment to the teachings of the Bible. Thus, a belief arising in a religious context and held with only modest conviction may tend to reinforce itself and develop into an unshakable conviction. It would hardly be surprising then, if, in this context, some ordinary natural event were seen as a miracle.

Finally, it might be the case that what we thought were strictly deterministic laws are in fact statistical laws. Since the latter are compatible with rare occurrences of uncaused events, the events designated as miracles may be wrongly labeled since they may be uncaused; that is, they may be neither naturally or supernaturally determined. Advocates of the miracle hypothesis, then, must show that the existence of miracles is more probable than the existence of some uncaused events.

In summary, supporters of the view that Jesus performed miracles (H_m) must show that H_m is more probable than the following:

H_p = Jesus brought about the allegedly miraculous events in question but this will be explained by future scientific progress when more scientific laws are discovered.

H_s = Jesus seemed to bring about the allegedly miraculous events in question but did not.

H_r = The allegedly miraculous events in question were uncaused.

There is no easy way to assess the comparative probabilities that are involved. However, as we have already seen, the progress of science, the history of deception and fraud connected with miracles and the paranormal, and the history of gullibility and misperception all strongly suggest that H_p and H_s are better supported than H_m.

Thus, the obstacles involved in supposing that Jesus performed miracles have not been met.

It is less clear what one should say about the comparative probability of H_m and H_r. Both seem unlikely in the light of the evidence but it is certainly not clear that H_r is less likely than H_m. On the one hand, science already allows indeterminacy on the microlevel, for example, in quantum theory. On the other hand, macroindeterminacy, the sort that would be relevant to explaining miracles, is no less incompatible with the present scientific worldview than it is with H_m. At the very least, one can say that there is no reason to prefer H_m over H_r on probabilistic grounds.

Did Jesus Perform Allegedly Miraculous Acts?

I have just argued there is good reason to suppose that it is less likely that Jesus performed miracles than that he only seemed to perform them. But is there reliable historical evidence to indicate that he seemed to perform miracles?

If Jesus performed what seemed like miracles, then it is likely that there would be evidence of this in Jewish and pagan sources. As we have already seen, although Josephus in the Testimonium Flavianum indicates that Jesus did perform miracles, this passage must be set aside as a later Christian interpolation. The other, less controversial, passage in Josephus's *Antiquities* does not indicate that Jesus performed any miracles. Furthermore, pagan sources surveyed in Chapter 2 give no indication that Jesus performed miracles.

If Jesus performed what seemed like miracles, then one would expect that Paul and other early Christian writers would have claimed that he performed them. But they do not. Paul gives no indication that Jesus worked any miracles in his lifetime even where this would seem natural to do if he believed that Jesus had. He refers to miracles that are associated with the Christian ministry as "gifts of the spirit" (1 Cor. 12:10, 28) and says that among the "signs of a true apostle" are "signs and wonders and mighty works" (2 Cor. 12:12). One would have thought that he would have cited Jesus' own "mighty works" at this point but he does not. Other early Christian writers are equally silent about Jesus' miracles.[53]

This does not necessarily mean that Jesus, if he existed, did not perform what seemed like miracles. But it does indicate that this is unlikely. On the other hand, if he did not work miracles, this does not necessarily mean that he was not the Son of God, for he might have wanted to live a life of obscurity. However, given the improbability of the Virgin Birth, the Resurrection, and the Second Coming, if he did not work miracles, one of the few remaining important traditional sources of evidence for his being the Son of God must be discounted. The only remaining source would be his ethical teachings and his example.

The Evidence of Jesus' Ethical Teachings and Example

If Jesus' ethical teachings and moral example were perfect, would this entail that he was the Son of God? The answer is no. The perfection of Jesus' morality and example is compatible with alternative explanations: for example, with Jesus being the son of some morally perfect but finite god or with Jesus being endowed with moral perfection by God as an example to humankind and yet having none of the other properties of a deity including any supernatural powers such as the ability to work miracles. Nor would Jesus' moral perfection make the hypothesis that he is the Son of God more probable than not. The expectation of his moral perfection on the alternative theories is just as high as on the theory that he is the Son of God and these alternatives seem a priori no less probable than the theory that Jesus is the Son of God.

What if it turns out that Jesus was not an ideal model of ethical behavior and that some of his teachings were dubious? This would not prove conclusively that he was not the Son of God. However, combined with the other evidence we have cited it would surely make his divinity unlikely. One would expect that the Son of God would not act in morally questionable ways and expound ethical doctrines that are problematic. So it is important for this reason alone to examine Jesus' moral example and his ethical teachings. It is also important for independent reasons. His example has been thought even by extremely liberal Christians who reject both his divinity and his historicity to be the best model of ethical behavior available and his teachings the best code of conduct produced by humankind. Thus, in chapter 6 I will examine Christian ethics.

CONCLUSION ON THE TRUTH OF THE INCARNATION

Belief in the Incarnation is clearly unjustified. Not only is the evidence for the Incarnation lacking but it is incoherent and conceptually problematic. The truth of other doctrines of Christianity—the Resurrection, Virgin Birth, and the Second Coming—that are used to support the truth of the Incarnation have been shown to be probably false and this undercuts much of the traditional support for the Incarnation. In addition, in this chapter we have seen that the miracles allegedly connected with Jesus' life provide no evidence for the Incarnation and that, even if Jesus was morally perfect, this would not constitute very strong evidence that he was the Son of God. These results, combined with the conceptual problems discussed here, present a strong case against believing that Jesus was the Son of God. As I argued in Chapter 1, there is a strong presumption that a theory that has no empirical support should not be believed. However, when a theory lacks such support *and* has serious conceptual problems— including a prima facie incoherency—there is a *very* strong presumption that it should not be believed. Further doubt will be cast on the truth of the Incarnation when Jesus' ethical behavior and teachings are considered.

One aspect of the Incarnation has not been mentioned thus far: the doctrine of the Atonement, the doctrine of the reconciliation of sinful human beings to God. This doctrine is closely related to why God became incarnated as Jesus, died, and was resurrected. Theories that provide answers to this question not only link the Incarnation with the Christian doctrine of salvation but also purport to provide a rationale for the Resurrection. Unlike the doctrine of the Incarnation there has never been anything like an official theory of the Atonement that has been accepted by most Christians and whose nonacceptance would put them beyond the fold. It is significant that none of the official creeds of Christendom state explicitly why there was an incarnation, why Jesus as the incarnation of the Son of God died on the cross, why he was resurrected from the dead, and why in order to be saved one must have faith in him. This lack of creedal acknowledgment and sanction of a theory of the Atonement suggests an unwillingness among Christians to be committed to some one theory.

There have been many theories of atonement presented by the greatest thinkers of Christendom that have attempted to explain the conceptual links between the Incarnation, the Resurrection, and salvation. Despite their noncanonical nature it is important for our purpose to consider them and we examine the major theories of the Atonement in Appendix 2. These theories attempt to provide a rationale for otherwise puzzling and inexplicable ideas. If the major theories of the Atonement do not provide a plausible account of the Incarnation, the Resurrection, and salvation, the credibility of Christianity is weakened even further and we have still less reason to accept it. If after nearly two centuries the greatest minds of Christendom have not produced an acceptable theory that connects the Incarnation, the Resurrection, and salvation *and* these doctrines have problems in their own rights, this surely is a most powerful indictment against Christianity. Dubious doctrines that remain unexplained are surely less credible than dubious ones that have been explained.

NOTES

1. For the historical background to this debate within Christianity see Aloys Grillmeier, *Christ in Christian Tradition* (New York: Sheed and Ward, 1965); J.N.D. Kelly, *Early Christian Doctrine*, rev. ed. (New York: Harper and Row, 1978).

2. Thomas V. Morris, *The Logic of God Incarnate* (Ithaca, N.Y.: Cornell University Press, 1986).

3. Ibid., p. 20.

4. Nicholas Lash, "Jesus and the Meaning of 'God': A Comment," in *Incarnation and Myth: The Debate Continued*, ed. Michael Goulder (Grand Rapids, Mich.: Eerdmans, 1979), p. 42. Quoted in Morris, *The Logic of God Incarnate*, p. 13.

5. Keith Ward, review of *Incarnation and Myth*, ed. Michael Goulder, *Theology* 82 (1979): 452. Quoted in Morris, *The Logic of God Incarnate*, p. 13.

6. Morris, *The Logic of God Incarnate*, p. 63.

7. Ibid., p. 64.

8. Ibid., p. 65.

9. Ibid.

10. Ibid., p. 144.

11. Ibid., p. 23.

12. Ibid., p. 66.

13. Ibid., p. 145.

14. Ibid.

15. Ibid., p. 38.

16. Ibid., p. 39.

17. Ibid.

18. Ibid., p. 38.

19. Ibid., p. 41.

20. Ibid., p. 102n. 20.

21. Ibid., pp. 102–3.

22. Ibid., p. 103.

23. Ibid.

24. Ibid.

25. Ibid., p. 105.

26. Ibid., p. 148.

27. Ibid., p. 149.

28. Ibid., p. 150.

29. Ibid., p. 146.

30. On the other hand, it seems narrower than the account given by Jesus, who seemed to maintain that someone who even looks at women with lust has committed adultery (Matt. 5:27). One wonders whether Morris's broad understanding of adultery carries over to other sins. For example, on Morris's view would someone be considered a murderer if he or she only had murderous intentions and never committed the actual physical act? This makes a difference in how one assesses the possibility of a morally perfect being trying to sin. If the intention to do a moral wrong is itself considered morally wrong, then on Morris's theory a morally perfect being could not even try to sin because trying to do x presumably involves the intention to do x.

31. *The Random House Dictionary*, ed. Jess Stein (New York: Ballantine Books, 1978), p. 909.

32. See Eleonore Stump, review of *The Logic of God Incarnate*, by Thomas Morris, *Faith and Philosophy* 6 (1989): 220.

33. Ibid., p. 222.

34. See Bruce Langtry, review of *The Logic of God Incarnate*, by Thomas Morris, *Australasian Journal of Philosophy* 65 (1987): 501–3.

35. Morris, *The Logic of God Incarnate*, p. 157.

36. Ibid., p. 70.

37. Morton Smith, *Jesus the Magician* (San Francisco: Harper and Row, 1978); Michael Grant, *Jesus: An Historian's Review of the Gospels* (New York: Charles Scribner's Sons, 1977).

38. The only other theory that Morris takes seriously in attempting to show that the Incarnation is incoherent is the kenotic theory. In this theory God temporarily divested himself of all of the divine properties that are "not compossibly exemplifiable with human nature" (*The Logic of God Incarnate*, p. 89). For example, the Son of God would temporarily divest himself of omniscience when he became incarnate as Jesus. Morris rejects this theory for two reasons. First, Morris argues that the Son of God is necessarily omniscient; hence, the Son of God cannot divest Himself of omniscience. Although he considers the possibility of giving up this strong modal claim, he is hesitant to do so unless there is no alternative theory. However, he believes that there is an alternative theory, namely the one defended in his book. Second, the kenotic theory is incompatible with the immutability of God. A divine being

cannot cease to be divine and, hence, cannot cease to have the properties that are essential to a divine being. The most sophisticated way of reconciling the immutability of God and God divesting himself of omniscience would be to say that God is not omniscient but is omniscient-unless-freely-and-temporarily-choosing-to-be-otherwise. Consequently, God could still be immutable and temporarily divest himself of his omniscience. Morris believes that although this theory would give up the standard analysis of God's attributes it might be necessary if there were no alternatives. But he sees his own two mind theory as a viable alternative. A third problem that Morris points out is sometimes raised against the kenotic theory that he does not endorse. Kenotic theory entails a view of the Trinity that is controversial. Since during the period that God the Son is incarnated he is neither all-knowing nor all-powerful some other divine being must be supporting the existence and operation of the physical universe. But this doctrine has been branded as polytheism (ibid., p. 93).

In sum, one can understand why Morris prefers his own theory over the kenotic theory and why other Christian thinkers might as well. Kenotic theory would entail giving up strong modal claims about God, giving up the claim that God is omniscient, and rejecting the standard interpretation of the Trinity. But since his theory is unsuccessful the kenotic theory may be the next best alternative. However, given the problems just specified it seems clear that the Incarnation can only be made plausible by modifying Christian doctrine in a way that would not be acceptable to many Christians.

39. Ibid., p. 199.

40. Ibid., p. 200.

41. Ibid., p. 201.

42. Ibid., p. 202.

43. Ibid., p. 203.

44. Ibid., p. 204.

45. As I argued in Chapters 3 and 4, the Incarnation neither entails the Virgin Birth and Resurrection nor makes them likely.

46. Criticisms similar to this were raised by the eighteenth-century deists Thomas Woolston and Thomas Chubb. See R. M. Burns, *The Great Debate on Miracles* (Lewisburg, Pa.: Bucknell University Press, 1981), pp. 77–79.

47. See James Randi, " 'Be Healed in the Name of God!' An Exposé of the Reverend W. V. Grant," *Free Inquiry* 6 (1986): 8–19. See also James Randi, *The Faith Healers* (Buffalo, N.Y.: Prometheus, 1987).

48. See James Randi, "The Project Alpha Experiment: Part I. The First Two Years," *Skeptical Inquirer* 7 (Summer 1983): 24–33; James Randi, "The Project Alpha Experiment: Part 2. Beyond the Laboratory," *Skeptical Inquirer* 8 (Fall 1983), pp. 36–45.

49. Cf. Gary G. Colwell, "Miracles and History," *Sophia* 22 (1983): 9–

14. Colwell argues that one finds in Luke 24:1–11 and John 20:24–29 examples of skeptical humanity among Jesus' followers who were forced to accept his miracles from love of truth. But it is unclear why Colwell accepts these biblical stories as true since there are many inconsistencies in the story of the Resurrection where the examples of skeptical humanity are supposed to be found. Furthermore, Colwell ignores the independent evidence we have from contemporary faith healers that indicates the difficulty of being skeptical when one is deeply involved in a religious movement. See Paul Kurtz, *The Transcendental Temptation* (Buffalo, N.Y.: Prometheus, 1986), pp. 153–60, for an analysis of these inconsistencies and Randi, *The Faith Healers*, for the lack of skepticism in the context of faith healing.

50. Carl Friedrich Bahrdt, a German theologian of the Enlightenment, suggested that Jesus walked on floating pieces of timber. For a discussion of Bahrdt's views see Ernst Keller and Marie Luise Keller, *Miracles in Dispute* (Philadelphia: Fortress Press, 1969), pp. 69–70. The Kellers raise two objections to Bahrdt's explanation. They argue that according to Scripture the boat was not near the shore, and in any case Jesus' disciples would have noticed the timber. However, it is by no means clear that Scripture is correct about the location of the boat or even if the incident took place at all. In any case, if we substitute rocks for timber, the location of the boat according to Scripture can be accepted. Rocks below the surface of the water may extend for many furlongs out to sea. The Kellers mention Bahrdt's not implausible explanation of the failure of the disciples to notice. "They were 'held prisoner' by the prejudices of their own miracle-believing age—with constantly inflamed imaginations—always saw more in phenomena than was there in reality" (p. 71).

51. See Smith, *Jesus the Magician* (New York: Harper and Row, 1978).

52. See, for example, A. Daniel Yarmey, *The Psychology of Eyewitness Testimony* (New York: Free Press, 1979).

53. See G. A. Wells, *The Historical Evidence for Jesus* (Buffalo, N.Y.: Prometheus, 1982), p. 211–12.

6

Christian Ethics

*T*he case against Christianity would not be complete without an evaluation of Christian ethics. Since Jesus' ethical conduct and teachings are an important source of evidence for the Incarnation, it would certainly seem to count against the view that he is the Son of God if his ethical example was not completely exemplary or his ethical teachings were implausible. In addition, my analysis of the meaning of being a Christian in Chapter 1 indicated that part of being a Christian is believing that Jesus' life provides a model of ethical behavior to be emulated and that his ethical teachings provide rules of conduct to be followed. Indeed, I suggested that this belief constitutes the entire content of some forms of Liberal Christianity. It is essential, therefore, to evaluate it.

Our first job is to try to become clear on what Jesus' teachings were. As we shall see, this is not as easy as it may seem. Once we have some idea of Jesus' ethics we must consider his gospel impartially and ask: Do Jesus' teachings provide a workable ethics? Would a sensitive moral observer agree with what he taught? We must also look beyond his explicit ethical pronouncements in two ways. We must ask: Did Jesus' actual conduct exemplify his teachings? Was Jesus an ideal moral model? Would a sensitive moral person do what Jesus did? In addition, we must ask how Christian ethicists have interpreted Jesus' sayings. In so doing we must determine how Christian ethics differ from plausible systems of secular ethics and if Christian ethics have clear advantages over these secular systems.

What Ethical Principle Did Jesus Teach?

One initial problem is that even if one supposes that Jesus did exist it is unclear exactly what moral principles he was supposed to have taught and what moral ideal his conduct was supposed to exemplify.

As I noted in Chapter 2, the early Christian writers say nothing about Jesus' ethical pronouncements. Even when it would be to their advantage to do so, Paul and other early Christian writers do not refer to Jesus' teachings as stated in the Gospels.

The apparent ignorance of these early Christian writers about the ethical teachings of the Gospels certainly raises serious questions about whether Jesus really did teach what they say he did. How could it be that *all* of these early writers failed to invoke Jesus' views when it would have been to their advantage to do so? One obvious explanation is that the teachings are a later addition and were not part of the original Christian doctrine. If this explanation is accepted, there is no good reason to suppose that so-called Christian ethics is what Jesus taught. However, most Christians seem to ignore this problem and take the synoptic Gospels as the basis of Christian ethics. I follow this convention in this chapter.

The Ethical Teaching of the Synoptic Gospels

If one expects to find a fully developed and coherent ethical theory in the synoptic Gospels, one will be disappointed.[1] Jesus is reported in these Gospels to have said many things about ethical conduct, some of which are unclear and others of which do not seem to cohere well with his ethical pronouncements in another places. Yet although an entirely satisfactory account of Jesus' ethical teachings must elude us, some progress can be made in formulating an account of them.

Richard Robinson has developed a useful formulation of Jesus' ethical teaching in terms of certain commandments.[2] The primary commandment of Jesus is to love God: "You shall love the Lord your God with all your heart, and with all your soul, and with all your mind. This is the great and first commandment" (Matt. 22:37–38). However, as it was understood by Jesus, this commandment had an urgency, harshness, and otherworldly quality about it that is hardly conveyed by this simple statement. Jesus believed that the Kingdom of God was at hand (Matt. 4:17) and, indeed, that this Kingdom would come into power within the lifetime of some of the people he was addressing (Mark 9:1). Because of the nearness of the Kingdom of God, he was not concerned with worldly problems. Saying, "Sell all that you have and distribute to the poor, and you will have treasure in heaven; and come, follow me" (Luke 18:22) he neglected his family for his gospel (Matt. 12:46–50), predicted that preaching his gospel could result in brother betraying brother and in parricide (Matt. 10:21), maintained that his disciples should hate members of their family and their own lives (Luke 14:26), and said that anyone who did not renounce all that he had could not be his disciple (Luke 14:33). Jesus also threatened great punishment for those who rejected his teachings (Matt. 10:14–15).

The Faith in Jesus Commandment is closely related to the Love of God Commandment.[3] In the synoptic Gospels Jesus is portrayed as demanding faith in himself and maintaining that it is a sin not to have it. What exactly is one to believe in believing in Jesus? What precisely is one to have faith in? Insofar as an answer is given, it is "Jesus is the anointed," "Jesus is the son of God," and "Jesus is the Son of Man." However, Jesus is often portrayed as being hesitant to give these answers himself. For example, when the priests asked him "Are you the Son of God, then?" Jesus' answer was merely, "You say that I am" (Luke 22:70). This Faith in Jesus' Commandment is perhaps the most novel of Jesus' for while commentators have shown that his other commandments were anticipated in earlier Jewish literature, there obviously was no anticipation of this one.[4]

According to Jesus, the second most important commandment is: "You shall love your neighbor as yourself" (Matt. 22:39). This commandment was not, of course, original with Jesus; it is found in the Old Testament. (Lev. 19:18). Nevertheless, he seemed to believe that he was extending this commandment to include love of one's enemies (Matt. 5:38–48; Luke 6:27–36).[5] He also seemed to regard this commandment as entailing nonresistance to evil: "But I say to you, Do not resist one who is evil. But if any one strikes you on the right cheek, turn to him the other also; and if any one would sue you and take your coat, let them have your cloak as well; and if anyone forces you to go one mile go with him two miles" (Matt. 5:39–41). He also linked the Love Your Neighbor Commandment with generosity, forgiveness, and the Golden Rule. For example, with respect to forgiveness he says: "If your brother sins, rebuke him, and if he repents, forgive him; and if he sins against you seven times in the day, and turns to you seven times, and says, 'I repent', you must forgive him" (Luke 17:3–4).

Although Jesus did not explicitly formulate as a separate commandment that we are to regulate our thoughts, feelings, and language as well as our actions the Purity of Heart and Language Commandment seems to play an important role in his ethical thinking. He said: "You have heard that it was said to the men of old, 'You shall not kill; and whoever kills shall be liable to judgment.' But I say to you that every one who is angry with his brother shall be liable to judgment; who ever insults his brother shall be liable to the council and whoever says: 'You fool!' shall be liable to the hell of fire" (Matt. 5:21–22). He opposed swearing of various kinds (Matt. 5:34–36). He also said: "You have heard that it was said 'You shall not commit adultery.' But I say to you every one who looks at a woman lustfully has already committed adultery with her in his heart" (Matt. 5:27–28).

Again, although the Commandment of Humility does not figure as an explicitly formulated separate commandment, the idea that one should humble or lower one's self plays an important role in Jesus' ethical thought. For him this involved avoiding displays of superiority, not caring about prestige, not demanding honors or recognition, not judging others. It involved serving others, even in lowly ways (Luke 22:26) for he said: "For every one who exalts himself will be humbled, but he who humbles himself will be exalted" (Luke 18:14), and "for he who is least among you all is the one who is great" (Luke 9:48). Being humble for Jesus seemed also to entail both giving alms (Matt. 6:4) and praying in secret (Matt. 6:6).

The Moral Practices of Jesus

In the synoptic Gospels Jesus not only makes pronouncements about what should and should not be done. His practices yield insights into his moral character, ones that sometimes sit uneasily with his actual commandments and conflict dramatically with our idealized picture of Jesus, the Son of God and the Christian model of ethical conduct. In Chapter 5 we saw that Jesus the Son of God is alleged to be morally perfect. Although he can be tempted to sin he cannot actually sin. Moreover, we have been taught that Jesus is gentle, forgiving, full of compassion and universal love, offering universal salvation and redemption. Given this understanding of Jesus it is hardly surprising that part of being a Christian is believing that Jesus' life provides a model of ethical behavior to be emulated.

Yet his actual behavior does not live up to the idealized picture and in fact seems at times to contradict his own teachings. For example it is quite clear that he believed that people who did not embrace his teachings will be and should be severely punished. Thus, he said to his disciples: "And if any one will not receive you or listen to your words, shake off the dust from your feet as you leave that house or town. Truly, I say to you, it shall be more tolerable on the day of judgment for the land of Sodom and Gomorrah than for that town" (Matt. 10:14–15). Moreover, although he preached forgiveness, he maintained that "whoever blasphemes against the Holy Spirit never has forgiveness and is guilty of an eternal sin" (Mark 3:29). Indeed, it is clear that Jesus sanctioned the eternal punishment of the fires of hell for those who sinned (Matt. 25:41, 46). "You serpents, you brood of vipers, how are you to escape being sentenced to hell?" (Matt. 23:33)

In some places the synoptic Gospels teach universal salvation. For example, in Luke it is proclaimed that "all flesh shall see the salvation of God" (3:6). However, in other passages in the synoptic Gospels Jesus is not portrayed in this way. Rather, he is shown as conceiving of his mission as narrowly sectarian, namely, that of saving the Jews. He thus said to his disciples: "Go nowhere among the Gentiles and enter no town of the Samaritans, but go rather to the lost sheep of the house of Israel" (Matt. 10:5–6). Clearly believing that he was the *Jewish* Messiah, he said: "Think not that I have come to abolish the law and the prophets; I come not to abolish them but to fulfill them" (Matt. 5:17). He said to a Canaanite women whose daughter was possessed by a demon and who begged for his help: "I was sent only to the lost sheep of the house of Israel." Only after the women pled with him and made a brilliant reply to his justification for his refusal to help did he heal the daughter (Matt. 15:22–28). It seems clear, then, that without her mother's perseverance and quick wit the Canaanite women's daughter would not have been healed by Jesus although a Jewish women's daughter would have been.

Although he preached nonresistance to evil he did not always practice it. He used force and drove out "those who sold and those who bought in the temple, and he overturned the tables of the money changers and the seats of those who sold pigeons" (Mark 11:15). He made no effort to win over the wrongdoers by love. In other cases, Jesus' action is far less than compassionate and gentle. Not only did he not say anything against the inhumane treatment of animals but in one case his actual treatment of them was far from gentle and kind. He expelled demons from a man and drove them into a herd of swine who thereupon rushed into the sea and drowned (Luke 8:28–33). It has been noted that Jesus could have expelled the demons without causing the animals to suffer.[6] The story of the fig tree is hard to reconcile with Jesus' teachings and our idealized picture of him. On entering Bethany he was hungry and seeing a fig tree in the distance, he went to it to find something to eat. But since it was not the season for figs the tree had no fruit. Jesus cursed the tree and later it was noticed by Peter that the tree had withered. (Mark 11:12–14, 20–21). Jesus' action is not only in conflict with his Purity of Heart and Language Commandment, it also suggests a mean-spiritedness and vindictiveness that is incompatible with his alleged moral perfection.

Jesus' practice has an additional problem. He does not exemplify important intellectual virtues. Both his words and his action seem to indicate that he does not value reason and learning. Basing his entire ministry on faith, he said: "unless you turn and become like children, you will never enter the kingdom of heaven" (Matt. 18:3). As we know, children usually believe uncritically whatever they are told. Jesus seldom gave reasons for his teachings. When he did they were usually of one of two kinds: he either claimed that the Kingdom of Heaven was at hand or that if you believed what he said you would be rewarded in heaven whereas if you did not, you would be punished in hell. No rational justification was ever given for these claims. In short, Jesus' words and actions suggest that he believed that reasoning and rational criticism are wrong and that faith, both in the absence of evidence and even in opposition to the evidence, is correct. Rational people must reject Jesus' example that values blind obedience and that forsakes reason.

What Jesus' Practices and Teachings Neglect

Many Christians profess to find in the moral teachings of Jesus answers to all the moral questions of modern life. Needless to say, he explicitly addressed few of the moral concerns of our society today. For example, he said nothing directly about the morality or immorality of abortion, the death penalty, war, slavery, contraception, or racial and sexual discrimination. Unfortunately, it is not clear what one can deduce about these topics from his sayings and his practice. His doctrine of not resisting evil suggests that he would be against all war yet his violent action in driving the money changers from the temple suggests that he might consider violence in a holy cause justified. His Love Your Neighbor Commandment, which entailed love of your enemies, suggests that he would be opposed to the death penalty yet his threats of hellfire for sinners suggest that at times he might deem death or worse to be an appropriate punishment.

Jesus makes no explicit pronouncements on moral questions

connected with socialism, democracy, tyranny, and poverty and what one can infer from some things he says seems to be in conflict with other things he says. Consider his attitude toward poverty. His advocacy of selling everything and giving it to the poor (Luke 18:22) may suggest that he was opposed to poverty and wanted it eliminated. Yet when a women who poured expensive ointment on his head that could have been sold and given to the poor was rebuked for this by his disciples, Jesus defended her by saying that you always have the poor with you (Matt. 26:11). He also seemed to advocate material poverty by maintaining that a rich man cannot enter the Kingdom of Heaven (Matt. 19:23–24), and, as in Luke's version of the Beatitudes, that the poor are blessed and that theirs is the Kingdom of Heaven (Luke 6:20).

In some cases, Jesus' silence on the morality of a practice can only be interpreted as tacit approval. For example, although slavery was common in Jesus' own world, there is no evidence that he attacked it. As Morton Smith has noted:

> There were innumerable slaves of the emperor and of the Roman state; the Jerusalem Temple owned slaves; the High Priest owned slaves (one of them lost an ear in Jesus' arrest); all of the rich and almost all of the middle class owned slaves. So far as we are told, Jesus never attacked this practice. He took the state of affairs for granted and shaped his parables accordingly. As Jesus presents things, the main problem for the slave is not to get free, but to win their master's praise. There seem to have been slave revolts in Palestine and Jordan in Jesus' youth (Josephus, *Bellum* 2. 55–65); a miracle-working leader of such a revolt would have attracted a large following. If Jesus had denounced slavery or promised liberation, we should almost certainly have heard of his doing it. We hear nothing, so the most likely supposition is that he said nothing.[7]

Moreover, if Jesus had been opposed to slavery, it is likely that his earlier followers would have followed his teaching. However, Paul (1 Cor. 7:21, 24) and other earlier Christian writers commanded Christians to continue the practice of slavery.[8]

Unfortunately, Jesus' apparent tacit approval of slavery is obscured in the Authorized and Revised Versions of the New Testament by a translation of the Greek word for slave *doulos* as "servant." For example, in the Revised Standard Version Jesus says that a servant is like his master (Matt. 10:25). A more accurate translation would be that a slave is like his master.

Evaluation of Jesus' Ethics

THE LOVE OF GOD AND FAITH IN JESUS
COMMANDMENTS

The harsh otherworldly aspect of the Love of God Commandment is accepted by few Christians today. For example, only sects
such as the Jehovah's Witnesses hold doctrines approximating to the
view that the Kingdom of God is at hand, that one should not be
concerned about the future, that one should give up everything,
including one's family, to follow Jesus. Although these are clear
messages of Jesus they are ignored by most Christians.

Consider Jesus' idea that one should not be concerned about the
future. There is, of course, at least one way of interpreting Jesus'
injunction that may have some point. It is possible in our personal lives
to be so concerned about the future that we neglect to enjoy the
simple pleasures of living. If this is all that Jesus' message entails,
many might agree. Unfortunately, it is not. Since his injunction seems
to be based on the belief that God will provide for us, even many
theists seem to reject it. Indeed, any rational person who is concerned
about a just and healthy society must reject Jesus' injunction because
the evidence indicates that careful planning for the future is necessary
for such a society. In fact, some of the most serious problems of the
modern age—for example, overpopulation, atmospheric pollution, and
energy shortages—are partially the result of our not planning carefully
for the future.

The Faith in Jesus Commandment presupposes the truth of the
Incarnation. Since, as I have shown in Chapter 5, there are serious
conceptual and factual problems with that doctrine, serious obstacles
stand in the way of a rational person's following this commandment.

THE PURITY OF HEART AND LANGUAGE
COMMANDMENT

Jesus' stress on controlling one's thoughts, emotions, and desires
has been deemphasized and in many cases nearly eliminated from
modern discussions of Christian ethics.[9] Today those who oppose the
commandment usually give two reasons. First, people who are sympathetic with depth psychology argue that since most of our emotions
and desires are involuntary and cannot be controlled, to condemn
them as wrong and sinful causes unnecessary guilt and psychological
harm. Thus, Jesus' teachings would result in the repression of feelings

that we must be in contact with for reasons of our psychological health. [10] Moreover, if Jesus' injunction is interpreted as a command not to contemplate any evil actions at all, it has been maintained that it thwarts our imagination and forbids the contemplation of evil, for example, in art and literature. However, it may be argued that such contemplation discourages wrong actions more than it encourages them. [11] For those who are sympathetic with Jesus' injunction it may be argued that it can be interpreted as simply advising us not to encourage dangerous emotions or desires, such as anger with one's brother or sexual desire for a forbidden person. On this interpretation, his injunction would be justified in terms of its preventing violent or unacceptable social practices.

However, both modern critics and defenders assume that the commandment should be judged in terms of the consequences of following it; that is, in terms of the consequences of controlling thoughts and emotions. Whether this is how Jesus saw the injunction is at least doubtful. He may well have believed that certain thoughts or emotions were bad in themselves independently of their consequences. If this was his view, there is little reason to suppose it is true. Emotions, desires, thoughts, and feelings do not seem to be good or bad in themselves. The crucial ethical issue is whether they lead to beneficial or harmful actions. This is not easily determined but in *some* cases there is good reason to suppose that thoughts, emotions, and feelings may well cause social harm. For example, there is some evidence now to suggest that exposure to violent pornography stimulates rape fantasies in males and increases aggression. [12] In other words, thoughts and emotions can indeed have a harmful effects. In this respect, at least, modern defenders of the injunction are correct. Thus, it is not necessarily mistaken to suppose that certain thoughts and feelings should be discouraged, rather than encouraged, for example, by education and increased public awareness. However, we are far from knowing under what conditions this should be done, and how it can best be done without causing harmful psychological repression. In this respect the modern critics of the injunction are right.

Jesus' injunction against certain uses of language should be evaluated in the same way as his injunction against having certain thoughts. There is little reason to suppose that any use of language is evil per se. If Jesus thought otherwise, then his view is unjustified. The issue turns again on the consequences of the use. For example, there is good reason to suppose that the use of sexist language indirectly has harmful effects on women and thus should be avoided. However, calling someone a fool does not deserve hell's fire, as Jesus thought, and although in most cases it would be the wrong thing to say even if it was true, on some occasions saying it would be correct and cause more good than harm. Again, swearing may not be appropriate in many contexts and circumstances but in others it expresses emotions and feelings that could not perhaps be expressed in other ways and may have no harmful effect.

THE COMMANDMENT OF HUMILITY

If Jesus' Commandment of Humility meant simply that one should not be proud or arrogant, it is excellent advice. However, this commandment is usually given a more radical interpretation and Jesus seems to have intended it in a stronger way. As we have seen, it involves serving people in lowly ways, not caring about prestige, not demanding honors or recognition, not judging others, giving alms, and praying in secret. But taken to this extreme his advice seems questionable. It is important to know one's own strengths and weaknesses and to act accordingly.[13] Sometimes this will involve putting oneself forward, sometimes not. Sometimes taking a lowly position would not only serve no useful purpose, it would be morally undesirable. If, for example, the pilot of an airplane has a sudden heart attack, you are an experienced pilot, and without your taking over the plane will crash, is it not your moral obligation to put your knowledge into operation even if this involves an overt display of superiority? In this circumstance being humble and insisting on some lowly role would seem to be insanity.

As we have seen, for Jesus being humble involved praying and giving alms in secret. Is he correct to insist that one should be humble in this way? It will depend on the motive. For example, a person who gives a large sum of money to the poor might make a public announcement of this in order to impress people and increase his or her social standing. However, the motive could be completely altruistic. The person might believe that knowledge of the donation will encourage others to contribute and, indeed, it might if the person is well respected in the community. Thus, sometimes public displays of ostensibly altruistic actions—ones that could have been done privately—may be done for completely altruistic motives. Jesus may have wrongly supposed otherwise.

Being humble for Jesus also involved not judging others. If this means that we are never to make judgments about whether someone has done something wrong or whether some person has certain moral flaws, it is unacceptable because it would involve abandoning legal procedure as we now understand it. It would also mean that we could not assess other people's moral character and know whom to trust and rely on. However, such knowledge is surely important and our lives would be difficult without it.

This is not to say that the injunction not to judge others could not be interpreted in a weaker and more justifiable way. However, it is unclear that this more acceptable construction is what Jesus meant. One might interpret the injunction to mean that it is a mistake to dwell on the faults of others and to neglect our own. In our own personal lives we may be much better off spending more time engaging in rigorous self-criticism and less time criticizing our neighbors. Moreover, it could be maintained that to respect others despite their faults is a virtue that should be cultivated. Surely its cultivation would help to smooth personal relations, promote the common good, and bring about world peace. Any sensible person should be for Jesus' injunction if this is what it means.

THE LOVE YOUR NEIGHBOR COMMANDMENT

Whatever problems there may be with the ethical teachings and practice of Jesus as they are portrayed in the synoptic Gospels, many Christians would insist that the essential core of the Christian message is the commandment to love your neighbor.[14] Let us sample some of the interpretations of this commandment that have been provided by recent Christian ethical theorists and see if it is acceptable.[15] It should be clear in what follows that some of these contemporary interpretations of Christian ethics have come a very long way from Jesus' obscure and questionable pronouncements in the Gospels. Indeed, stripped of its theological gloss, recent Christian ethics has a considerable overlap with secular ethical theory. Thus, the question arises of why it should be preferred.

Paul Ramsey's Basic Christian Ethics

One of the clearest and most thoughtful interpretations of contemporary Christian ethics is Paul Ramsey's *Basic Christian Ethics*. Ramsey says that he "endeavors to stand within the way the Bible views morality"[16] and he argues that "the basic principles of Christian ethics cannot be understood except from a study of the New Testament and by studying the great theologians of the past in whose reflections on moral issues Christian themes are 'writ large.' "[17]

Ramsey begins his book by maintaining that Christian ethics cannot be separated from its religious foundations. In particular, Christian ethics is based on what he calls the righteousness of God; that is, the loving-kindness and mercy that is involved in his saving of humankind. God's unswerving love for his creatures is the model of how we should act toward our neighbors. Christian ethics, according to Ramsey, is deontological; it specifies what one has an obligation to do, not what it is good to do. In one of his later books he says: "The Christian understanding of righteousness is . . . radically non-teleological. It means ready obedience to the *present* reign of God, the alignment of human will with the Divine will that men should live together in covenant-love no matter what the morrow brings, even if it brings nothing."[18] This, says Ramsey, is the core of Old Testament ethics and it carries over into the New Testament where Jesus, the embodiment of God's righteousness in his life, teaches this righteousness in his commandment to love your neighbor. The Love Your Neighbor Commandment is the basic rule or principle of Christian morality, Ramsey says: "Everything is quite lawful, *absolutely everything* is permitted which love permits, everything without a single exception."[19] God demands total concern with neighbor need: "The biblical notion of justice may be summed up in the principle: To each according to the measure of his real need, not because of anything human reason can discern inherent in the needy, but because his need alone is the measure of God's righteousness towards him."[20]

Ramsey points out that many people have discerned a problem in Christian ethics in that some aspects of Jesus' neighbor love are based on a belief that the Kingdom of God was at hand. Since, according to Jesus, this commandment implies that people are not to resist evil, Ramsey says, it seems to "suit only an apocalyptic perspective."[21] For example, according to Ramsey, Jesus was not so naive as to believe that all evil could be overcome by love: he thought evil would be destroyed by God's righteous vengeance in the forthcoming apocalypse. However, since even most Christians do not suppose that God's righteous vengeance is near, Ramsey asks how Christians should act. What relevance does neighbor love have in a nonapocalyptic world? He stresses that it would be a mistake to suppose that just because Christian ethics has its origins in an apocalyptic worldview, it has no validity. Because of Jesus' apocalyptic vision this focus of his ethics was on one particular other person here and now. However, Ramsey maintains that the focus on a here-and-now, bipolar relationship has relevance even when divorced from its apocalyptic setting because it provides a norm for all one-to-one relationships. As one commentator on Ramsey's work puts it: "Thus the love commandment provides a kind of heuristic norm which impinges on each bipolar human relationship."[22]

Ramsey maintains that Christian ethics is both deontological and completely altruistic. As a Christian, you must always be concerned with your neighbor's welfare, never directly with your own. Concern with your own welfare is only permitted if this is relevant to your neighbor's.[23] The implications of this view are brought out by considering examples of when you do and do not have an obligation to resist physical attack on yourself and others. If you see person A being physically attacked by person B you have an obligation to protect A even if this necessitates your killing of B. Your concern should be with your neighbor's welfare; that is, with A's welfare. Suppose you are physically attacked by B, however, and the welfare of A depends on your surviving the attack. Again you have an obligation to resist B even if this means killing B. But now suppose that you are attacked by B and no one else's welfare is adversely affected if you do not survive. Ramsey's position seems to be that you should not defend yourself *even by nonviolent means,* even if this means your death.[24]

What is your neighbor's welfare? If your concern must always be with your neighbor's welfare, what values determine this? Ramsey tries to remain neutral on this question, saying:

> Christian ethics raises no fundamental objection to definitions of *value* given by any school of philosophical ethics. Hedonism, for example, or the theory that pleasure alone is the good, may be incorrect on philosophical grounds, but if true there would be nothing unchristian about it. . . . [Christianity's] concern is to turn a hedonist who thinks only of his own pleasure into one who gives pleasure (the greatest good he knows) to his neighbors.[25]

Thus Ramsey claims that there are two great questions in ethics. "*What* is good? and *Whose* good shall it be when choice must be made between mine and thine?"[26] The first question, Ramsey says, is the main concern of philosophical ethics. The second question "is the main, perhaps the only, concern of Christian ethics."[27]

Ramsey distinguishes his brand of Christian ethics from both a utilitarianism based on self-interest and one centered on values. Some utilitarians, for example Jeremy Bentham, have maintained that social relations and laws should be constructed in a way that takes advantage of our selfish nature. Properly arranged these would indirectly induce each human being to bring about the social good as a means of looking after his or her own welfare. However, Ramsey argues that although this strategy will work for people operating within such a system it may not work for the legislators who create this system. They could make laws tailored to their own advantage rather than the common good. In any case, he maintains that even if a community of enlightened, self-interested persons would work, this presupposes that a community with common interests could be created. "This is the work of Christian love, the work of reconciliation. Only Christian love enters the 'no man's land' where dwell the desperate and despised outcastes from every human community, and bring community with them into existence."[28]

Ramsey considers J. S. Mill's utilitarianism value-centered because it holds that one should bring about the greatest amount of happiness. He raises the standard criticism that Mill's theory can give no plausible account of the distribution of value. Thus, if action X brought about more happiness to the lower classes and less to the privileged classes than action Y, but X and Y resulted in the same amount of total happiness, there would be no way in principle for Mill's theory to decide between X and Y. Yet Ramsey argues that classical utilitarianism gave greater concern to the distribution of happiness than was ever justified by its theory; that is, utilitarians tended to favor X over Y. This inconsistency was praiseworthy and showed utilitarianism's "fundamental dependence on the Christian heritage of regard for others for their own sake."[29]

Although a complete analysis and evaluation of Ramsey's system is not possible here, it should be clear that many aspects of Jesus' original views have dropped out of Ramsey's ethical views as they are presented in *Basic Christian Ethics*. For example, Ramsey says nothing about Jesus' threats of hellfire for those who do not accept his views. Jesus' mercy and kindness is stressed; his vindictiveness and vengefulness is ignored.

Although Ramsey stresses the Love Your Neighbor Commandment it is important to see that Jesus gave us very little analysis or explanation of what he intended by this commandment. Because of this vagueness and uncertainty it is hardly surprising that Ramsey's interpretation of Christian ethics is by no means shared by all Christians. Ramsey interprets Jesus to have believed that the Neighbor Love Commandment entails that one should not resist evil, not even resist it by nonviolent means. But he interprets this to apply to only purely selfish action. According to Ramsey Christian ethics allows you to kill in order to protect others, for example, in times of war. But this interpretation would be rejected by Christian pacifists, for example Tolstoy, who are opposed to all killing related to war. Ramsey, in *Basic Christian Ethics*, makes no serious attempt to show that his interpretation is more justified in terms of biblical scholarship than other interpretations. Further, his view that Jesus cannot be plausibly interpreted to have advocated nonviolent resistance would undoubtedly be denied by Martin Luther King and other Christian advocates of its use. Whether nonviolent resistance is a plausible technique of social change is another issue.[30]

Non-Christians and even humanists can in principle accept Ramsey's ethical teachings when they are divorced from their theological underpinnings, and despite Ramsey's claim that Christian ethics cannot be separated from its religious foundation, they can be. There seems to be no reason why non-Christians and secularists could not hold Ramsey's view about, for example, self-defense and the problems of utilitarianism. The crucial question is whether there would be any justification for them to do so.

However, Ramsey's position on self-defense is unjustified. There seems to be no good reason why a person A should not defend himself or herself against violent attack even by nonviolent means if in so doing this would not be beneficial to other people. At least nonviolent self-defense from violent attack where no other-regarding interest is present would be approved of by a person who was fully informed, unbiased, and disinterested, that is, by an ideal observer. I am also inclined to suppose, although with less confidence, that violent self-defense, so long as the violence is no more than is necessary to repel the attack, would also be approved of by an ideal observer. Furthermore, I do not see that Ramsey's prohibition on nonviolent self-defense follows from the Love Your Neighbor Commandment even as he understands it. If you can defend yourself nonviolently from your neighbor's attack, you are not doing anything that harms your neighbor. A conflict with the Love Your Neighbor Commandment interpreted as Ramsey does would only appear when self-defense involved harming your neighbor.

Whether utilitarianism can give an adequate account of justice is part of an extensive, ongoing philosophical debate.[31] Ramsey's criticism adds nothing to what critics of utilitarianism have already said.[32] Indeed, depending on how one interprets the love commandment, it may be no better off than utilitarianism with respect to the problem of distributive justice. Consider the view of William Frankena, one of few recent philosophical critics of utilitarianism who is concerned to relate his theory to the Christian ethics of love.[33] Frankena argues that "the clearest and most plausible view, in my opinion, is to identify the love of law [the commandment to love your neighbor] with what I have called the principle of beneficence, that is of doing good, and to insist that it must be supplemented by the principle of distributive justice or equality."[34] On the other hand, if one builds distributive justice into the law of love as Ramsey seems to do, then Frankena argues that "the law of love . . . is really a twofold principle, telling us to be benevolent to all and to be so equally in all cases." In this case, he argues that the law of love is "identical with the view I have been proposing,"[35] that is, a moderate deontological theory that consists of a principle of beneficence combined with a principle of justice.[36] Frankena's nonreligious ethics seems very close indeed to Ramsey's theory. For example, one statement of Frankena's principle of justice is that one ought to help people in proportion to their needs and abilities. As we have seen, Ramsey sometimes states the principle of neighbor love as the principle of treating people according to their needs.[37] Furthermore, it has been pointed out that the principle of neighbor love overlaps with the principle of justice as this is sometimes stated.[38]

One wonders, then, whether the problems of utilitarianism are any better illuminated by Ramsey's ethics of neighbor love than by some statements of the principle of justice. For example, Ramsey is no doubt correct that in order to have a community of enlightened self-interest it is necessary to have a community with common interests. But is he correct that only Christian love can bring about community in a population in which there is none? Why could not the spirit of utilitarianism tempered with justice do the same thing? This is in part an empirical issue concerning the factors that can bring about community. Surely there have been communities where there was a strong sense of community and where Christian love was absent. One thinks, for example, of native American communities before the coming of the Christian missionaries. In any case, no evidence has been provided by Ramsey for his claim that Christian love is an essential factor in the creation of community, but if there is such evidence, then a nonbeliever might have good reason to adopt a secular version of Christian ethics.

One final caveat. Ramsey claims that Christian ethics are deontological. At times he only seems to mean by this that Christian ethics impose obligations and not specify what it is good to do, but this is a misleading sense of "deontological." Indeed, on this account some forms of utilitarianism are deontological theories since according to them one has an obligation to bring about the greatest good. At other times Ramsey seems to mean that the commandment of neighbor love demands some sort of action or way of life in the present with no thought of the consequences this action or way of life might have in the future.[39] But this cannot be right. One can conceive of circumstances in which any action or forbearance that we would normally suppose was our Christian duty would be wrong because of the indirect consequences.[40] A good Samaritan who helps someone in need surely would have done the wrong thing, and we would venture to say an unchristian act, if his or her help was highly likely to indirectly result in a full-scale nuclear war and the destruction of the human race.[41] Thus, someone who wishes to follow the Love Your Neighbor Commandment must be prepared to take indirect consequences of typical Christian practice into account despite what Ramsey seems to suggest. In this respect followers of Christian ethics have a duty that is similar to that of followers of utilitarianism.[42] Perhaps Ramsey would not wish to deny this. But then, it is unclear in what sense Christian ethics would be deontological in Ramsey's view.

Reinhold Niebuhr's An Interpretation of Christian Ethics

In *An Interpretation of Christian Ethics*, Reinhold Niebuhr attempts to explain how the ethics of Jesus, an ethics that Niebuhr believes specifies an impossible ethical ideal, can have relevance to the modern world. According to Niebuhr, the ethics of Jesus, with its ideal of love,

> ha[ve] the same relation to the facts and necessities of human experience as the God of prophetic faith has to the world. it is drawn from, and relevant to, every moral experience. It is immanent in life as God is immanent in the world. It transcends the possibilities of human life in its final pinnacle as God transcends the world. It must, therefore, be confused neither with the ascetic ethic of world-denying religions nor

with the prudential morality of naturalism, designed to guide good people to success and happiness in this world.[43]

Although the ethics of Jesus have relevance to every moral experience these ethics, Niebuhr says, do not deal with the immediate problems of every human life, namely, "the problem of arranging some kind of armistice between various contending factions and forces. It has nothing to say about the relativities of politics and economics, nor of the necessary balance of power which exist and must exist in even the most intimate social relationships."[44] He says:

> The absolutism and perfectionism of Jesus' love ethic set itself uncompromisingly not only against the natural self-regarding impulses, but against the necessary prudent defenses of the self, required because of the egoism of others. It does not establish a connection with the horizontal points of a political or social ethic or with the diagonals which a prudential individual ethics draws between the moral ideal and the facts of a given situation. It is only a vertical dimension between the loving will of God and the will of man.[45]

Niebuhr maintains that Jesus' injunctions against prudential concern over our health and welfare, all forms of self-assertion, and his commandment to forgive our enemies do not take into account our natural impulses or social consequences. Consequently, Jesus' ethics "is not an ethic which can give us specific guidance in the detailed problems of social morality where the relative claims of family, community, class, and nation must be constantly weighed."[46] Despite this Niebuhr maintains that "the ethic of Jesus may offer valuable insights to and sources of criticisms for a prudential social ethics which deals with present realities."[47] The Christian must compromise by "creating and maintaining tentative harmonies of life in the world in terms of the possibilities of the human situation, while yet at the same time preserving the indictment upon all human life of the impossible possibility, the law of love."[48]

Niebuhr holds that we cannot live up to the ethical ideal of Jesus because of our human nature. Although human beings are natural creatures they are also spiritual and as such they are connected with a reality that transcends the natural. "Man as a creature of both finitude and the eternal cannot escape his problem simply by disavowing the ultimate."[49] This dual nature of human beings is captured in what Niebuhr calls the myth of the Fall. According to this myth sin came into the world through human responsibility and cannot be attributed to God. Although this myth is not to be taken literally, Niebuhr maintains that it gives us insight into the nature of sin; that is, into the tension between our natural and our spiritual natures. For Niebuhr, this dual nature entails that science, which can only study the natural aspect of our being, will never be able to describe the area of human freedom in which moral choices are made. This area of human freedom and spirituality can only be disclosed by introspection of an intense type of religious experience where choices are made between good and evil.

The myth of the Fall not only gives us insight into moral responsibility it also gives us clues to the character of moral evil, Niebuhr says. According to the myth, original sin is rebellion against God where God's creatures try to become God. If this myth is not taken literally as a description of some distant historical event, it amounts to this: Finite humans by their very nature seek to make themselves infinite; egoism is, thus, the driving force behind sin. It is possible for humans to be saved from this sinful pretension by recognition of their inability to become infinite and to become reconciled to God through their resignation to their finite condition. Niebuhr sees no hope for this in "the collective life of mankind" for such a life "offers men the very symbols of pseudo-universality which tempt them to glorify and worship themselves as God."[50]

How is what Niebuhr calls the impossible possibility, the law of love, relevant to the real world where competing interests must be balanced and human egoism is rampant? First, he argues that the minimal moral standards one finds in all moral systems, for example, injunctions against the taking of human life, are grounded in the law of love. He maintains that minimal standards cannot be fully explained by considerations of rational prudence. Furthermore, he argues that as higher systems of morality are developed where there are more than merely negative prohibitions, for example, where principles of justice are constructed that enable humans fair opportunities to secure goods to sustain life, the law of love is implicitly the guiding maxim. As Niebuhr puts it: "Equality is always the regulative principle of justice; and in the ideal of equality there is an echo of the law of love, "Thou shalt love thy neighbor as THYSELF."[51] The principle of equal justice is an approximation to the law of love in our imperfect world: in a perfect world without competition and conflict there would be no need for such a principle.

The moral progress of civilization from penal reforms to the considerations of special needs in education, Niebuhr argues, is guided by the ideal of love. To be sure, this ideal will never be realized completely and a compromise with sinful human nature must be made. He argues, however, that both Christian liberalism and Christian orthodoxy have impeded moral progress. Christian liberalism has not understood the sinful nature of human beings and Christian orthodoxy used humans' sinful nature as an excuse for "the complacent acceptance of whatever imperfect justice a given social order had established."[52]

Unlike liberal Christianity, what Niebuhr calls prophetic Christianity realizes that human egoism, which is the basis of sin, can never be broken and that harmonies must be achieved by playing one egoistic interest against another. However, Niebuhr says that prophetic Christianity, unlike naturalism, does not adopt a complacent attitude toward egoism. Criticizing naturalists like John Dewey, he says that Dewey's theory of naturalism presupposes "a greater degree of rational transcendence over impulse than actually exists and a natural obedience impulse to the ideal which all history refutes."[53] In particular, he maintains that nothing in Dewey's theory can explain why nations have not realized the goal of universal peace.

Although Niebuhr ties his ethical view closely to Christian religious doctrines there is no a priori reason to do so. Thus, a non-Christian and even a secularist could maintain that although the ethics of Jesus is an impossible ideal, it nevertheless provides insights about and serves as a source of criticisms of actual ethical systems. Of course, a secularist would have to justify this impossible ideal on nontheological grounds. However, there is no obstacle in principle to doing so. For example, a utilitarian might maintain that using this ideal as a source of insight and criticism is justified on grounds of utility. Despite what Niebuhr at times seems to suggest, there is no reason why a secularist could not appeal to an ethical ideal that far transcends all present moral systems and attempts to approximate such an ideal while realizing full well that the ideal can never be realized completely. Furthermore, despite Niebuhr's frequent use of the phrase "the prudential morality of naturalism," naturalistic morality need not be prudential where this means a morality that is based on self-interest.

Indeed, there is no a priori reason why a secularist could not appeal to the myth of the Fall to provide insights into human nature, as Niebuhr does, but interpret these nontheologically. Divorced from its theological language, the myth of the Fall suggests that human beings have an egoistic nature that will prevent them from ever completely achieving an altruistic ideal. Unlike Niebuhr, whose theory of sinful human nature seems to be based on introspection and scriptural interpretation, secularists could attempt to justify this theory by an appeal to history and the findings of social science. History, if it is appealed to at all by Niebuhr, is used to illustrate his theory of human nature. He gives us no clue as to what conceivable historical evidence would tend to count against it. Even secularists may be willing to admit that the law of love has implicitly provided an ideal for every social reform and, in particular, that in the ideal of equal justice there is "the echo of the law of love."

However, although a secularist *could* take this tack, there are alternatives that may be more appealing. Minimal moral standards such as the injunction against the taking of a human life can be justified, as H. L. A. Hart has argued, in terms of the human impulse for survival and simple truisms about human beings.[54] Further, as John Rawls's work suggests, it is possible to base a principle of justice on what rational egoists would choose under certain conditions.[55] There may be reason to suppose, therefore, that minimal ethical constraints and even the construction of an ethically plausible principle of justice do not need to appeal to the law of love for their guiding inspiration.

I have suggested that even secularists could accept the view that human beings are fundamentally egoistic and attempt to base their belief on the findings of history and the social sciences. However, I am skeptical that this attempt would be successful. Although the findings of history and social science provide much evidence of human beings acting selfishly there is little reason to suppose that selfish human action is innate and unchangeable or that altruism on a worldwide scale is impossible. There is, after all, ample evidence of human beings acting on purely altruistic motives. We are far from knowing when and under what conditions, however, human beings act with unselfish motives and how altruism can be promoted.

In light of what we know about human nature, even secularists can still hope that radical changes in society and education can bring about a world that is closer to the Christian ideal than Niebuhr would admit. However, although they would not be justified in believing on the basis of the evidence that the realization of this ethical ideal is impossible, they might be justified in believing that it is unlikely and extremely hard to achieve. Naturalism is compatible, thus, with a hardheaded realism about moral progress. In this regard I believe that

Niebuhr is wrong to suppose that Dewey had a complacent attitude toward egoism and a naive view about the possibility of human progress. He seemed perfectly aware that social progress would not be easy and that there would never be a time when all human action would be morally right.[56] But even if Dewey was overly optimistic, this is not inherent in naturalism.

As I have suggested, even secularists can accept the law of love as an ethical ideal without its theological trappings. However, before they do so they should be sure they know what this ideal amounts to. Unfortunately, as commentators have pointed out, Niebuhr does not spell out very clearly what the impossible possibility involves.[57] What exactly would a society be like that was governed completely by the law of love? Niebuhr's statements are suggestive but elusive. For example, he says:

> The basic rights to life and property in the early community, the legal minima of rights and obligations of more advanced communities, the moral rights and obligations recognized in these communities beyond those which are legally enforced, the further refinement of standards in the family beyond those recognized in the general community—all of these stand in an ascending scale of moral possibilities in which each succeeding step is a closer approximation of the law of love.[58]

However, it is not clear what exactly the goal of Niebuhr's moral progress is. Perhaps the closest Niebuhr comes to a definition of the law of love is "the obligation of affirming the life and interests of the neighbor as much as those of the self."[59] But if this is what the law of love amounts to, it is difficult to understand without further clarification why Niebuhr's characterization of moral progress in the above quotation approaches it.

Nor without further clarification does it seem possible to know in even the simplest cases what approximating the law of love entails. For example, suppose it is in my neighbor's interest to live and in my interest to live but the circumstances are such that I can live only if my neighbor dies and my neighbor can live only if I die. How do I come close to the law of love in such a case since, according to Niebuhr, I have an obligation to affirm my life and my interests, as well as those of my neighbor? As far as I can determine, nothing in Niebuhr's account provides an answer. Naturally, if there are difficulties in knowing how to approximate to the law of love even in such a simple case, to know how to approximate to it in the complex cases that prevail in modern society will prove even more difficult.

With further elaboration and clarification Niebuhr's interpretation of the law of love may well provide important insights for non-Christian and secularist ethics, but without elaboration and clarification it has little utility.

Gene Outka's Agape: An Ethical Analysis

Perhaps the most systematic analysis of the Neighbor Love Commandment to date has been developed by Gene Outka in *Agape: An Ethical Analysis*. Outka not only provides an analysis of recent theological writings on Christian love (agape) but attempts to relate theological discussions on this topic to contemporary analytic ethics.

According to Outka, one of most important aspects of agape is the regard for "every person qua human existent."[60] This regard is independent of special traits, actions, and so on that distinguish one person from another. Thus, the law of love says that we have an obligation to care for our neighbor for his or her own sake and not for any benefit to ourselves. This entails that we ought to have regard for our neighbors no matter what they might do, no matter what their social status is, no matter what their moral character, personality, and the like may be. Our regard must be permanent and unwavering.

The regard for every human being qua human being that is entailed by the Commandment of Neighbor Love Outka calls "equal regard" but this does not mean treating every one identically. One should care for one's neighbor's appropriately in terms of their needs and abilities. Consequently, different people may have to be treated differently. Self-sacrifice is sometimes cited as another essential aspect of the Neighbor Love Commandment; indeed, it is sometimes considered to be its highest manifestation. Outka, however, rejects this interpretation of agape. He maintains that if agape is considered as self-sacrifice, it would "provide no way of distinguishing between attention to another's needs and submission to his exploitation and no warrant for resisting the latter."[61] He considers self-sacrifice only to have instrumental value. Self-sacrifice may be useful, for instance, in promoting the welfare of others, he says, but it is not the highest manifestation of agape.

Mutuality has also been construed by some Christian ethical theorists as essential to agape. Thus, they argue that in order for a person to have agape love for a neighbor, the neighbor must return the agape love. Outka rejects this view although he does maintain that genuine regard for one's neighbor should involve concern about how the neighbor responds to your regard because the neighbor's response is symptomatic of his or her well-being. For example, if your neighbor, Jones, does not show concern for you after you have come to her aid, her lack of concern should be a concern for you because Jones apparently lacks an important trait necessary for harmonious human relations. This lack of concern on Jones's part may thus prompt you, out of neighborly love, to make a special effort to induce care in Jones not only for you but for everyone. [62]

Although agape is to be distinguished from various concepts of justice, Outka argues that it has the most overlap with equalitarian justice. Just as agape as equal regard does not entail treating everyone identically, so equalitarian justice does not. [63] In order to apply the principle of equalitarian justice one must take into account each person's needs and abilities. For Outka the two are not identical. Agape is a more inclusive notion than equalitarian justice. It plays a large role in intimate personal relations, friendship, and parenthood where "the giving and taking need not be measured out very carefully." [64] Furthermore, agape refers to an agent's basic loyalties; in particular, it refers to the self-giving element in devotion to God. In order to describe this devotion, "justice" is not the right word. "Love" is.

Outka considers various theological schemes for justifying agape but since they all presume the existence of God, it is not necessary to consider them here. One problem with the schemes Outka considers should, however, be mentioned. Religious attempts to justify agape face the problem of the is-ought gap. Theological statements are ostensibly factual statements specifying what is the case whereas the Neighbor Love Commandment specifies what should be the case. Since is-statements do not entail ought-statements, how can the Neighbor Love Commandment be derived from theological statements? One solution Outka mentions but does not defend is to suppose that theological assertions implicitly include moral values and therefore are not merely factual assertions. Consequently, there is no gap between is and ought. Another solution is to argue that although the statement "God is love" does not entail "You ought to love," it would be bizarre and unintelligible for one to accept the first statement and reject the second, especially given the metaphysical background that is involved in belief in God.

Outka maintains that "certain believers and non-believers do not wish to see the justificatory case for agape stand or fall altogether on explicitly religious or theological grounds."[65] Consequently, he considers possible nontheological grounds for agape. In particular, he considers the conditions ethical philosophers have specified for a principle's being a moral principle. On the one hand, it has been argued that the very minimal requirement of universalizability is a necessary condition. Some philosophers have gone well beyond this minimal consideration, however, to maintain that for a principle to be a moral principle it must be adopted for the good of everyone alike.[66] In this latter case, equal concern for each individual—one of the foundation stones of agape on Outka's view—appears to be implicitly involved.

Outka seems to admit that in some philosophical formulations of the conditions of moral principles there is a considerable overlap with agape. However, he maintains that there is no widespread consensus among philosophers on even the minimal requirement of universalizability and that the less than minimal requirement has been attacked as enshrining a particular code under the guise of spelling out the formal properties of moral principles.

Outka next considers philosophers who give "nonreligious reasons which specify still further in an other-regarding direction."[67] For example, Gregory Vlastos has given an account of equalitarian justice based on a doctrine of universal rights that overlaps significantly with agape.[68] Arguing that valuers, persons, are ends in themselves and have irreducible value, Vlastos maintains that we make a category mistake if we praise a man as a man rather than as a teacher, parent, actor, and so on. He attempts to justify this equalitarianism in terms of the capacity of human beings to experience the same values, for example relief from acute pain.

This argument has been challenged by Kai Nielsen, who denies that "there is any conceptual impropriety in praising a man as a man."[69] Outka says that those theologians who are skeptical of philosophical arguments may regard "a challenge such as Nielsen's as confirmatory. They may see it as one more indication that such appeals will always remain inconclusive, with new disagreements constantly erupting."[70] On the other hand, theologians who appeal to common moral reasoning and yet who "do not regard religious belief as a mere addendum, may wish to say something like the following about nonreligious or humanist cases for agape:"[71]

First, agape as a full-dress concept in the theological literature has features built into it and beliefs backing it which by definition a humanist version could not include (e.g., the intrinsic goodness of communion with God and the correlative treatment of witness, the belief that each man's irreducible value connects with his being a creature of God, and so on). Second, the question of whether a humanist version may be compatible or simply identifiable with parts of agape is still left open. Likewise undetermined is whether one can formulate a humanist scheme in which it makes sense to speak of each man as irreducibly valuable and where one person's well-being is as valuable as another's.[72]

I see no a priori reason why even secularists could not accept a large part of Outka's specification of the content of neighbor love insofar as such content does not entail belief in God. Although it may be true, as Outka says, that agape is a wider notion than equalitarian justice, one wonders how much wider it is when the latter is combined with other principles that are often embraced by secular moralists. Consider, for example, what Frankena calls the principle of beneficence: the principle that one should bring about the greatest balance of good over evil.[73] This principle plays a large role in making moral decisions in intimate personal relations, friendship, and parenthood where "the give and take need not be measured very carefully." One wonders if when theological elements are excluded, there are any real differences between agape, as Outka understands it, and some principle of equalitarian justice *combined* with a principle of beneficence. Unfortunately, he does not consider this question.

Outka leaves open the question of whether a nonreligious justification for an ethics that closely approximates an ethics of agape can be found. What reservations he has seem to be based on the disagreement among philosophers. Thus, the disagreement between Vlastos and Nielsen, he suggests, would confirm the beliefs of theologians who are skeptical of philosophical arguments and be one more indication of the inclusiveness of such arguments.

I certainly do not wish to maintain that philosophical arguments are not often inconclusive or that there is wide agreement on most issues. However, one should not exaggerate the agreement among Christian theologians about the correct interpretation of Christian ethics. There is in fact widespread disagreement among them on almost every aspect of Christian moral teaching.[74] If disagreement among philosophers can be used as a justification for doubting whether an equivalent to an ethics of agape could be founded on secular grounds, why not use disagreement among theologians as justification for doubting whether agapistic ethics could be founded on religious grounds?

As I pointed out above, there is a general problem involved in supposing that the law of love can be founded on theological grounds, namely, the is-ought gap. This has nothing to do with disagreement among theologians. As we have seen, Outka suggests two ways of solving this problem. Both solutions are problematic. First, if a religious assertion such as "God exists" implicitly includes moral values, then in order to hold such a statement rationally, ethical arguments would have to be appealed to as well as, for example, traditional arguments for the existence of God. Even if traditional arguments for God were sound, this would still not be enough to justify believing that the statement "God exists" is true since the ethical values included in the statement would still be unproven. Theists who suggest this solution to the is-ought gap surely place a greater burden than ever on those who wish to establish the rationality of belief in God. Second, I do not see why it would be bizarre or unintelligible to maintain that God is love and, even given the metaphysical background beliefs of theism, question if we should love. Of course, it may seem bizarre and unintelligible to religious believers to do so because they tacitly assume an ethical statement such as: "If God is love, we ought to love." Yet this statement is not entailed by the statement "God exists" or by any other statements that are part of the metaphysical background of theism.

Another reason that it may seem bizarre and unintelligible to theists to believe that God is love and yet to question if one should love is that they tacitly assume some version of the Divine Command Theory of morality, something not explicitly considered by Outka. On this theory the Commandment of Neighbor Love would follow from a certain metaethical theory combined with the assumption that God commanded neighbor love. Since, however, this theory in its various forms has serious problems, it cannot be used as a way of bridging the gap between is and ought. [75]

Of course, one who wishes to adopt a secular version of agapistic ethics may also have the is-ought problem on their hands. If secularists rely on some form of ethical naturalism, the key question is how one can deduce ought statements about the secular equivalent of agape from statements specifying certain states about the natural world. As I argue in Appendix 1, in some forms of naturalism there are fewer problems in so doing than in any version of the Divine Command Theory. Further, as I have argued elsewhere, there are secular schemes of rational ethical justification that are not based on ethical naturalism,[76] and it is possible that a secular equivalent of agapistic ethics can be justified on them.

I conclude, then, that nothing that Outka has said throws any more doubt on the possibility of constructing a secular equivalent to an agapistic ethics than on the possibility of constructing a religious one. Furthermore, independent metaethical considerations suggest that it may be easier in principle to base the secular equivalent to an agapistic ethics on nonreligious grounds than to base agapistic ethics on religious grounds.

Nevertheless, Outka is surely correct that the question is still open of how much overlap there is between religious agapism and its secular equivalent. He is correct for the wrong reason, however. We should leave the question open not because of any disagreement among philosophers, but because of the lack of empirical evidence and a certain conceptual unclarity in the notion of agape itself.

In the light of our present evidence we simply do not know with any clarity what actions will best realize the goals of a secular equivalent of agapism. Suppose, for example, that someone has adopted Frankena's normative ethical system in which the principle of justice and the principle of beneficence serve as a close secular equivalent to agapism.[77] It is conceivable that these two principles may make certain actions obligatory that do not appear agapistic. For example, it is possible that the best way to realize these two principles in certain circumstances is to act selfishly.[78] Thus, it is conceivable that according to Frankena's ethics, in some circumstances acting selfishly may be an appropriate ethical action. Just as Outka considers self-sacrificial actions instrumentally, on Frankena's scheme we may consider unselfish actions instrumentally. Unselfish actions should be performed only if they have certain results. However, it is an empirical question if unselfish actions do have these results. Consequently, it is an empirical question under what conditions it would be ethically appropriate to act unselfishly and under what ones it would be appropriate to act selfishly; this is not something to be settled by armchair speculation. However, in the light of our present evidence we are far from knowing with any certainty in what circumstances people should, for example, act selfishly.

A crucial question for religious ethical theorists in the agape tradition that is seldom considered, let alone answered, is whether one would ever be morally required to act selfishly: that is, to not be concerned with one's neighbor's welfare. As the Commandment of Neighbor Love is usually understood it might seem that this sort of action is excluded and that one must always be concerned with the welfare of one's neighbors. But one might wonder on reflection why agapism is committed to this. Paradoxically stated, on occasions may it not be that not acting to further the welfare of one's neighbors is the best way to further their welfare?[79] Put nonparadoxically, on some occasions if you act from selfish motives, might you not indirectly bring about your neighbor's welfare? For example, people with a strong disposition to look after their neighbors' welfare in everyday situations may so exhaust themselves that they are prevented from helping them in grave emergencies. It might have been better for their neighbors if they usually had given no thought to them. A mother who loves her children so much that she neglects developing her own talents and interests may provide a bad role model for them. The children might have been better off in the long run if she had been more selfish. In reply, the questions can be raised of whether this would not involve double-thinking or some form of self-deception. Would one not have to pretend to be doing certain actions for selfish motives but in the back of one's mind still be doing them out of love for one's neighbor? Not necessarily. In certain situations it might be best in terms of neighbor love not to think about the welfare of others even indirectly. Calculation of indirect consequences and pretense of selfishness may be psychologically harmful and incapacitating.

This brings up the question of whom the love commandment is directed at, or to put it differently, whose practice it should be guiding. As it is usually understood, it is directed at everyone and should be guiding everyone's practice. However, it may be argued that on occasions this would be a mistake. On occasions perhaps it should only be the guiding principle of people such as social planners, lawmakers, and educators who have a significant influence on the behavior of large numbers of people. They would direct, encourage, and teach others to act in nonagapistic ways that would indirectly bring about the greatest welfare of everyone. For example, although it might be a mistake for mothers themselves to calculate the indirect effect of developing their own talents on their children's welfare this would be an appropriate consideration for the educators of women.

Now if religious agapism countenanced this understanding of the

Neighbor Love Commandment, there might be a very close correspondence between the actions religious agapism would make obligatory and those a secular scheme like Frankena's would. However, it is uncertain that many religious agapists would countenance this understanding and the theory is simply not clear enough so that the issue can be decided by analyzing its formulation. Some religious agapists might insist that there is something intrinsically valuable about actions directed toward the welfare of others. Consequently, they would not agree that Christian ethics could ever allow purely selfish actions: that is, ones in which the actor is not at least indirectly concerned with the welfare of others.[80]

If so, religious agapism and a secular equivalent, such as the normative ethical theory of Frankena, would not in principle overlap in certain possible worlds where a wide class of purely selfish actions brings about ethically desirable results. However, in our world, given our present knowledge, the degree of overlap is uncertain. This is because we do not know with any certainty whether there are any purely selfish actions that bring about desirable ethical results. In our world such actions might be rare and, consequently, in our world there is a wide overlap between religious agapism, when this is interpreted to exclude purely selfish action, and secular equivalents.

Conclusion

Assuming that Jesus' ethical teachings are contained in the synoptic Gospels—a dubious assumption given the evidence of the early Christian epistle writers—a large part of his teachings seem irrelevant or indefensible to morally sensitive people or even to many contemporary Christians. Jesus' otherworldliness, harshness, demand of blind obedience, and vindictiveness are not only morally unacceptable but in conflict with the claim that he is morally perfect. Further, his extreme emphasis on purity of heart and language and humbleness is also objectionable. Moreover, his tacit approval of slavery and the unclarity of his teaching concerning other matters (for example, poverty) makes him an inappropriate ethical model. To be sure, plausible interpretations can be found for some of Jesus' more questionable and excessive pronouncements but they conflict with or at least temper what Jesus seemed to intend.

Even if we waive these problems and concentrate on what is considered by many to be the essence of Jesus' teachings, namely, the

Love Your Neighbor Commandment, there are obstacles. The unclarity of the commandment allows it to be interpreted in different ways. Some of these such as Ramsey's have unacceptable implications: one cannot defend one's self even with nonviolent means if one does this for purely selfish motives. Other interpretations such as Niebuhr's are so unclear that it is impossible to discern what the commandment entails. Still others such as Outka's are so close to secular systems of ethics that allow both a principle of equalitarian justice and a principle of beneficence that it is difficult to understand the difference. Furthermore, some of the claims made for the Love Your Neighbor Commandment, for example, that principles of justice and minimal moral restraints on conduct implicitly appeal to it, are questionable.

I have argued that it is possible to develop a plausible secular equivalent to the Christian ethics of neighbor love that in this world at least may well have significant overlap with it. Uncertainty on this score reflects our ignorance over the consequences of our actions and the unclarity in the concept of neighbor love itself.

NOTES

1. I am indebted in what follows to Richard Robinson, *An Atheist's Values* (Oxford: Basil Blackwell, 1964); George H. Smith, *Atheism: The Case Against God* (Buffalo, N.Y.: Prometheus, 1970); Bertrand Russell, "Why I Am Not a Christian," in *Philosophy and Contemporary Issues*, ed. John R. Burr and Milton Goldinger (New York: Macmillan, 1984), pp. 115–26.

2. Robinson, *An Atheist's Values*, pp. 140–49.

3. My account here is particularly indebted to Robinson's analysis in *An Atheist's Values*, pp. 145–46.

4. See, for example, John Piper, *Love Your Enemies* (Cambridge: Cambridge University Press, 1979), for some anticipations of the commandment to love one's enemies in Jewish and Greek sources.

5. For a critique of the thesis that Jesus' formulation was an extension of the Old Testament commandment see Michael Arnheim, *Is Christianity True?* (Buffalo, N.Y.: Prometheus, 1984), pp. 161–62.

6. Russell, "Why I Am Not a Christian," p. 123.

7. See Morton Smith, "Biblical Arguments for Slavery," *Free Inquiry* 7 (Spring 1987): 30.

8. Ibid.; see also Edward A. Westermarck, "Christianity and Slavery," in *A Second Anthology of Atheism and Rationalism*, ed. Gordon Stein (Buffalo, N.Y.: Prometheus, 1987); pp. 427–37.

9. For example, see Paul Ramsey, *Basic Christian Ethics* (New York: Charles Scribner's Sons, 1950). Ramsey barely mentions this aspect of Jesus' teachings.

10. Smith, *Atheism*, p. 153.

11. Robinson, *An Atheist's Values*, p. 153.

12. See, for example, E. Donnerstein, "Pornography and Violence Against Women: Experimental Studies," *Annals of the New York Academy of Science* 347 (1980): 277–88; E. Donnerstein, "Pornography Commission Revisited: Aggression-Erotica and Violence Against Women," *Journal of Personality and Social Psychology* 39 (1980): 267–77.

13. See Robinson, *An Atheist's Values*, pp. 153–55.

14. Some scholars have argued that Jesus' ethics are so tied to his eschatology that they have no relevance for contemporary thought. See Jack T. Sanders, *Ethics in the New Testament* (Philadelphia: Fortress Press, 1975).

15. For some other interpretations not considered here see Richard H. Hiers, *Jesus and Ethics: Four Interpretations* (Philadelphia: Westminster Press, 1968).

16. Ramsey, *Basic Christian Ethics*, p. xi.

17. Ibid., p. xiii.

18. Paul Ramsey, *Deeds and Rules in Christian Ethics* (New York: Charles Scribner's Sons, 1967), pp. 108–9.

19. Ramsey, *Basic Christian Ethics*, p. 89.

20. Ibid., p. 14.

21. Ibid., p. 35.

22. David H. Smith, "Paul Ramsey, Love and Killing," in *Love and Society: Essays in the Ethics of Paul Ramsey*, ed. James T. Johnson and David H. Smith (Missoula, Mont.: Scholars Press, 1974), p. 5.

23. Ramsey, *Basic Christian Ethics*, pp. 157–71.

24. Ramsey had developed his position on the moral obligation to defend others in his later works in attempting to morally justify war. See, for example, Paul Ramsey, *War and the Christian Conscience: How Shall Modern War Be Conducted Justly?* (Durham, N.C.: Duke University Press, 1961).

25. Ramsey, *Basic Christian Ethics*, pp. 112–13.

26. Ibid., p. 114.

27. Ibid., p. 114–15.

28. Ibid., p. 242.

29. Ibid., p. 239.

30. It has been maintained, for example, that an entire nation can be defended by a population trained in such techniques. See, for example, Gene Sharp, *The Politics of Nonviolent Action: Part 2—The Methods of Nonviolent*

Action (Boston: Porter Sargent, 1973). However, whether these techniques can be used to eliminate injustice and to bring about social good and as defenses against aggression both domestic and nondomestic is still debated. Some argue that the technique of nonviolent resistance might be a very useful technique for ethical change and defense but only in certain contexts and under certain conditions. For example, it has been argued that these techniques worked fairly well in India when they were used by the followers of Gandhi against the British and in the civil rights movement in the South when they were used by the followers of Martin Luther King. However, it is alleged that they would not have been effective if they had been used against Nazi oppression in World War II. See Michael Walzer, *Just and Unjust Wars* (New York: Basic Books, 1977), pp. 329–35. On the other hand, advocates of these techniques point to cases where they were used against Nazis with some success. See Duane L. Cady, *From Warism to Pacifism* (Philadelphia: Temple University Press, 1989), pp. 103–4. Other studies suggest that nonviolent resistance methods would prove unsuccessful in stopping many cases of domestic violence and rape. See Pauline B. Bart and Patricia H. O'Brien, "Stopping Rape: Effective Avoidance Strategies," *Signs* 10 (1984): 83–105. One can conclude that the effectiveness of methods of nonviolence resistance is controversial and unclear and its evaluation depends on empirical evidence that is often lacking. Consequently, any blanket approval of it at present is unjustified. If Jesus did advocate its use, he was unjustified.

31. For contemporary utilitarian literature attempting to justify a principle of equal distribution see Peter Singer, "Famine, Affluence, and Morality," *Philosophy and Public Affairs* 1 (1972): 229–43; Richard Brandt, *A Theory of the Good and the Right* (Oxford: Clarendon Press, 1979), pp. 311–16; Henry West, "Justice and Utility," in *Moral Philosophy*, ed. Joel Feinberg and Henry West (Encino, Calif.: Dickenson, 1977), pp. 328–43.

32. See, for example, Harlan Miller and William Williams, *The Limits of Utilitarianism* (Minneapolis: University of Minnesota Press, 1982); Samuel Scheffler, *The Rejection of Consequentialism* (Oxford: Clarendon Press, 1982).

33. See, for example, William Frankena, *Ethics*, 2d ed. (Englewood Cliffs, N.J.: Prentice-Hall, 1973), pp. 56–59.

34. Ibid., p. 58.

35. Ibid.

36. Christian ethics may also be construed as an ethics of virtue rather than one of obligation. See William K. Frankena, "The Ethics of Love Conceived as an Ethics of Virtue," *Journal of Religious Ethics* 1–2 (1973–1974): 21–36.

37. Ramsey, *Basic Christian Ethics*, p. 14.

38. Gene Outka, *Agape: An Ethical Analysis* (New Haven, Conn.: Yale University Press, 1972), p. 91.

39. This deontological interpretation of Christian ethics should be con-

trasted with the teleological interpretation of Joseph Fletcher in *Situation Ethics: The New Morality* (Philadelphia: Westminster Press, 1966).

40. For a theoretical discussion of how in some cases if several people act to achieve a good aim, this aim will be worse achieved, see Derek Parfit, *Reasons and Persons* (Oxford: Clarendon Press, 1984), chaps. 2, 4.

41. Cf. Kai Nielsen's discussion of what he calls Christian absolutism in *Ethics Without God* (Buffalo, N.Y.: Prometheus, 1973), chap. 4.

42. See, for example, Larry Alexander, "Pursuing the Good—Indirectly," *Ethics* 95 (1985): 315–32.

43. Reinhold Niebuhr, *An Interpretation of Christian Ethics* (New York: Meridian Books, 1959), p. 43.

44. Ibid., p. 45.

45. Ibid.

46. Ibid., p. 54.

47. Ibid., p. 55.

48. Ibid., p. 61.

49. Ibid., p. 68.

50. Ibid., p. 85.

51. Ibid., p. 101.

52. Ibid., p. 129.

53. Ibid., p. 187.

54. H.L.A. Hart, *The Concept of Law* (Oxford: Clarendon Press, 1961), pp. 189–95.

55. John Rawls, *A Theory of Justice* (Cambridge, Mass.: Harvard University Press, 1971), chap. 3.

56. For a defense of Dewey against Niebuhr's criticism see Morton White, *Social Thought in America: The Revolt Against Formalism* (Boston: Beacon Press, 1957), pp. 250–57.

57. See, for example, Outka, *Agape: An Ethical Analysis*, pp. 26–27. In some of Niebuhr's other works Outka finds Niebuhr characterizing the law of love in terms of frictionless harmony. However, frictionless harmony is compatible with brainwashing and thought control. In order for such an ideal to be acceptable it needs qualification and elaboration.

58. Niebuhr, *An Interpretation of Christian Ethics*, p. 103.

59. Ibid.

60. Outka, *Agape: An Ethical Analysis*, p. 9.

61. Ibid., p. 275.

62. This is my example, not Outka's. However, I believe it is in the spirit of his thesis.

63. See Frankena, *Ethics*, pp. 49–52.

64. Outka, *Agape: An Ethical Analysis*, p. 310.

65. Ibid., p. 195.

66. See Kai Nielsen, "On Moral Truth," *Studies in Moral Philosophy*,

American Philosophical Quarterly, Monograph no. 1, p. 13. Cited in Outka, *Agape: An Ethical Analysis*, p. 199.

67. Outka, *Agape: An Ethical Analysis*, p. 201.

68. See Gregory Vlastos, "Justice and Equality," in *Social Justice*, ed. Richard B. Brandt (Englewood Cliffs, N.J.: Prentice-Hall, 1962), pp. 49–51.

69. Outka, *Agape: An Ethical Analysis*, p. 203. See Kai Nielsen, "Skepticism and Human Rights," *The Monist* 52 (1968): 586.

70. Outka, *Agape: An Ethical Analysis*, p. 205.

71. Ibid.

72. Ibid., pp. 205–6.

73. Frankena, *Ethics*, p. 45.

74. For example, consider the disagreement over Fletcher's situation ethics interpretation. See John C. Bennett et al., *Storm over Ethics* (Philadelphia: United Church Press, 1967); Harvey Cox, ed., *The Situation Ethics Debate* (Philadelphia: Westminster Press, 1968). Furthermore, some interpretations play down the idea of neighbor love that is so stressed in other interpretations. See, for example, Garth L. Hallet, *Christian Moral Reasoning: An Analytic Guide* (Notre Dame, Ind.: University of Notre Dame Press, 1983), where Christian moral reasoning is characterized in terms of value balancing, and agape, neighbor love, and so on seem to play a relatively small role.

75. See Appendix 1.

76. See Martin, *Atheism: A Philosophical Justification* (Philadelphia: Temple University Press, 1990), Introduction.

77. See Frankena, *Ethics*, pp. 56–58.

78. Cf. Parfit, *Reasons and Persons*, chap. 1; Alexander, "Pursuing the Good—Indirectly," *Ethics* 95 (1985): 315–32.

79. Ibid.

80. This seems to be Ramsey's view.

7

Salvation by Faith

A central doctrine of Christianity is that one is saved through faith in Jesus. Thus, the Athanasian Creed says explicitly that "whosoever who earnestly desires to be saved must above all hold the Catholic Faith" and it is further affirmed that unless one keeps this faith whole and undefiled "he shall perish in eternity." The Catholic Faith, according to the creed, is the content of the creed itself. The Nicene Creed is less explicit. However, it certainly suggests that salvation comes through faith in Jesus when it affirms belief in one Lord Jesus Christ, the only-begotten Son of God, "who for us men and our salvation came down from heaven," who died on the cross, was resurrected, ascended to heaven, and will come in glory and in judgment. The creed does not explicitly say in what this belief in "one Lord Jesus Christ" consists although it is natural to infer that a necessary condition for salvation through faith in Jesus is belief in the content of the creed itself. Although the Apostles' Creed is the least explicit and in fact says nothing directly about salvation, given what we understand of the use of the creed by Christian churches, it is natural to suppose that believing it is considered by most Christians to be at least a necessary condition for salvation through Jesus Christ.

Commentators have also stressed the importance of salvation through Jesus to Christianity. Thus, Jaroslav Pelikan argues in an article on Christianity in the *Encyclopedia of Religion*:

> Neither the belief in God as Trinity nor the dogma of Christ as divine and human in nature nor the doctrine of humanity as created in the image of God but fallen into sin is, however, an end in itself for Christian faith. As a religion of redemption, Christianity presents itself as the message of how, through Christ, reconciliation has been achieved between the holiness of God and the sin of fallen humanity.[1]

And John Hick maintains in the *Encyclopedia of Philosophy*:

> At its primary level of belief Christianity claims that by responding to God's free forgiveness, offered by Christ, men are released from guilt of their moral failure (justification) and are drawn into a realm of grace in which they are gradually recreated in character (sanctification). The basis of this claim is the Christian experience of reconciliation with God, and, as a consequence, with other human beings, with life's circumstances and demands, and with oneself.[2]

Although the importance of the doctrine of salvation to Christianity is undeniable, what exactly is it? Is there one clear doctrine of salvation? Or are there several that are incompatible? What are the problems with the Christian view(s) of salvation?

Biblical Doctrines of Salvation

Clearly the source of the Christian doctrine of salvation is the New Testament. But what does the Bible teach? There are important differences between the synoptic Gospels, John, and Paul's letters and unclarities in all of these accounts. Indeed, one can discern four different views of salvation in the New Testament.

1. Although Jesus' message about salvation in the synoptic Gospels is not completely clear, he teaches both that one can be saved by following a very strict moral code and that one can be saved by giving up everything and following him. Let us consider these ideas in more detail.

The first three gospels teach that salvation is closely connected with belief in the imminence of the Kingdom of God (Luke 10:9; Mark 13:30). What will the Kingdom of God consist of? Although the account is sketchy these gospels indicate that God will rule the Earth, the Son of man will come and pronounce judgment, the dead will be resurrected, and Satan and the demons will lose their power.[3] But how is one to participate in this coming Kingdom of God? How is one to be saved? Is belief in Jesus sufficient for salvation? Is it necessary?

It is not clear according to these gospels if belief in Jesus is either sufficient or necessary for salvation. Some of the pronouncements of Jesus indicate that much more is involved and, indeed, that even exemplary moral conduct independent of faith can be sufficient. For example, in the Sermon on the Mount Jesus proclaimed that in order to enter the Kingdom of Heaven not one of the commandants must be relaxed and a person's righteousness must exceed that of the scribes and the Pharisees (Matt. 5:10–20). He suggested that those who will find salvation are few since following what he teaches is so very hard (Matt. 7:13–14). Yet he said that those who hear his words and do not follow them are like a house built on sand and will fall down in times of floods, rain, and wind (Matt. 7:24–27). Indeed, when Jesus was later asked by a young man what one must do to have eternal life he replied "if you would enter life, keep the commandments" (Matt. 19:17). Yet when he was pressed to specify what commandants he went beyond the commandants by saying that one must sell what one possesses and give to the poor. And he proclaimed to his disciples that it will be easier for a camel to go through the eye of a needle than for a rich man to enter the Kingdom of Heaven (Matt. 19:21–24; cf. Luke 18:18–25).

These passages certainly suggest that it is possible to enter the Kingdom of God by simply adopting a strict moral code that few people indeed can follow (Luke 13:24); in fact they suggest that it is impossible to enter the Kingdom without adopting such a code. Yet although it is unclear why this interpretation is not commonly adopted by New Testament scholars perhaps commentators have been unduly influenced by the doctrines of salvation of John and Paul.[4] In any case, in some parts of the synoptic Gospels salvation through faith in Jesus is, to say the least, not well developed and the favored doctrine is salvation through following a strict moral code.

2. Other passages in the synoptic Gospels suggest that salvation can be achieved by renouncing everything and following Jesus and that behaving according to a strict moral code is not necessary to salvation.[5] After hearing Jesus' proclamation about the impossibility of entering the Kingdom of Heaven if one is rich, the disciples are dismayed and ask, "Who then will be saved?" (The import of the question seems to be that Jesus' ethical standards for salvation are so high that no one, including the disciples, can meet them.) Jesus answers that with men this is not possible but with God all things are possible. Peter points out that they have given up everything and followed him. Jesus assures them that everyone who has left family and lands "for my name's sake" will enter eternal life (Matt. 19:25–29; Mark 10:29). Jesus then tells the parable of the householder and vineyard workers. The workers are paid the same amount of money whether they work the whole day or a part of it and the workers complain about the unfairness of this. But the householder argues: "Am I not allowed to do what I choose with

what belongs to me? Or do you begrudge my generosity?" (Matt. 20:15).

Exactly how this passage should be interpreted is not clear. One obvious reading is that to give up everything and follow Jesus is sufficient for salvation. God, like the householder, can choose whom to reward. Just as the vineyard laborers who have worked all day may get no more earthly reward than those who have only worked part of a day, people who have followed a strict code of ethics all of their life may get no more heavenly reward than those who have only recently given up everything and followed Jesus. On the other hand, there is nothing in what he says to indicate that those following the strict code that Jesus specifies will not be saved.[6] Jesus can be interpreted as saying that following this code is not the only way to be saved.

Thus, according to the synoptic Gospels, salvation is a two-track affair. It can be obtained through adhering to a strict moral code that few can follow or by following Jesus. This second track is also difficult but in a different way. It involves great personal sacrifice but not the rigors of following a strict moral code.

There is, however, at least one problem with this interpretation. As we saw in the last chapter, although Jesus is often considered to be a universal Savior, he is sometimes portrayed in the synoptic Gospels in narrow, sectarian terms as a Jewish savior. This narrow sectarianism of the synoptic Gospels seems to conflict with Jesus' statements that people who follow his strict moral code will be saved. It also conflicts with his statement to his disciples that because of their sacrifice they will be saved. Presumably, people other than Jews could follow his strict moral code and make great sacrifices in becoming disciples. To say the least, it is difficult to make sense of all this. Of course, on the narrow, sectarian interpretation the two tracks were open *only* to Jews. In this interpretation whether non-Jews could be saved, and if so, how, was not something with which Jesus was concerned.

3. Both John and Paul indicated that salvation is achieved only through faith in Jesus. However, even here there are differences in what they assume this faith consists of.

We have seen that the Athanasian Creed maintains that unless one keeps the faith "whole and undefiled" one shall perish in eternity. This idea is clearly taught in John's Gospel except that for John the content of faith is different from the Athanasian Creed. John does not seem to demand belief in the Trinity:

For God so loved the world that he gave his only Son, that whoever believes in him should not perish but have eternal life. For God sent the Son into the world, not to condemn the world, but that the world might be saved through him. He who believes in him is not condemned; he who does not believe is condemned already, because he has not believed in the name of the only Son of God. . . . He who believes in the Son has eternal life; he who does not obey the Son shall not see life, but the wrath of God rest upon him." (John 3:16–36)

In many other passages in John this same message is given: One is only saved through Jesus. "I am the way, and the truth, and the life; no one comes to the Father, but by me (John 14:6). What does believing in Jesus involve? In Jesus' reply to Nicodemus, he indicated that in order to enter the Kingdom of God one must be born anew (John 3:7). But is being born again the result of believing in Jesus? What exactly does it consist in? It is not implausible to suppose that John taught that being born again is the result of believing in Jesus and that it involves some sort of ethical transformation. Jesus says that "he who believes in me will do the works that I do" and "if you love me, you will keep my commandments" (John 14:12–15). "This is my commandment, that you love one another as I have loved you" (John 15:12).

Thus, there is no suggestion in John, as there is the synoptic Gospels, that salvation can be achieved by following a strict ethical code. Indeed, no strict ethical code is suggested. Nor is it implied directly that if one sacrifices everything to follow Jesus one is saved independently of following some strict code of ethics. One is saved only by believing in Jesus, which seems to involve some spiritual rebirth that may involve an ethical transformation in which one manifests the love that Jesus manifested for his disciples. There is no suggestion in John that Jesus had narrow, sectarian goals of salvation as there is in parts of the first three Gospels. On the other hand, John, like the synoptic Gospel writers, threatens punishment. He indicates that the wrath of God will rest on anyone who disobeys the Son of God.

Salvation by following a strict ethical code seems to be completely foreign to Paul's understanding: "For we hold that a man is justified by faith apart from works of the law" (Rom. 3:28) "Therefore, since we are justified by faith, we have peace with God through our Lord Jesus Christ. Through him we have grace in which we stand and we rejoice in our hope of sharing the glory of God" (Rom. 5:1–2). Paul argues that because of Adam's sin everyone became a sinner but because of Jesus' death we are given the gift of being free from sin and we are reconciled to God. Paul sometimes seems to be saying that faith in Jesus makes it impossible for us to sin. He maintains that our old sinful self was crucified with Jesus and we are no longer in bondage to sin (Rom. 6:6–11). On the other hand, he urges Christians not to sin (Rom. 6:12–16).

But what, according to Paul, is one supposed to believe when one has faith in Jesus Christ? It is not completely clear. He certainly thought that Jesus was resurrected on the third day. But, as we know, there is no reason to suppose that Paul had knowledge of the details of the Gospel story of the trial and crucifixion. So if faith in Jesus involved belief in his Resurrection, for Paul this involved less in terms of the content of belief than it did in the creeds. Nor is there any reason to think that Paul believed in other doctrines specified in the traditional creeds of Christianity. Thus, Paul probably did not believe in the Virgin Birth since he does not mention this. Indeed, some scholars have argued that it is not completely clear whether Paul believed that Jesus was the Son of God[7] although there is little doubt that he believed that Jesus and God were closely related. Consequently, it is not clear that for Paul, in contrast to the creeds and John, faith in Jesus involved belief in the Virgin Birth and the Incarnation.

4. Paul seems to suppose that *until* Jesus came men were under the law but the coming of Jesus annulled the law. "So that the law was our custodian until Christ came, that we might be justified by faith. But now that faith has come, we are no longer under a custodian" (Gal. 3:24–25). This suggests that people before Jesus *could* have been saved by strictly following the Jewish law but afterwards they could only be saved through Jesus. This seems to conflict with Jesus' statement in the synoptic Gospels that more than following the Jewish law is needed for salvation but that by following a strict moral code that goes beyond the Jewish law salvation can be achieved. But what about the people who did not hear of Jesus after he came? In Romans Paul asks: "But how are men to call on him in whom they have not believed? And how are they to believe in him of whom they have never heard? And how are they to hear without a preacher?" (10:14). Paul seems to assume that people have now heard since the voices of preachers have "gone out to all the earth and their words to the ends of the world" (10:18).

There are at least four ideas of salvation suggested by the creeds, the Gospels, and Paul's letters. The first, presented in the synoptic

Gospels, is that one is saved by following a strict ethical code that goes beyond the Jewish laws. According to the second, which was also presented in the synoptic Gospels, one is saved by making great sacrifices in following Jesus. The third, maintained by Paul and John, is that one is saved by having faith in Jesus. Paul seems to suppose that this is sufficient and necessary only for those people who lived after Christ came. The fourth, suggested in Paul's letters, is that one can be saved before Christ came by following the Jewish laws. The first, second, and fourth routes to salvation seem to be salvation by works. The third involves salvation by faith alone. Certainly the third route is the one most commonly associated with Christianity. However, it is unclear exactly what besides belief it involves. Even when one concentrates only on the cognitive dimension of faith there are unclarities. The creeds seem to demand belief that defines Orthodox Christianity, everything from the Virgin Birth to the Second Coming, from the Resurrection to the Incarnation. On the other hand, John seems to demand only belief in the Incarnation while Paul seems to demand only belief in the Resurrection. Neither John nor Paul, unlike the creeds, demands belief in the Virgin Birth or the Trinity.

Evaluation of the Doctrine

THE DEPENDENCY ON OTHER CHRISTIAN DOCTRINES

One fundamental problem with the doctrine of salvation by faith in Jesus is its close dependency on questionable doctrines such as the Incarnation, the Resurrection, the Virgin Birth, and the Second Coming. If the arguments in the earlier chapters are correct, there is good reason to suppose that Jesus was not the Son of God, was not resurrected from the dead, was not born of a virgin, and will not come again. However, salvation through faith certainly presupposes that at least *some* of these doctrines are true and must be believed if one is to be saved. Thus, the Athanasian Creed proclaims that Jesus is the Son of God and that in order to be saved one must believe this. John maintains that unless one believes in Jesus one is condemned and belief in Jesus presumably involves belief that he is the Son of God. Paul's idea of salvation through Christ certainly presumes belief in the Resurrection.

Furthermore, the two routes to salvation suggested in the synoptic Gospels only make sense if some of the basic doctrines of Christianity are assumed. The route to salvation by following a strict

ethical code that goes beyond following Jewish law is indirectly dependent on dubious Christian doctrines. As we have seen, many
aspects of this strict ethical code outlined by Jesus make sense only if
it is presumed that the end of the world was near. Of course, if we had
independent reason to suppose that this code was proclaimed by the
Son of God, then perhaps we might have grounds for following it. But
this would presuppose an another dubious assumption of Christianity,
namely, that Jesus *is* the Son of God. The second track to salvation of
giving up everything and following Jesus also presupposes dubious
Christian doctrines. It would be irrational to give up everything and
follow Jesus if the basic doctrines of Christianity are improbable.

THE INCOMPATIBILITY WITH BELIEF IN AN
ALL-GOOD GOD

It is important to see that to reject the four routes to salvation
outlined above is compatible with belief in an all-powerful, all-knowing, and all-good God. Indeed, there is good reason to suppose that
salvation by these routes is incompatible with such a belief.

Surely an all-good God would not want his creatures to follow
the implausible, strict, ethical code laid down by Jesus. How could a
good God want us to have no concern for the future since many of the
most serious problems of our time, for instance, world hunger and
environmental pollution are in part the result of lack of concern? How
could an all-good God condemn people for being angry with someone
or punish a person with the fires of hell for calling someone a fool?
(Matt. 5:21–22). Nor would it seem that an all-good God would want
people to sacrifice in the name of Jesus if the evidence indicates that
he is not what Christians claim. Surely an all-good God does not
demand irrational action.

There is also another issue that calls into question the compati-
bility of the Christian doctrine of salvation with an all-good God. The
four routes to salvation outlined above neglect the status of people
who have not had the opportunity either to follow Jesus' strict moral
code, or to sacrifice in Jesus' name, or to have faith in Jesus, or to
follow the Jewish laws. People might lack these opportunities for many
different reasons, the most obvious being that they were born in the
wrong time or the wrong place. A Chinese woman in the second
century B.C., a native American living in the eighth century A.D., and
a black living in Africa in the second century A.D. would have had no
opportunity to be saved in any of the ways outlined above. They would

not have heard of Jesus' strict ethical code; they would not have known about Jewish law; they would have had no opportunity to sacrifice in Jesus' name since they would have never heard of Jesus; they would have had no opportunity to have faith in Jesus even if that involved only believing that Jesus existed.

Paul was clearly wrong to suppose that news of Jesus had reached the ends of the earth by his time. Even today there are many people in the world who have little or no exposure to Christianity or to the Jewish laws. For these persons also salvation is apparently impossible. Furthermore, there is also the possibility of intelligent extraterrestrial life. Indeed, some astronomers suggest that the existence of such life is extremely likely somewhere in the vastness of the galaxy. Such creatures would not have the opportunity of being saved and this also is unfair and is incompatible with an all-good God.

Morris's Solutions

Thomas Morris points out that what he calls the scandal of particularity is an old theological worry: How can humans who either lived and died before the time of Christ or lived since the time of Christ in different religious cultures and traditions be held accountable for not responding to him?[8] Concern about the salvation of extraterrestrial, intelligent beings, Morris argues, is simply a variant of this problem. He offers four different possible solutions.

Morris first suggests a solution favored by Eastern church fathers in which the Incarnation "somehow metaphysically transformed our nature." This process, known as deification, would be not transmitted by any physical causation and could touch any rational creature "whatever their location in the space-time continuum. One divine incarnation would serve for the salvation of all the universe."[9] Morris admits that this model "has not been a very popular understanding of salvation made available by Christ. Dominant models of salvation have required a response on the part of the created individual being saved."[10] Surely he is correct that this is not a very popular understanding of the Christian salvation. But he fails to note that the reason why it is unpopular is that it seems to be out of keeping with what the Bible teaches.

The second solution Morris proposes is based on his rejection of what he takes to be the questionable assumption that it would be necessary for God to save all rational creatures through the Incarnation of Christ.

In principle, it seems that a Christian could hold that the divine economy is such that we human beings are offered salvation through the incarnation of God as Jesus, but that other rational beings may be offered salvation through some completely different sort of means not involving a divine incarnation at all. [11]

Morris's argument has several problems. First, he seems to be talking in this passage only about the possibility of alternative means of salvation for extraterrestrial beings. For his solution to work it must also hold for human beings—earthlings—who have not had the opportunity to have faith in Jesus. Second, as we have seen, there is scriptural evidence that Paul and John understood salvation of human beings to occur *only* through Jesus. In Paul's case this was tempered by the stipulation that salvation was possible without Jesus before he came by following Jewish law. The two routes specified in the synoptic Gospels would also exclude members of other religious cultures and ancient times from salvation. If there were alternative means open to members of different cultures, then one would have supposed that Jesus and his disciples would have said so. Once we start postulating alternative means of salvation why not suppose that even people raised in Christian homes could be saved without faith in Jesus? But if this is allowed, what is the point of the Incarnation? Third, Morris gives no reason to suppose that there *are* alternative means that are available to people in different religious cultures and ancient times. He only implies that such means are possible. But what reason do we have to suppose that in fact some means of salvation was available to, say, a fourteenth-century Australian aborigine? What could it have been?

The third solution that Morris suggests is that knowledge of the Incarnation may not be propagated by natural causes and may not be had in this life. God may either offer knowledge of the Incarnation directly to his rational creatures or offer it in the next life. Now it is, of course, possible that God could give his rational creatures knowledge of the Incarnation directly. But there seems to be no reason to suppose that in general this has happened or is happening. For example, we have no evidence that Chinese of the third century B.C. had knowledge of the coming Incarnation of Christ. Furthermore, it seems likely that this amazing knowledge would have been recorded in Chinese history if it were at all widespread.

This leaves us with the afterlife. There is no way we can here and now determine what we will know in the afterlife or even whether there is an afterlife. But the proposal that a rational creature who did not know of the Incarnation in this life would be informed in some later life and be provided with the opportunity to be saved seems to be an act of desperation to protect the doctrine of Christian salvation from refutation, not a serious proposal. In any case, why would God wait until the afterlife to provide people with this opportunity? Certainly there is no scriptural support for the view that such knowledge will be provided in the afterlife.

The fourth solution offered by Morris is that God could have been incarnated many times and thereby have given every rational creature an opportunity for salvation. Thus, God could have been incarnated in all of the planets inhabited by rational creatures and in all of the great civilizations of the earth. Using his two minds theory and the rest of the apparatus discussed in Chapter 5 Morris argues that there are no logical obstacles in multiple incarnations. Indeed, he suggests that perhaps multiple incarnations on other inhabited planets would be necessary, because in order for God to save his creatures through being incarnated, he must share all of the kinds of experiences that they experience. Consequently, in order to save extraterrestrials who are likely to have different sensory apparatus, different brains, and radically different experiences multiple incarnations might indeed be necessary.

The same conceptual problem with his two minds theory that we noted earlier reappears in the incarnation of God in an alien body on another planet. In addition to the conceptual problems there is the factual issue. Is there any reason to suppose that extraterrestrial incarnations have occurred? Unfortunately one must wait for interstellar space exploration to verify the hypothesis that extraterrestrial cultures have been blessed with divine incarnations. However, it should be noted that Morris's suggestion is in principle capable of such verification. Presumably if such incarnations had occurred they would be likely to be believed by the creatures of these cultures and evidence would be cited to justify their beliefs.

But there is a more immediate problem. Morris suggests that in order to save human beings God through the incarnation of his Son must experience all the trials, tribulations, temptations, and suffering of human beings. But how could God have been successful in doing this in one single incarnation here on Earth? Relatively speaking Jesus experienced very little of the intense suffering that human beings have undergone. For example, a Jew in a concentration camp, a starving mother and her child, or a person dying from cancer without pain killers surely experience more and different kinds of suffering than Jesus did. Jesus knew nothing personally of the degradation experienced by women and minorities, of the horrors of war, of the terrors of Nazism. In order for Jesus to have really experienced the many and varied sufferings of humanity God would have had to be incarnated many times in human form. Once is simply insufficient. Yet surely there is no evidence that he has been incarnated more than once in human form. Indeed, all of the evidence suggests that he was not. Consequently, this way of handling the scandal of particularity is not viable.

Finally, it should be noted that Morris seems only to consider salvation through faith in Jesus. However, as we have seen, the New Testament offers at least four salvation tracks. The difficulty of reconciling the goodness of God with the means to salvation is inherent in all of these salvation tracts. At best Morris provides solutions to the problem inherent in one of these. In fact, either his solutions do not succeed or else they succeed only by changing the original doctrine of Christian salvation. I conclude that Morris's defense of the Christian doctrine of salvation is not successful.

Catholic Defense

The Catholic church has given much thought to the salvation of infidels. The crucial question is whether Catholic thinkers have been able to interpret the Christian doctrine of salvation in such a way that infidels are not unjustly relegated to hell without at the same time making the Incarnation irrelevant. Maurice Eminyan, in his comprehensive study of this subject, maintains that the church's doctrine of the salvation of infidels can be divided into two parts: from the origin to the discovery of North America and from then to the present day.[12] During the first period the church was concerned about how the millions of people that lived before Christ could be saved. According to Eminyan the church fathers utilized a passage from Paul. "Ever since the creation of the world his invisible nature, namely, his eternal power and deity, has been clearly perceived in the things that have been made. So they are without excuse" (Rom. 1:20). According to Eminyan they concluded from this that "the chosen people, therefore, were not the only beneficiaries of God's divine plan of salvation. The same argument was used in regard to the pagans who lived after Christ, although these were even more inexcusable, for, insisted the early Apologists, the echo of the Gospel preaching had already reached the farthest limits of the earth."[13] Saint Thomas "also believed that at least an echo of the Gospel had reached the farthest limits of earth in his time. If, by any chance, there should yet be any person still invincibly ignorant of the truths that are necessary for salvation, God would send him a missionary to teach him these truths."[14]

However, with the discovery of North America theologians were again faced with the concrete problem of salvation of the infidels. Reformers such as Luther and Calvin held that explicit faith was absolutely necessary for salvation. According to Eminyan: "For Luther, the absence of a missionary among infidels was a sure sign of their reprobation. Calvin went further: in order to render infidels more deserving of condemnation God has left them a few traces of truth."[15] The Catholic doctrine was different. The doctrine of the Council of Trent as interpreted by theologians such as Suarez was that explicit faith in Christ and the Trinity is strictly speaking necessary for salvation. However, since the obligation to believe in these two doctrines "derives from a positive law promulgated by the Gospel, faith *in voto* (i.e., implicit faith)" in these two doctrines will suffice for salvation whenever "the Gospel itself has not yet been divulged and there is therefore invincible ignorance."[16]

Although there have been some movements in the church that have proclaimed that infidels cannot be saved at all, these have been condemned as heresies and there has been a tendency away from the doctrine of explicit faith. Eminyan cites as an example of this tendency Father Perrone, a professor at the Roman College, who in the nineteenth century "advocated the opinion that the American Indians before the sixteenth century were in exactly the same situation as the Romans were before the Christian era: their implicit faith in Christ the Mediator was contained in their adherence to a providence capable of coming to man's rescue."[17]

More recent Catholic theologians who have wrestled with the problem of the salvation of infidels have proposed similar solutions. Infidels can be saved by having implicit faith. They have been provided revelation in some hidden ways that they can accept or reject.[18] What these hidden ways involve seems to vary from theologian to theologian. For example, for some the hidden ways involve merely providing supernatural and positive values in their otherwise false religions; in others it involves knowledge of the ultimate human end at the dawn of human reason; in others it involves a divine offer of salvation in the instant of death; in still others it involves an interior inspiration in the minds of good infidels.

There are several problems with the Catholic doctrine. First, the utilization of Paul's statement in Romans seems strained. The rest of the passage says that "for although they knew God they did not honor him or give thanks to him but became futile in their thinking and their senseless minds became darkened" (Rom. 1:21). It is certainly unclear that Paul was suggesting that people could be saved simply by honoring God and giving thanks to him although he may have thought this was necessary for salvation. After all, if this is all that was necessary, what was the point of the Incarnation?[19] Further, it is surely overly optimistic to suppose that all of the people who existed before Christ "clearly perceived God's eternal power and deity in the things that have been made." Saint Thomas's view that the echo of the Gospel had reached the farthest limits of the earth in his time was mistaken as was his view that God will send a missionary to any infidels who have not heard of the Gospel. After all many millions of native Americans died *before* missionaries were sent.

Although Luther's and Calvin's doctrines concerning the infidels were harsh, they certainly seemed to reflect the implications of the New Testament doctrine better than the Catholic official doctrine of faith *in voto*. The emptiness of the doctrine is illustrated well in Father Perrone's claim that one has implicit faith so long as one believes "in a providence capable of coming to man's rescue." What infidels are excluded from this doctrine of salvation? Perhaps only atheists, agnostics, and skeptics. If so, one wonders why? These people may have good reasons for not accepting a beneficent providence. Why should they not be saved? In any case why should only infidels who have not heard of the gospel be allowed to be saved in the way Father Perrone suggests? People in our time and in Christian societies may have good reasons for not accepting the Gospel. Indeed, if the argument of this book is correct, they should have. Why should they not be saved by faith *in voto*? On the other hand, if this is allowed why did God come to earth? Surely we have come a long way from Peter's worried question in Matthew 19: Who then will be saved? If Father Perrone is taken seriously neither the rich man nor Peter need have worried. Belief in a beneficent providence would have sufficed.

Recent Catholic theological thought that allows for the salvation of infidels for a wide variety of reasons goes even further than Father Perrone in diluting the idea of Christian salvation, and the same problems about it can be raised. There is no New Testament justification for this broad interpretation of salvation. There is no good reason why only infidels and not wayward Christians are provided with these alternative means of salvation. It is unclear that even this broad doctrine applies to all worthy infidels. An atheist could be an extremely moral person and yet not accept supernatural values, not believe that humans have any ultimate end, reject the offer of salvation at death because he or she believes there are good reasons for supposing it is illusory, and not respond to some spiritual inspiration for similar reasons. But why should such a person not be saved? After all, his or her response is rational and honest.

In sum, either the Catholic doctrine of faith permits too many people to be saved, making the Incarnation unnecessary, or forbids the salvation of too many, calling into question the infinite goodness of God. Thus, this doctrine inadequately explains how the Christian doctrine of salvation can be reconciled with belief in an all-good God without seriously modifying the doctrine.

Conclusion

The Christian path or (if my interpretation is correct) paths to salvation have serious problems. They presume at least some of the dubious doctrines of Christianity that were examined in earlier chapters. Furthermore, the doctrine of salvation is incompatible with an all-good God. Rational creatures who lived before Jesus as well as ones who lived after Jesus but were not exposed to his teaching would not be saved. On the other hand, if one alters the doctrine in order to solve the problem of particularity, one wonders why anyone needs to have faith in Jesus to be saved.

NOTES

1. Jaroslav Pelikan, "Christianity: An Overview," *Encyclopedia of Religion* (New York: Macmillan, 1987), vol. 3, p. 356.

2. John Hick, "Christianity," *Encyclopedia of Philosophy*, ed. Paul Edwards (New York: Macmillan and Free Press, 1967), vol. 2, p. 107.

3. Werner Georg Kümmel, *The Theology of the New Testament* (Nashville, Tenn.: Abingdon Press, 1973), pp. 34–35.

4. See, for example, Alan Richardson, *An Introduction to the Theology of the New Testament* (New York: Harper and Brothers, 1958), pp. 79–83.

5. G. Ryder Smith, *The Bible Doctrine of Salvation* (London: Epworth Press, 1946), p. 144, seems to suppose that the actions that Jesus recommended to the young man for salvation and the actions of the disciples that will gain them salvation amount to the same thing. To be sure, the disciples have given up their wealth in following Jesus and a rich young man is advised to give up his wealth. But the young man has not been advised to follow Jesus and the disciples are not advised to follow the commandments strictly.

6. Leon Morris, *New Testament Theology* (Grand Rapids, Mich.: Academie Books, 1986), p. 128, maintains that the parable teaches that one does not merit salvation by good works. However, Jesus says that if the rich man followed the commandments and gave up everything to the poor, he would be saved, that in *this* case his good works would bring about salvation. I am inclined to think therefore that Jesus was advocating in this passage *two* ways to salvation.

7. Ibid., p. 48.

8. Thomas V. Morris, *The Logic of God Incarnate* (Ithaca, N.Y.: Cornell University Press, 1986), pp. 170–86.

9. Ibid., p. 176.

10. Ibid.

11. Ibid., p. 177.

12. Maurice Eminyan, S.J., *The Theology of Salvation* (Boston: Daughters of St. Paul, 1960), p. 19.

13. Ibid.

14. Ibid., p. 20.

15. Ibid.

16. Ibid., p. 21.

17. Ibid., p. 22.

18. Ibid., p. 28.

19. Cf. Charles Watts, "The Death of Christ," reprinted in Gordon Stein, *An Anthology of Atheism and Rationalism* (Buffalo: Prometheus, 1980), p. 217.

8

Christian Responses

We have seen in the preceding chapters that the major doctrines of Christianity should not be believed. What responses could Christians make to our arguments? Although I cannot begin to canvass all possibilities, let us consider some of the most plausible ones.

Nonliteralism

A Christian might maintain that the arguments and evidence presented in this book do undermine Christianity *if* one takes its doctrines literally. These doctrines need to be reinterpreted in a way that brings out their deeper meaning, it might be said. This strategy is typical of many sophisticated, contemporary believers. Unwilling to accept traditional Christianity and yet reluctant to abandon it completely, they attempt to reinterpret its doctrines in such a way that they can accept them without being irrational. Given this reinterpretation, they maintain, one can be a Christian *and* a person committed to reason, the truths of history, and scientific inquiry. There are several problems with this approach, however.

It is not clear what counts as a legitimate reinterpretation. How can one tell whether some particular reinterpretation really does get at some deeper meaning? Why is one interpretation correct and another not? Nor is it clear what is left of Christianity that is recognizably Christian after the reinterpretation. In addition, it may be the case that after such a reinterpretation of Christianity the basic doctrines are still unjustified. Do the reinterpreted doctrines also need to be based on faith?

Let us examine three representative attempts to reinterpret Christianity: Boslooper's interpretation of the Virgin Birth, Bultmann's

demythologizing of Christianity, and Braithwaite's noncognitive interpretation of Christianity.

THE SYMBOLIC MEANING AND THE VIRGIN BIRTH

After maintaining that the Virgin Birth "is a 'myth' in the highest
and best sense of the word"[1] Thomas Boslooper, in *The Virgin Birth*,
argues:

> The virgin birth of Jesus ought to be maintained and believed in the
> twentieth century as it was in the first and second, as an expression of
> Christology which formulates for the popular, primitive mind worthy
> and edifying Christian doctrine. This belief and the creedal confession
> of it are basic to the expression of Christianity as community. The
> absence of the virgin birth in the contemporary Christian World Mission
> is unthinkable. The acceptance and understanding of the virgin birth is
> imperative. . . . The myth of Jesus' origin and the accompanying legends
> perform a didactic, evangelizing, eclectic, and universalizing function in
> the church's attempt to communicate to many audiences many signifi-
> cant Christian truths. . . . The story of the virgin birth represents in
> mythical form two of Christendom's principal logical propositions: that
> God acted in history and that monogamous marriage is civilization's
> most important social institution.[2]

To say that this interpretation is surprising perhaps underesti-
mates the problem of its arbitrariness. It is not clear why Boslooper
believes that one of Christendom's principle logical propositions is that
monogamous marriage is civilization's *most* important social institution. Surely not even most Christians believe this. Moreover, even if
this claim is correct, why does he suppose that the story of the Virgin
Birth represents in mythical form *this* proposition rather than any
number of others? He gives no reason to justify his interpretation.

In addition, Boslooper's reinterpretation seems to denude Christianity of its uniqueness. Christianity is the only major world religion
besides Buddhism in which a virgin birth plays an important role.[3]
Indeed, the Virgin Birth is one of the aspects of Christianity that
distinguishes it from most other faiths. However, on his interpretation
this uniqueness disappears. According to Boslooper the Virgin Birth
represents in mythical form the proposition that God acts in history.
But this belief is found in most world religions including Judaism and
Islam. The Virgin Birth also represents in mythical form, according to
Boslooper, the proposition that monogamous marriage is civilization's
most important social institution. If this belief was widely held by

Christians, it might well be a unique feature of Christianity. However, as I have already suggested, it is dubious that it is. Of course, we could attenuate Boslooper's rhetoric and say that monogamous marriage is *one* of civilization's most important social institutions. Then perhaps it would be true to say that it is believed by most Christians. But this proposition is also held by most people in some non-Christian religions.

Boslooper appears to be maintaining that the beliefs a Christian should hold about the Virgin Birth must be determined by the person's level of sophistication. The Virgin Birth is not to be taken as literally true by sophisticated believers; it should be understood as a myth. Nevertheless, they are to use the idea of a literal Virgin Birth in communicating the Christian message to unsophisticated persons—people with "primitive" minds. Such a myth has great power, Boslooper suggests, in maintaining the Christian community and in furthering its evangelistic purposes. However, the assumption that the only way to communicate with unsophisticated people is through myths should be rejected. There is no reason why people could not be educated to understand and accept the falsehood of the Virgin Birth.

Could Boslooper's interpretation be justified on beneficial grounds? Perhaps he might argue that unsophisticated people should believe in the Virgin Birth because it is beneficial to do so. There are two reasons why this approach should be rejected. First, as I argue in Chapter 1, there is a prima facie epistemic duty to believe what seems to be true in the light of the evidence and, in addition, there are general beneficial reasons for believing only what the evidence indicates. This creates a strong presumption that one should only believe that something is true on the basis of epistemic reasons. In addition, there is a presumption that beneficial reasons will only be used when there is no epistemic reasons for disbelief. Although there are circumstances in which this presumption can be defeated, they are rare and unusual. Applied to the case of the Virgin Birth this creates a strong presumption for not believing on beneficial grounds since there are good epistemic reasons for disbelief.

DEMYTHOLOGIZING AND ESCHATOLOGY

Perhaps the important variant of the nonliteralist approach is the demythologizing of Rudolf Bultmann and his followers. Although a complete analysis of Bultmann's work cannot be attempted here, it is possible to consider some of its fundamental difficulties.[4]

The basic problem Bultmann addresses is that of reconciling Christianity with twentieth-century thought. The position he takes in *Jesus Christ and Mythology* is typical of much of the rest of his writing.[5] There he classifies as mythological the traditional Christian doctrines of the Resurrection, the Virgin Birth, and the Second Coming because they conflict with "the conception of the world which has been formed and developed by science" and "the modern study of history."[6] In this world, unlike that of the New Testament, there is no supernatural intervention in the natural course of events. He recommends that the statements of Christianity be reinterpreted rather than eliminated, thus revealing a "deeper meaning which is concealed under the cover of mythology."[7]

Consider Bultmann's reinterpretation of eschatology. He argues that today we "no longer share the mythological conception of eschatology as a cosmic event at the end of time." Although the New Testament conceptions are no longer intelligible "they do express the knowledge of the finiteness of the world and of the end which is imminent to us all because we all are beings of this world."[8] The myth of a cosmic end of the world hints at deeper truths—the finiteness of human existence and human responsibility to the will of God. "To use nonmythological terms, the finiteness of the world and of man over against the transcendent power of God contains not only warning, but also consolation."[9] The warning, Bultmann suggests, is to perform the will of God; the consolation is that of salvation and eternal bliss.

Since Bultmann continues to speak of God as acting, for example in bestowing grace, one might suppose that he has not escaped completely from the use of mythological language. However, he maintains that there are two ways of understanding God as acting. In the traditional sense God intervenes in the course of natural events by breaking the causal link. Bultmann rejects this as mythological. However, God can act "within" natural events. The action of God "is hidden from every eye except the eye of faith. Only the so-called natural, secular (worldly) events are visible to every man and capable of proof."[10]

How does Bultmann's concept differ from pantheistic piety? He says that pantheism is a general worldview in which one is convinced in advance that God is working within nature. On his view the person of faith believes here and now (not in advance) in some particular event (not in general) that God is working within nature. Bultmann calls this "the paradox of faith." There is no room for God's working, yet faith "nevertheless" understands God's action here and now as an event that "is completely intelligible in the natural or historical connection of events."[11] Bultmann insists, however, that this does not mean that God is a subjective phenomenon or that he does not exist apart from faith.

Bultmann denies that demythologizing rationalizes the Christian message and destroys the mystery of God: "On the contrary demythologizing makes clear the true meaning of God's mystery."[12]

> The attempt to de-mythologize begins with this important insight: Christian preaching, in so far as it is preaching the Word of God by God's command and in His name, does not offer a doctrine which can be accepted either by reason or by a *sacrificium intellectus*. Christian preaching is *kerygma*, that is, a proclamation addressed not to the theoretical reason, but to the hearer as a self. . . . De-mythologizing will make clear this function of preaching as a personal message, and in doing so it will eliminate a false stumbling block.[13]

Why should one accept this reinterpretation of the biblical myth of Christian eschatology? What are the criteria for a correct interpretation? According to Bultmann they are personal and practical. He maintains that every interpreter of Scripture must have guiding presuppositions. These are in part based on one's own relation to the text; that is, on one's own psychical life and background. One's interest in interpreting the Bible is not purely historical, however, but it is to hear "what the Bible has to say for our own actual present, to hear what is the truth about our life and about our soul."[14] Bultmann maintains that "the Bible becomes for me a word addressed personally to me, which not only informs me about existence in general, but gives me real existence."[15]

How does Jesus fit into Bultmann's scheme? Bultmann asks: If one must speak of God as acting here and now in personal relations, "can we still believe that God has acted once for all on behalf of the whole world?" He answers that "God meets us in His Word, in a concrete word, the preaching instituted in Jesus Christ."[16] However, "the Word of God is not a timeless statement but a concrete word addressed to men here and now."[17] The living message of God is not invented by human beings but "rises up in history." It has as its origin a historical event. "This event is Jesus Christ."[18]

However, the historical person, Jesus of Nazareth, cannot be seen as the external Logos, the Word, by an objective historian. One must understand Jesus Christ "in a manner which is beyond the categories by which the objective historian understands world-history, if the figure and the work of Jesus Christ are to be understood as the divine work of redemption."[19] Bultmann calls this a paradox.

The redemption provided by Jesus Christ should not be looked on as a future event. "The eschatological event which is Jesus Christ happens here and now as the Word is being preached."[20] The "once for all" of God's acting in the historical event of Jesus Christ is, in Bultmann's view, always present in the proclaimed word. "Certainly the Word says to me that God's grace is a prevenient grace which has already acted for me; but not in such a way that I can look back on it as a historical event of the past."[21]

All of the problems inherent in nonliteralism are manifested in Bultmann's demythologizing in *Jesus Christ and Mythology*. First, he says that the Christian prophecy of a cosmic end of the world that conflicts with science should be replaced with a deeper truth, namely, that human beings are finite and are responsible to the will of a transcendent God in which they have their salvation. The myth also conveys, according to Bultmann, the meaning that one should be open to God's future, which is imminent in everyone. But why is this reinterpretation of the traditional Christian doctrine better than an indefinite number of others?[22] Bultmann admits that the criteria for reinterpretation are personal and practical. Given another psychic life and background and different practical concerns, an entirely different interpretation could be generated. But then, a Christian antinuclear pacifist might interpret the "deeper truth" of the myth to be that unless one strives for peace the world will end in a nuclear holocaust. Even if one agrees with Bultmann that existentialism is an appropriate tool of biblical interpretation, this leaves open an indefinite number of possible interpretations. A deep concern with the loneliness of human existence and the anxiety of freedom and responsibility is surely compatible with any number of reinterpretations of Christian myths including the interpretation of antiwar pacifists. Indeed, it's hard to see which reinterpretations existentially influenced categories of reinterpretation would rule out.

Second, not much that is recognizably Christian is left of Christianity after Bultmann's reinterpretation. The Virgin Birth, the Resurrection, and the Second Coming are all myths that at most have symbolic meanings although Bultmann does not say what these are. The historical Jesus of Nazareth seems to have little importance for him. His future coming is a myth and his past existence according to objective history is that of a mere man. Although Bultmann maintains that in the eyes of the faithful the Jesus of history is not a mere man, it is not clear exactly what in their eyes he thinks Jesus is supposed to be. Is he all-powerful and all-knowing? Since such properties would conflict with science and history it would seem that Jesus could have none of the properties usually associated with him. Indeed, from Bultmann's perspective it is not clear what Jesus can be to the faithful except an "eschatological event" that is somehow present "here and now" when the Word is proclaimed, enabling one, with God's grace, to be reborn and realize what it means to exist authentically.

This brings us to the last problem. After Christianity is demythologized Christians are still asked to believe something on pure faith, for example, that Jesus is more than a mere human being. Why should one believe that Jesus was anything more than what is justified by the historical evidence? Indeed, in one important respect a Christian was better off before Bultmann's reinterpretation. Before demythologizing a Christian was asked to believe that Jesus was born of a virgin, was resurrected from the dead, and will come again in glory. In the light of the evidence a rational person could not believe these things but at least such a person was fairly clear about *what* he or she was being asked to believe, namely that certain miracles had occurred and will occur. After demythologizing one is not asked to believe in miracles, but what one is asked to believe is far less clear than before.

Why is it less clear? It is difficult to see how Christian beliefs are different from non-Christian beliefs. According to Bultmann there are no miracles in the sense of God's interrupting the natural course of events; God's actions are all "within" natural events. However, he says that God's actions are not capable of empirical proof or verification. In other words, there is no empirical difference between God working within nature and there being no God at all. Nevertheless, in his view a person of faith can correctly believe in some particular case that God is working within nature. Further, when Jesus is considered from the point of view of objective history, he was a mere man. But a person with faith believes that Jesus was more than a mere man and this belief is supposedly different from the non-Christian beliefs. However, there is no empirical difference in believing that Jesus is a mere man and believing that he is more than a mere man, that is, that Jesus is the Christ. It is difficult to see what a Christian's belief in Christ comes to.

Bultmann admits that such a view is paradoxical. But why? Perhaps he senses that the factual meaning of an expression and its empirical confirmation are related. However, if the factual meaning of an expression is closely connected with its empirical confirmation, then Bultmann's view must be rejected. For then there would be no difference in factual meaning between believing that Jesus was a mere man and believing that Jesus was the Son of God. But we need not press verificationism here.[23] Even if the factual meaning in two cases is different why should anyone believe that Jesus is Christ? Why in particular should one believe that he was the eschatological event that is present here and now when the Word is proclaimed?

Not only are we asked to believe something that is obscure. We are asked to believe something for which there is no evidence and for which there *could* be no evidence. If belief is permissible in this sort of case, belief in almost anything is permissible. Why not believe that Appolonius was the eternal Logos, the Word? Why not believe that Appolonius is an "eschatological event" that is present here and now when *his* doctrines are proclaimed? Why not believe the same thing about Reverend Moon? Once faith is uncontrolled by evidence anything goes.

NONCOGNITIVISM AND AGAPE

Richard Braithwaite, in his *An Empiricist's View of the Nature of Religious Belief*, adopts a verificationist theory of factual meaning: the factual meaning of a statement is given by its method of verification.[24] According to this theory, religious as well as moral statements have no factual meaning; that is, they are neither true nor false. Although moral statements have no cognitive meaning, they guide our conduct and hence, according to Braithwaite, have a meaning "in some sense of meaning."[25] Braithwaite adopts the meaning-as-use theory to account for the meaning of moral statements. The meaning of a moral statement is given by the way in which it is used.

The problem for an empiricist, says Braithwaite, is to explain "how a religious statement is used by a man who asserts it in order to express his religious conviction."[26] Braithwaite argues that religious assertions are used primarily as moral assertions. How are moral assertions used? According to Braithwaite, "the primary use of a moral assertion is that of expressing the intention of the asserter to act in a particular sort of way specified in the assertion."[27] Religious assertions then also express one's intentions to act in a particular way. However, in religious assertions, unlike in ethical assertions, there is no explicit ethical course of action that is specified. In order to determine what ethical course of action is being expressed by a particular religious assertion, Braithwaite argues, one must consider the body of assertions of which this particular assertion is a representative member:

> If what is wanted is not the meaning of the religious assertions made by a particular man but what the set of assertions would mean were they to be made by anyone of the same religion (which I will call their *typical* meaning) all that can be done is to specify the form of behaviour which is in accordance with what one takes to be the fundamental moral principles of the religion in question. Since different people will take different views as to what these fundamental moral principles are, the typical meaning of religious assertions will be different for different people.[28]

In Braithwaite's view the fundamental moral principle of Christianity is to follow an agapeistic way of life. Christian religious assertions then express a person's intention to follow such a way of life, and on the meaning-as-use theory this is their typical meaning. There are other differences between moral and religious statements, Braithwaite says, beside the fact that the behavior policy intended by religious statements is not specified by one statement in isolation. First, the moral teachings of religions are conveyed by concrete examples. Second, the moral principles of the higher religions are concerned with internal as well as external behavior. Christianity, Braithwaite maintains, involves agapeistic behavior as well as an agapeistic frame of mind.

How does Braithwaite distinguish one religion from another? The important difference, he argues, is found in the fact that the intentions to pursue some ethical policy are associated with different stories or sets of stories. By "story" he means a proposition or set of propositions "which are straightforwardly empirical propositions capable of empirical test and which are thought of by the religious man in connection with his resolution to follow the way of life advocated by his religion."[29] Braithwaite says that what he calls a story could be called a parable, fairy tale, allegory, fable, tale or myth. On the assumption that both Christianity and Buddhism advocate an agapeistic way of life the difference between them then is in the stories associated with them.

Braithwaite argues that religious stories need not be believed and need not be true because they are only psychologically relevant in pursuing a moral way of life. Many people find it easier to follow a way of life if their actions are associated with these stories even though they do not believe them. The religious person may interpret stories in whatever way is helpful in carrying out the morality of his or her religion. Braithwaite ends his essay by saying that the Christian religion demands a "personal commitment to a personal way of life" and that the questions "What shall I do" and "What moral principles should I adopt" are "of the very essence of the Christian religion."[30]

Even if some form of the verification theory of meaning can be defended as a criterion of factual meaning and the meaning-as-use theory is adopted as an account of noncognitive meaning, there are problems with Braithwaite's view. First, Braithwaite supposes that the primary function of religious language is to express one's intention to act in a particular ethical manner. However, there are surely many nonethical uses that religious statements might have. For example, religious statements might be used to call people's attention to supposed miracles either in order to induce nonbelievers to believe or to reinforce belief in the faithful; they might warn people that, for example, the end of the world is near; they might express group loyalty, for example, identification with the Catholic religion. Braithwaite is selective in considering only their ethical use.

Second, Braithwaite neglects all of the aspects of Jesus' ethical teaching that are unacceptable today; for example, his implicit approval of slavery, his condemnation of curses, his recommendation not to be concerned about the future, his strict ethical codes that entail turning the other cheek and giving all of one's wealth to the poor.

In a way, Braithwaite admits that he is selective. He admits that although in his view the fundamental moral principle of Christianity is to follow an agapeistic way of life, other people might have different views on what is the fundamental moral principle of Christianity. Consequently, other people will take the typical meaning of Christian religious assertions to correspond to different fundamental principles. He does not attempt to argue that there is any correct view about the typical meaning of a religious assertion and, indeed, his words suggest that he believes that there is none. Thus his theory seems to introduce a radical relativism and subjectivism into the reinterpretation of Christian statements. In this respect, Braithwaite's method leads to problems that are similar to the ones we just found in Bultmann's reinterpretations of Christian myths.[31]

Finally, as in the case of Bultmann, not much is left of traditional Christianity after Braithwaite's reinterpretation. Although it can be helpful to associate stories about Jesus' virgin birth, resurrection, second coming, and miracle working with one's attempt to lead a agapeistic way of life, one need not believe these stories. Jesus thus becomes at most a moral teacher who, along with Buddha, advocated agape. Most Christians will undoubtedly feel that Braithwaite's "Christianity" is no Christianity at all.

Other Possible Responses

What other responses could be made to the arguments considered in the preceding chapters? There are several other possible responses that could be made but these can be given briefer treatment than nonliteralism. Either they are not as important or else they have already been answered indirectly in earlier chapters.

RATIONALISM

A Christian might attempt to refute the argument that there are good reasons to reject the doctrines of Christianity by reevaluating both the historical and theological evidence and the arguments that I have presented. Thus, he or she might attempt to show that the evidence for the Resurrection or the Virgin Birth or the Incarnation is strong enough to justify rational belief. However, for the reasons already presented I am very skeptical that this attempt can succeed.[32]

HISTORICAL SUBJECTIVISM

A Christian could either deliberately or unwittingly avoid my historical argument by assuming that subjective "existential" standards of historical investigation are appropriate to biblical investigation. For example, some theologians have maintained that they "are relieved of the intolerable burden of anxiety concerning historical researches into the detail of Jesus' existence."[33] One common strategy is to make a distinction between "objective history" and "existential history" and to maintain that in existential history one is interested in a "personal grasp of meaning" and "revelation of alternative modes of human existence."[34]

Reinhold Niebuhr, for example, argues that it is the "revelatory depth" of the cross and the Resurrection that is the "primary concern of faith" and not the confirming of this past event "through specific historical details."[35] Indeed, Niebuhr seems to argue that it makes no difference that the Gospel writers altered the details of the Resurrection story, since they "apprehended the significance" of the Resurrection. "The story of this triumph over death is thus shrouded in a mystery which places it in a different order of history than the story of the crucifixion."[36] The real miracle is *belief* in the Resurrection, without which the church would not exist, and not the actual fact of Resurrection that is the concern of objective history.

However, as Ronald Hepburn has argued, if the revelatory depth of a fact is the primary concern of faith "we must already be sure that there *is* a fact (objective-historically) and that it *has* revelatory depth."[37] Niebuhr assumes but does not show that the New Testament writers interpreted the events of the resurrection "along *sound* lines."[38] One need not object to his point that history is important only if helps one grasp the significance of the past or if it helps one understand "alternative modes of human existence." But the question of what actually happened cannot be eliminated. If there is an enterprise such as existential history, it presupposes we can have knowledge of what actually happened; it cannot dispense with it.[39] However, as I have shown in the preceding chapters, in terms of the historical evidence there is good reason to suppose that the major doctrines of Christianity are false because there is good reason to suppose that the events assumed by these doctrines did not actually happen.

EXTREME FIDEISM OR IRRATIONALISM

A Christian could maintain that I am correct to argue that it is irrational to believe that Christian doctrines are true but nevertheless affirm that he or she will continue to believe despite all the counterevidence and arguments.[40] David Hume was perhaps referring to this stance when he said:

> [The] *Christian Religion* not only was at first attended with miracles, but even to this day cannot be believed by any reasonable person without them. Mere reason is not sufficient to convince us of its veracity; and whoever is moved by *Faith* to assent to it, is conscious of a continued miracle in his own person, which subverts all the principles of his understanding, and gives him a determination to believe what is most contrary to custom and experience.[41]

If this is the response taken to the arguments presented in this book, it cannot be debated. One can, of course, debate the virtues of being rational and of basing what one believes on evidence and arguments. But if a person is willing to engage in this debate, there would seem to be no good reason not to debate the truth of Christianity itself.

MODERATE FIDEISM

A Christian could admit that there is no good reason to believe the major doctrines of Christianity but hold that there is no good reason to *dis*believe them and, consequently, that one could believe on faith that does not go against the evidence.[42] However, in order for this strategy to work a Christian apologist would need to refute my arguments that there are good reasons to disbelieve the major Christian doctrines. For the reasons already given I am skeptical that this can be done but I would certainly encourage the attempt. It would be also be necessary to show that it is morally and epistemologically permissible to believe in Christian doctrines when there is no reason to believe them. Again, I doubt that this can be done.

CHRISTIAN FOUNDATIONALISM

A Christian might maintain that belief in the doctrines of Christianity are basic beliefs, ones that need no evidence or argument to justify them. For the reasons given in Chapter 1. I do not believe that religious foundationalism in general is a viable option. Christian foundationalism in particular has the additional problem of showing that there is no reason to reject Christian doctrines. This would involve at least refuting the arguments that I have given for believing that Christian doctrines are false.

LIBERAL REDUCTIONISM

A Christian can argue that the major doctrines of Christianity should be rejected in the light of the evidence but that the moral teachings of Jesus should be retained. Indeed, it might be argued that the moral teachings of Jesus are really the heart of Christianity and that the other doctrines are relatively unimportant; thus, it is possible to reduce Christianity to its ethics without great loss. However, as we have seen, there are serious problems with this position. Moreover, if, as many modern Christian ethical theorists maintain, the essence of Jesus' moral teachings is the commandment to love your neighbor, it is uncertain that Christian ethics is an improvement over some secular ethical systems. In addition, it is surely dubious that Christianity can be reduced to its moral teachings without great loss. Indeed, many

Christians would justifiably feel that such a reduction would remove what is vital and unique to Christianity.

Conclusion

There are alternatives to rejecting Christianity but either they do not seem promising or else they transform Christianity beyond recognition. It would be far more straightforward and rational to reject Christianity outright rather than to attempt to salvage it. However, for most of the 1.6 billion Christians in the world rejection is not at the present time a practical possibility. They are either unaware of the problems of the Christian faith or because of their training and background, they are believers nevertheless. I have no recommendations to make here about what can or should be done about this regrettable situation.

NOTES

1. Thomas Boslooper, *The Virgin Birth* (London: SCM Press, 1962), p. 21.
2. Ibid., pp. 232–34.
3. Zarathushtra (Zoroaster) was also supposed to have been born of a virgin, but Zoroastrianism is not considered a major world religion. See David Adams Leeming, "Virgin Birth," *Encyclopedia of Religion* (New York: Macmillan, 1987), vol. 15, pp. 272–76.
4. See Ronald W. Hepburn, "Rudolf Bultmann," in *The Encyclopedia of Philosophy*, ed. Paul Edwards (New York: Macmillan and Free Press, 1967), vol. I, pp. 424–26; Schubert M. Ogden, *Christ Without Myth: A Study Based on the Theology of Rudolf Bultmann* (New York: Harper and Row, 1961); David Cairns, *A Gospel Without Myth?* (London: SCM Press, 1960); John Macquarrie, *The Scope of Demythologizing: Bultmann and His Critics* (New York: Harper and Row, 1960).
5. Rudolf Bultmann, *Jesus Christ and Mythology* (New York: Charles Scribner's Sons, 1958).
6. Ibid., p. 15.
7. Ibid., p. 18.
8. Ibid., p. 25.
9. Ibid., p. 27.

10. Ibid., p. 62.

11. Ibid., p. 65.

12. Ibid., p. 43.

13. Ibid., p. 36.

14. Ibid., p. 52.

15. Ibid., p. 53.

16. Ibid., p. 78.

17. Ibid., p. 79.

18. Ibid., p. 80.

19. Ibid.

20. Ibid., p. 81.

21. Ibid., p. 82.

22. Cf. Walter Kaufmann's critique of some of Bultmann's reinterpretations in *Critique of Religion and Philosophy* (New York: Harper and Brothers, 1958), pp. 141–57.

23. See Michael Martin, *Atheism: A Philosophical Justification* (Philadelphia: Temple University Press, 1990), chap. 2.

24. Richard Braithwaite, *An Empiricist's View of the Nature of Religious Belief*, reprinted in *The Logic of God*, ed. Malcolm L. Diamond and Thomas V. Litzenburg (Indianapolis: Bobbs-Merrill, 1975), pp. 127–47.

25. Ibid., p. 133.

26. Ibid.

27. Ibid., p. 134.

28. Ibid., p. 138.

29. Ibid., pp. 140–41

30. Ibid., p. 147.

31. Some commentators claim to find even closer similarities between Braithwaite and Bultmann. See, for example, Alasdair MacIntyre, review of *History and Eschatology*, by Rudolf Bultmann, *Philosophical Quarterly* 10 (1961): 92–93. Moreover, Braithwaite's approach has been seen to have a close similarity to the program of radical demythologizing carried out by Fritz Buri. See Macquarrie, *The Scope of Demythologizing*, p. 141.

32. I would consider Gary Habermas and Thomas Morris rationalists in this sense.

33. D. D. Williams, *Interpreting Theology, 1918–1952* (London: SCM Press, 1953), p. 105. Quoted in Ronald W. Hepburn, *Christianity and Paradox* (London: Watts, 1958), p. 96.

34. Hepburn, *Christianity and Paradox*, p. 97.

35. Reinhold Niebuhr, *Faith and History* (London: Nisbet, 1949), p. 167. Quoted in Hepburn, *Christianity and Paradox*, p. 97.

36. Niebuhr, *Faith and History*, p. 166. Quoted in Hepburn, *Christianity and Paradox*, p. 98.

37. Hepburn, *Christianity and Paradox*, p. 101.

38. Ibid., p. 99.

39. For further criticisms of the "flight from history" in recent theology see Hepburn, *Christianity and Paradox*, chap. 6, 7.

40. See Richard H. Popkin, "Fideism," *The Encyclopedia of Philosophy*, ed. Paul Edwards (New York: Macmillan and Free Press, 1967), vol. 3, p. 201. According to Popkin, Tertullian, Pierre Bayle, Kierkegaard, Félicité Robert de Lamennais, and L. I. Shestov are extreme fideists.

41. David Hume, *Essay Concerning Human Understanding*, ed. L. A. Selby-Bigge (Oxford, 1951), p. 131. Quoted in Richard Popkin, "Fideism," vol. 3, p. 201.

42. See Popkin, "Fideism," p. 201. Popkin classifies Augustine and Pascal as moderate fideists.

Appendix 1
THE DIVINE COMMAND THEORY

The Divine Command Theory is a metaethical theory according to which moral truths do not exist independently of God's will. A human action is morally obligatory because God commands it; God does not command it because it is morally obligatory. Thus, morality is not discovered by God but is created by him. The Divine Command Theory thus makes moral knowledge directly dependent on theological knowledge in that without knowledge of what God commands, one could not claim to know what one's moral duties are.

An examination of Christianity would be incomplete without an evaluation of this theory, which has a long and distinguished history. It has been advocated in various forms in the past by Ockham, Augustine, Duns Scotus, and Calvin[1] and in our time by Brunner, Buber, Barth, Niebuhr, and Bultmann.[2] Although the Divine Command Theory is not strictly speaking entailed by Christianity—one could consistently be a Christian and reject it—it is commonly associated with it. Indeed, it is the metaethical theory of choice for many sophisticated Christians for the following reasons. If one believes that God is all-powerful and the creator of the Universe, it is natural to assume that he created moral truths and that their existence depends on his will. Thus, in order to preserve God's unlimited power, it seems plausible to many theists that God is the creator of moral truths. The Divine Command Theory, then, can be used either to support indirectly or to undermine Christianity. On the one hand, if Christianity is true *and* certain assumptions are made about God's power and creative scope, then the Divine Command Theory follows. But if that theory is a plausible theory and the assumptions are acceptable, then it is indirectly supported. On the other hand, if the theory has serious problems and the assumptions are acceptable, then it should be rejected.

Furthermore, the theory is often cited by its advocates as being superior to secular metaethical systems. Indeed, on the basis of this theory Christians sometimes maintain that if there were no God, then moral anarchy would follow. One often-cited advantage of the Divine Command Theory over secular theories, then, is that according to it moral truths are objective and absolute.[3]

Varieties of the Radical Divine Command Theory

In its most extreme form the Divine Command Theory maintains that God's command that some action be done constitutes the complete reason why this action is morally required. In weaker versions, God's command is simply a necessary part of the complete reason. The remainder might be, for example, that God is the creator of the Universe and its creatures; hence, God's creatures have an obligation to obey their creator's command just as children have an obligation to obey their parents' commands. Let us consider some of the varieties of this extreme form of the theory.

One way of understanding the most extreme version of the theory is that it provides an analysis of the meaning of moral terms. On this construal, advocates of the theory would be claiming that one can define the meaning of expressions such as "morally required," and "morally permitted" in terms of the theological expression "God commands." Thus, the theory would maintain that:[4]

(1) It is morally required that p = God commands that p.

Analyses of related ethical terms would follow similar lines, for example:

(2) It is morally permitted that p = It is not the case that God commands that ~ p.

(3) It is morally forbidden that p = God commands that ~ p.

It should be noted that, in order to capture the intent of the theory, the right-hand side of the definitions (1), (2), and (3) must be understood as conceptually prior to the left-hand side; that is, the moral term is explained by the theological term and not the reverse. Thus, the analyses provided in (1), (2), and (3) reduce moral terms to theological terms; they do not reduce theological terms to moral terms.

In contrast to what I will call the Linguistic Actual Divine Command Theory, consider the Linguistic Hypothetical Divine Command Theory. In this interpretation moral obligation is defined in terms of what God *would* command *if* God existed. There is no assumption that God does exist. The basic analyses of the theory can be stated in this way:

(1') It is morally required that p = If there were a God, God would command that p.

(2′) It is morally permitted that p = It is not the case that if there were a God, God would command that ~ p.

(3′) It is morally forbidden that p = If there were a God, God would command that ~ p.

In order to contrast this hypothetical analysis of ethical terms in terms of divine commands let us briefly consider another analysis of ethical terms: the Ideal Observer Theory.[5] According to the ideal observer theory, the meaning of "moral obligation" is analyzed in terms of the feelings of approval of an ideal observer, a person who is fully informed, unbiased, impartial, completely rational, and completely empathetic. Thus:

(1″) It is morally required that p = If there were an Ideal Observer, It would contemplate that p with a feeling of approval.

Analysis of related terms would follow similar lines:

(2″) It is morally permitted that p = It is not the case that if there were an Ideal Observer, It would contemplate that p with a feeling of disapproval.

(3″) It is morally forbidden that p = If there were an Ideal Observer, It would contemplate that p with a feeling of disapproval.

Although there are important similarities between this and the Linguistic Hypothetical Divine Command Theory, there are also crucial differences. Both theories attempt to analyze what certain ethical terms mean. The analyses of both are in terms of what some hypothetical beings would do. In addition, the hypothetical beings have some properties in common. For example, God and the Ideal Observer are fully informed.

The differences, however, are significant. The Linguistic Hypothetical Divine Command Theory defines moral expressions in terms of what God would command; the Ideal Observer Theory defines moral expressions in terms of what an Ideal Observer would have a feeling of approval or disapproval toward. Moreover, the Ideal Observer lacks certain properties that God is supposed to have. For example, God is all-powerful; the Ideal Observer need not be. Furthermore, depending on how one defines God, the Ideal Observer may have certain characteristics that God lacks. For example, the Ideal

Observer has complete powers of empathy; consequently, it can experience any human emotion or feeling. It is unclear whether this is true of God.[6]

A Nonlinguistic Actual Divine Command Theory has recently been presented by Phillip Quinn.[7] Its core is presented in three propositions:[8]

(T_{1a}) It is necessary that for all p it is morally required that p if and only if God commands that p.

(T_{1b}) It is necessary that for all p it is morally permitted that p if and only if it is not the case that God commands that $\sim$ p.

(T_{1c}) It is necessary that for all p it is morally forbidden that p if and only if God commands that $\sim$ p.

This version of the Divine Command Theory does not depend on an analysis of the meaning of ethical terms. Although T_{1a}, T_{1b}, and T_{1c} are supposedly necessary truths, they are not necessary because of the meaning of the terms involved. Consider T_{1a}. The necessity involved here is that in any possible world in which it is morally required that p, God commands that p and in any possible world in which it is God's command that p, it is morally required that p. One need not suppose that "moral obligation" is definable in terms of what God commands.

A Nonlinguistic Hypothetical Divine Command Theory and a Nonlinguistic Ideal Observer Theory could be developed as well.

Evaluation of the Radical Divine Command Theory

THE SEMANTICS PROBLEM
One important objection to the Linguistic Actual Divine Command Theory is semantic. It seems mistaken to suppose that this analysis captures what people usually mean by "moral obligation," "morally permitted," and "morally forbidden." For example, not all religious believers hold Definitions 1, 2, and 3. Some maintain, for example, that ethical expressions such as "morally obligatory" are not definable in terms of theological expressions. Thus, some ethical rationalists such as the British philosopher Richard Price (1723–1791), are also theists. According to Price, rightness and wrongness are as much objective properties of acts and situations as are properties such

as mass and hardness. He argues that the human understanding is competent to know such properties without knowing what God commands.[9]

Moreover, it seems unlikely that this is what nonbelievers and agnostics have meant by these terms. In general, nonbelievers have rejected moral anarchy although they are aware of the anarchistic implications of Definitions 1, 2, and 3. So it seems very unlikely that they would embrace these definitions. There is, of course, nothing inconsistent in an atheist advocating Definitions 1, 2, and 3. One who advocated them would simply be committed to moral anarchy. But atheism is compatible with moral anarchy.[10] Interestingly enough, nonbelievers can consistently embrace the Linguistic Hypothetical Divine Command Theory *without* accepting moral anarchy for they can accept Definitions, 1', 2', and 3' and yet not believe that everything is permitted. For even if God did not exist, they could maintain, certain actions would still be forbidden because *if* God existed, he *would* command that certain actions are forbidden.

The question might be raised how, if they did not believe that he exists, nonbelievers could know what God would command. One answer is that an atheist would try to approximate to the properties of God that are relevant for making commands about what is morally permitted and morally forbidden. For example, suppose it is logically necessary that if God exists, he is infinitely merciful and loving. Nonbelievers would attempt to determine what God would command if he were to exist by being as merciful and loving as they could be.

However, this suggestion has a problem. In some versions of the Divine Command Theory, God does not have any essential or necessary moral nature. Although he may be infinitely merciful or loving in this world, he is not in all possible worlds. What God commands is based on arbitrary fiat. Thus, approximating to the essential properties of God would not enable an atheist to determine what he would command if he were to exist. Since God has no essential moral properties, it would seem that what God would command would be unpredictable in principle. God himself could not even know what he would command in other possible worlds. Thus, although nonbelievers could embrace the Linguistic Hypothetical Divine Command Theory without commitment to moral anarchy, they could not know what God would command if God were to exist. The Divine Command Theory in hypothetical form would be useless in determining what should be done.

The Ideal Observer Theory does not have this problem since the Ideal Observer does have essential properties—unbiasedness, impartiality, unlimited powers of empathy, and being completely informed. An atheist can approximate to these properties and see whether, when contemplating the act in question, he or she has a feeling of approval or disapproval.[11]

One way of getting over the semantic problem of the Linguistic Actual Divine Command Theory would be to argue that the theory does not purport to capture the meaning of "morally obligatory," and so on in the discourse of nonbelievers and agnostics or even all Christians or Jews. The claim may be only that the analysis captures the meaning of these terms for most Christians and Jews. But this more restricted thesis also has problems.

Suppose an atheist says that it is morally obligatory that p and a typical theist—a person, let us assume, who would believe that ethical terms mean what the Linguistic Divine Command Theory maintains they mean—says that p is morally forbidden. These two people certainly seem to be contradicting each other. But on the present account they would not be—indeed, they could not be—in conflict. The theist would be saying that God commanded that $\sim$ p. But the atheist would certainly not be saying that God commanded that p. Thus, the restricted thesis being considered entails that these two people are not contradicting each other, appearances notwithstanding. Further, if an atheist asserts that it is morally forbidden that p and a typical theist asserts that it is morally forbidden that p, they appear to be agreeing. But they cannot be in this interpretation.

The seeming ability of nonbelievers and theists to agree and to contradict one another in moral matters suggests the present attempt to restrict the scope of the theory has implausible implications. Thus, without further evidence we are not justified in maintaining that most Christians and Jews mean by "morally obligatory", "morally permitted", and "morally forbidden" what Definitions (1), (2), and (3) claim they do.

The Nonlinguistic Actual Divine Command Theory does not have the semantic problems. But it can be accused of failing to capture what religious people mean by saying that morality is dependent on God. T_{1a} simply says that "It is morally required that p" and "God commands that p" are necessarily true or false together. But it does not follow from this that something is morally obligatory *because* God commands it. Consider the following possibility that seems perfectly compatible with T_{la}: God exists in every possible world; he is necessarily morally perfect in the sense that he would command what is morally required in all possible worlds because he is morally required to do so; there is a standard of what is morally independent of God's command. Although T_{la} would be true, morality would not be dependent on God's command in the sense that some religious believers maintain. Rather, God's command could depend on what is morally required. God who, by hypothesis, is morally perfect would command what is morally required in all possible worlds on the basis of this independent standard.[12]

Clearly, then, some further assumption is needed in order to capture the idea that God's command determines what is morally required. It is plausible to suppose that one must assume that God has no essential moral properties. For example, one must assume that it is possible that God could be cruel and unjust; it just so happens that God is just and kind. Quinn does, in fact, suppose that "God is free to command anything he chooses to command."[13] This in effect does assume that God has no essential moral properties that would constrain his choice. Indeed, given T_{la}, T_{lb}, and T_{lc} it is difficult to see what other assumption Quinn could make that captures the idea that God's commands determine what is morally required, morally permissible, and morally forbidden. The assumption that God has certain essential moral properties would be consistent with God's choice being based on some independent moral standard.

Given that God has no essential moral properties, it follows that:

(1) For every x, it is logically possible that God could have commanded x (where x is a variable ranging over every compossible set of actions).

But (1), combined with T_{la}, T_{lb}, T_{lc}, entails:

(2) There are possible worlds in which God commands cruelty for its own sake and this command is morally required.[14]

MORAL PROBLEMS

This brings us to the most infamous problem of the Divine Command Theory: it has morally outrageous consequences. This is seen clearly in the Linguistic Actual Divine Command version. By definition, if God commands cruelty for its own sake, this is morally required. By definition, if God commands people not to be kind to each other, then being kind to each other is morally forbidden.[15] In the Linguistic Hypothetical Divine Command Theory, the same problem arises. By definition, if there were a God and he would command cruelty for its own sake, then the practice of cruelty for its own sake would be morally obligatory.

The Nonlinguistic Actual Divine Command Theory has the same problem, although not in such an obvious or direct way as the linguistic variants. To many morally sensitive people the idea that there are possible worlds in which God commands cruelty for its own sake and that this command is morally required—an implication of the Nonlinguistic Actual Divine Command Theory of Quinn—would constitute a reductio ad absurdum of this version. Although Quinn argues that his theory does not have absurd implications, his rebuttal is weak. He maintains that our moral intuitions "fail to produce agreement about controversial issues, as recent actual cases involving abortion, euthanasia and similar problems show quite clearly."[16] The implication seems to be that the moral intuitions are always unreliable. But the intuition involved in the case at issue—cruelty for its own sake—is hardly controversial.

Quinn also argues that moral intuitions are especially unreliable when one is called on "to go beyond actual moral problems into the realm of the merely possible."[17] Since the case of God commanding cruelty for its own sake is a possibility, not an actuality, the implication seems to be that our intuitions concerning such a case would be especially unreliable. But, in fact, possible cases are usually less difficult to cope with than actual ones since actual cases involve disputes about the facts that in possible cases can be decided by fiat. Moreover, in possible cases one can simplify the situation to its essentials.[18]

In the case at issue—God's commanding cruelty for its own sake—one can make all the necessary simplifying assumptions. For example, there need be no problem of whether God really is commanding cruelty for some indirect human benefit. He is not. There is no complication that the apparent pain involved in the cruel act is illusory. It is not illusory. And so on. The complications involved in actual cases can all be eliminated by stipulation.

Quinn goes so far as to say that reliance on moral intuitions in order to refute the Divine Command Theory is merely moral dogmatism. He says there is "no reason why a divine command theorist should subscribe to a view which licenses moral dogmatism on the part of his critics."[19] This position seems to be based on the view that critics are relying on a controversial moral intuition. But, as I have already suggested, the judgment that cruelty for its own sake is morally wrong in scarcely controversial.

Furthermore, Quinn himself seems to rely on moral intuitions. He says that some possible world with the

> greatest over-all similarity to the actual world in which God commands what we call "gratuitous cruelty" might yet be very unlike the actual world, so dissimilar that intuition is an unreliable guide to what is required and what forbidden there. It might be, for example, that in such worlds what we call "gratuitous cruelty" provides cathartic release for its perpetrators without causing pain to its victims.[20]

This example seems to assume that people's moral intuitions about the "cruelty" would be in agreement if certain background circumstances were changed and made explicit. That is, he assumes that if we knew that what we called "gratuitous cruelty" involved cathartic release for people who committed it and did not cause harm to those against whom it was committed, then our moral intuitions would be in agreement that gratuitous cruelty would not be morally wrong. If Quinn relics on moral intuitions in this way in this case, surely the critics of the Divine Command Theory can do so in other cases. The critics must just be sure that the background circumstances on which their intuitions are based are made explicit.

It should be noted that Quinn's example does not tell at all against the argument where there is a genuine case of gratuitous cruelty, not one merely (wrongly) called "gratuitous cruelty." In Quinn's example, it is clear that there is no gratuitous cruelty. First, the "cruelty" is not gratuitous since there is a beneficial side effect. Second, it is unclear why one even speaks of "cruelty" in this case since the victims are not in pain. In the example adduced here, however, there was no beneficial side effect and people were in pain. It is significant that Quinn had to change the example in order to make his point.

THE EPISTEMOLOGICAL PROBLEM

Another fundamental problem of the Divine Command Theory is: How does one know what God commands? How, in particular, can one separate what are genuine commands of God from what are only apparent ones? This problem is serious for several reasons. First of all, there are several apparent sources of God's revelations to humans. In the Western tradition alone there is the Bible, the Koran, the Book of Mormon, and the teachings of Reverend Moon and many lesser known religious figures. Clearly it is impossible to follow the alleged commands found in all of these books and issued by all of those people claiming to speak for God because they are in conflict.

Furthermore, even within the same religious tradition, for example, Christianity, the same alleged command of God is interpreted in different ways. Thus, for example, the command "Thou shall not kill!" is said by some Christians to entail pacifism and by others not to, by some to justify abolishing the death penalty and by others not to. What *is* the correct interpretation of the command?

In addition, some apparent commands seem to many modern religious people, even those within the Christian tradition, to be morally questionable. Thus, for example, the Old Testament forbids male homosexual relations. The New Testament forbids divorce except for unchastity. Must modern Christians follow these apparent commands although they conflict with some of their deeply held moral judgments? One suggestion would be to reject any alleged divine command or any interpretation of a divine command as specious if it conflicts with one's own moral judgment. Thus, one must consider the following as an epistemological test:

(ET$_1$) An alleged divine command C should be judged as genuine, or an interpretation I of C should be judged as correct by person P IFF C or I of C agrees with person P's moral judgment.

There are, however, a number of problems with ET$_1$. First, since different persons have different moral judgments about the same thing, conflicting judgments of what is a genuine command of God would result. Person P$_1$ would be as well justified in saying that command C was genuine as person P$_2$ was in saying that C was not genuine. This would introduce a seemingly irreducible element of subjectivity into the theory. But, as we have seen, one alleged advantage of the Divine Command Theory over humanistic ethics is the objectivity it presumably brings into ethical deliberation.

Second, it is difficult to see how ET$_1$ could be justified unless it is assumed that a person's moral judgment is a reliable test of what God commands. Thus, one might assume that God had made humans in such a way that their moral judgments were reliable reflections of God's commands. This, however, is dubious on both factual and theological grounds. On factual grounds there is a lack of agreement about what is morally obligatory. On theological grounds to use one's own moral intuitions as a test of what God really commands smacks of hubris to many believers. Indeed, on at least one interpretation of the Bible, given the temptation of Satan and given humans' sinful nature, our own moral judgments are unreliable guides to divine commands.

Another suggestion would be to distinguish a genuine divine command from a specious one by appeal to historical scholarship and interpretation. Consider the following formulation of the epistemological test:

(ET$_2$) An alleged divine command C should be judged as genuine, or an interpretation I of C should be judged as correct, by person P IFF C or I of C agrees with the best supported historical scholarship and interpretation concerning the religious tradition in which C or I is found.

One difficulty with ET$_2$ is that it is dubious that historical scholarship can establish the supernatural origins of commands found in texts such as the Bible or those made by religious teachers. In fact, scholarship tends to reveal the all-too-human origins of the commands found in the holy books of the great world religions. Thus, from the standpoint of religious believers the use of historical scholarship to determine what is a genuine divine command could be dangerous. If, for example, there is little reason to suppose that Jesus is a genuine historical figure, the commands allegedly made by Jesus would have to be discounted. They could not be divine since there would have been no historical person either human or divine who issued them.

Distinguishing the correct from the incorrect interpretation of some allegedly divine command also seems to be beyond the powers of scholarship. Historical scholarship is capable of telling us which of various interpretations of a command were accepted by believers at some particular time, if some particular interpretation is inconsistent with some religious tradition, and if some term or phrase used in the command had a special meaning at a certain period in history. But it cannot determine whether some particular interpretation was intended by God. Thus, it is possible to tell if early Christians interpreted the commandment "Thou shall not kill!" in such a way that it entailed the abolition of the death penalty. But scholarship is incapable of determining if this entailment was intended by God.

THE CONCEPTUAL PROBLEM

This discussion has been assuming that the notion of a command of a transcendent God makes sense, but this may not be so. The notion of a command is ambiguous in that it is sometimes considered a certain kind of speech act and sometimes the content of this speech act. Thus, the content of the command to close the door is conveyed by an imperative sentence "Close the door!" and is the result of a speech act involving an utterance of the words "Close the door!" on a certain occasion. This ambiguity holds in religious contexts too. Thus, the content of the command to not kill is conveyed by the imperative sentence "Thou shall not kill!" and is presumably the result of a speech act involving the utterance of the words "Thou shall not kill!" But this creates a certain problem. If one interprets God as a nonspatial, nontemporal being without a body, what sense can one make of his performing a speech act? Such a being would seem incapable of an act that assumes, if not a body, at least some spatial and temporal point of origin. The only sense one can make of a divine command is to understand God in a nontranscendent way, as a being operating within space and time. But even this concession may not be enough, because it is unclear how a being within time and space could fail not to have a body or how such a being could issue commands. The existence of a voice issuing commands seems to presume some physical vocal apparatus; golden letters written in the sky would seem to presuppose some physical writing appendage. However, this understanding of God assumes an anthropomorphism rejected by sophisticated theologians. Moreover, since this anthropomorphic god is a being operating within time and space, it is subject to empirical investigation. Unfortunately, the available evidence no more supports the hypothesis of its existence than it supports the hypothesis that Santa Claus exists.

The advocate of the Divine Command Theory is, thus, presented with a dilemma. If God is transcendent, the notion of divine command seems difficult to understand. If God is construed in anthropomorphic terms, then the concept of divine command makes sense but the hypothesis that God exists becomes very improbable.

One could attempt to resolve the problem by supposing that God uses the physical body of humans to issue commands; that God, the transcendental being, does not speak himself, but through the mouth of Christ or Moses or Reverend Moon. But this only pushes the problem back one step. It is not clear how a transcendent being, a being without a body, a being outside of time and space can speak through a being in time and space.

In ordinary life we understand perfectly well how one person can speak through another. By speech or writing the first conveys information or desire to the second who then conveys it to others. The second person is explicitly authorized or is understood by convention to speak for the first person. This process involves a causal chain operating between bodies; in particular, it involves one person giving information, directions, or the like to another by voice or deed. But this clear familiar picture does not apply in the case of God. For God to convey information or instructions to Jesus, Moses, or Reverend Moon by voice or deed would require a body he does not have.

The only other possibility would be for God to convey commands to human beings via something analogous to telepathy or thought transference. Then presumably there would be no need for God to perform some speech act. There is still a serious problem, however, for God is outside space and on some accounts outside time. It is difficult enough to understand what it would mean to say that thought exists outside of space and time. It is incomprehensible how thoughts or desires could be transferred or conveyed to human beings in space and time. Transfer and conveyance suggest a temporal process occurring between two points in space; even instantaneous transference, assuming this even makes sense, involves at least two spatial points. But, in the case of transfer of information from a transcendent God to his spokespersons, there is no spatial point of origin. One might as well speak of a marriage involving only one person or a parent who never had any children.

A Modified Divine Command Theory

If the Divine Command Theory in its most extreme form does not work, might a modified version work? Some religious believers have argued that being a divine command is a necessary but not a sufficient condition for moral obligation. On this view the mere fact that God commands that p does not entail that p is morally required. Suppose, however, we add to the claim that God commands such and such that he is the creator of human beings. According to this modified version, children have a moral obligation to obey their parents. Insofar as we are to God as children are to their parents, human beings have an obligation to obey God just as children have an obligation to obey their parents. Thus, according to the modified divine command view, the claim that God commands that p *combined* with the assumption that God created humans entails that humans should obey that p.[21]

However, it is unclear that the modified view is correct for it is uncertain under what circumstances God the Creator's commands bring about a moral obligation to follow the commands. Consider a Modified Nonlinguistic Actual Divine Command Theory. Stated schematically the principle that would specify a sufficient condition of moral obligation would be:

(M) Necessarily if God commands that p under conditions C, then it is morally obligatory that p.

Conditions C would be those conditions found in a religious context that are analogous to the ones found in the context of ordinary life that create an obligation for children to follow the commands of their parents.

One obvious condition is that children only have an obligation to follow the commands of their parents if they are capable of doing so. Similarly for the children of God. Humans have an obligation to follow the commands of God only if they are capable of doing so. Stated more formally the general principle at work seems to be this:

(P) If X created Y and Y is capable of following commands and X commands that p, then Y has the moral obligation to do that p.

Given P and the alleged fact that God issues the command that p is morally required and that God created humans and that humans are capable of obedience, it follows that p is morally required.

One problem in the application of P, of course, is that parents can issue conflicting commands. If they do, their children will not be capable of following all their commands. A similar problem could occur in religious contexts. If it did, God's children would have no obligation to follow the commands of God since they would be incapable of doing do. In some instances the alleged commands of God seem to be in conflict. Consider a famous example presented by Richard Brandt:

Consider the Ten Commandments. One of them reads: "Remember the Sabbath day, to keep it holy. . . . In it thou shalt not do any work." Another reads: "Honour thy father and thy mother." These rules, which we assume may be taken as ethical statements (for example, "It is always wrong not to honour your father and mother.") are doubtless rather vague. There is one point, though, on which they are not vague: It seems that there is something we are *always* to do. These facts lead to difficulties. Suppose my father calls me on the phone on Sunday morning, tells me that a storm has blown off a piece of his roof the previous evening, and invites me to come and help him repair it before there is another rain. I seem to not be "honouring" my father if I refuse; I am breaking the rule about the Sabbath if I comply.[22]

Another problem with P is that it makes it obligatory to perform any apparently immoral acts that are commanded by a parent. Surely if a parent commands a child to kill an innocent person for the parent's pleasure, the child would have no obligation to do this. In a similar way, if God commanded one of his creatures to perform an immoral act, the creature would have no moral obligation to do so. Yet, according to P, they would.[23]

It seems implausible in the extreme to believe that humans have an obligation to follow immoral commands even if God did create them. Religious believers can attempt to overcome this problem by either denying that these commands are immoral, appearances notwithstanding, or denying that they are really the commands of God. The first attempted solution is implausible. Suppose that God commanded cruelty for its own sake. How could it be denied that this command is immoral? Surely humans would have no moral obligation to obey even though God created humans. The second solution assumes there is a plausible way of distinguishing the apparent commands of God from those that are genuine. But, as we have seen, no way is readily apparent.

It may be argued that P simply needs to be modified. Consider:

(P') If X created Y and Y is capable of following commands and X commands x and x is not immoral, then Y has the moral obligation to do x.

But even this may not be enough, for children may legitimately refuse to follow a parent's command that is not immoral if it conflicts with some stronger obligation and the same holds true for a religious context. Thus, although the alleged command of God not to steal is not immoral, it should be disobeyed if, for example, stealing would save a life.

Clearly P' will have to be weakened further. Consider:

(P″) If X created Y and Y is capable of following commands and X commands x and x is not immoral and Y has no stronger obligation, then Y has the moral obligation to do x.

But even this may not be enough. Imagine that Smith's parents command him to paint their kitchen. Suppose Smith has no stronger obligations but that his parents have ill-used him all his life and, in general, have been cruel toward him. Does Smith really have an obligation to obey his parents? It is doubtful that he does.

The relevance of this example to the religious context is fairly clear. If we follow through with the analogy with one's parents, it would entail that whether or not humans should feel obligated to follow God's, their creator's, commands should depend on how God has treated them. Here the problem of evil is relevant. This problem is traditionally posed as follows: Why believe that God exists given the existence of evil? For if God is all-good, he would want to prevent evil, and if God is all-powerful he could prevent evil, so why is there evil? One solution to the problem is to suppose that God is not good—at least not in our sense of "good." But, then, humans may just as legitimately refuse to follow the command of God as a child can refuse to follow the commands of a parent who has ill-treated him or her.

Perhaps the most that can be said is:

(P‴) If X created Y and Y is capable of following commands and X commands x and x is not immoral and Y has no stronger obligation and X has not ill-used Y, then Y has the moral obligation to do x.

It is unclear, however, if even this principle is acceptable. For example, why should a child follow his parents' command to paint their kitchen, even if he has no stronger obligation and the parents have treated the child well, if they can afford to hire someone to paint it or if the kitchen has recently been painted or if there are other children who are eager to help the parents. It is at least debatable in these circumstances that the child is morally obligated to follow his parents' commands.

Is there an analogue to this in the religious context? Suppose God commands Smith to start a church in order to save the world. Does Smith have a moral obligation to obey if there are other people better able to do so and more willing to help? Does Smith have an obligation to obey even though he can see no need for such a church and God does not explain to him why there is a need? If we take the child-parent, human-God analogy seriously, it is not clear that he does. Of course, religious believers might say that Smith has a moral obligation since he has been singled out by God and God moves in mysterious ways. But a child can be singled out by parents for some tasks and the parents' choice can appear mysterious to the child. The child has a right to know why he or she rather than some other child who seems more qualified and more eager is chosen and why the task needs to be done. Thus, if one follows through the analogy between parent and God to its ultimate conclusion, there is reason to suppose that even P''' fails. The only way that P''' (or P'' or P') would hold would be if one supposes that children have a blind obligation to obey their parents. They do not. If we take the analogy seriously, neither do God's children.

So far we have been unable to find a satisfactory formulation of condition C in M above. Thus, the obligation that children owe their parents and, by analogy, the obligation that humans owe God because he created them remains elusive. But let us suppose that a more subtle formulation of this obligation is satisfactory. A serious problem still remains.

In order to apply any of the above principles (or presumably a more subtle modification of them) it is necessary to have knowledge of one's moral obligation *independently* of them. For example, one must know both that the action under consideration is not immoral and that one has no stronger obligation in order to apply P'''. Thus, even if P''' is correct, it could not be applied without independent moral knowledge of what is immoral and of the other moral obligations one has. But the Divine Command Theory is supposed to tell us what is immoral and what our obligations are. Thus, the Modified Divine Command Theory does not seem capable of providing a sufficient condition for moral obligation without independent moral knowledge.

Now some advocates of the Modified Divine Command Theory believe that although the command of God is not a sufficient condition for moral obligation, it is a necessary condition. This would mean that necessarily if an action is morally obligatory, then God commands it. But there does not seem to be any reason to believe this. Even if God exists in this world, there could be possible worlds in which he does not exist, yet human beings have a moral obligation not to practice cruelty for its own sake. Many nonbelievers would maintain that our actual world is such a world. Thus:

(N) Necessarily, if it is morally obligatory that p, then God commands that p.

has no support.

In addition to the problems already raised, the Modified Nonlinguistic Divine Command Theory has all the conceptual problems of its more radical version. If it is unintelligible how a transcendent God can issue commands, it is no less unintelligible how a transcendent God can issue commands and can create human beings who are supposed to obey them. Giving commands and creating are both acts that it is difficult to understand how a nontemporal and nonspatial being can perform.[24]

Another attempt to develop a Modified Divine Command Theory maintains that what is morally forbidden is identical with what is contrary to what a *loving* God commands. (Presumably, similar accounts could be given of moral obligation and moral permissibility.) Let us consider the nonlinguistic version developed by R. M. Adams,[25] itself a modification of a linguistic version developed earlier by him.[26] Adams argues that properties like water and H_2O are necessarily identical although the identity cannot be known a priori; it is an empirical fact. In a similar way, the property of contrariety to a command of a loving God is, according to Adams, necessarily identical with the property of moral wrongness although this is not something one can know a priori; it is known a posteriori.

One advantage this theory has over the other the other modified divine command theory is that a loving God would not presumably command cruelty for its own sake. Thus, the theory would not have some of the outrageous moral implications discussed here. According to Adams, the theory has other advantages as well. He argues that his theory accords well with certain general characteristics that any plausible account of moral wrongness must have. For example, as the concept of wrongness functions in our thinking, the moral wrongness of an action is a property that an action has independently of what people think. Moral wrongness as identical with what is contrary to what God commands has this characteristic.

One basic problem with Adams's theory is that he seems to assume that although human knowledge of what is morally wrong is dependent on knowledge of God's commands, humans can have knowledge of certain values independently of God. This becomes clear when one asks why wrongness is necessarily identical with the doing of what is contrary to a *loving* God's commands, rather than what is identical with what is contrary to God's commands. Adams argues:

> But if wrongness is simply contrariety to the commands of God, it is necessarily so, which implies that it would be wrong to disobey God even if he were so unloving as to command the practice of cruelty for its own sake. That consequence is unacceptable. I am not prepared to adopt the negative attitude towards possible disobedience in that situation that would be involved in identifying wrongness simply with contrariety to God's commands. The loving character of the God who issues them seems to me therefore to be a metaethically relevant feature of divine commands. (I assume that in deciding what property is wrongness and therefore what would be wrongness in all possible worlds, we are to rely on our own moral feeling and convictions, rather than on those we or others would have in other possible worlds.)[27]

Suppose that someone claims that the following is a command of God:

(C) Commit acts of cruelty for their own sake!

Adams seems to be saying that because of the unloving nature of C, one can infer that C is contrary to the command of a loving God and, consequently, that C is not a command of God. Since God is loving, he would not command cruelty for its own sake. The crucial question one must ask here, however, is on what basis can one assert that God is loving or at least not cruel. One obvious answer is that we can judge that being loving is a property of God, perhaps even an essential property of God, because God is good and being loving is a property, perhaps an essential property, of a good person. But on what basis does one make such a judgment? Adams's statement in the quotation above suggests that one judges that the property of being loving is a good property in terms of our actual moral feelings and convictions. This, in turn, indicates that we can have knowledge of what is good and bad *independently* of God's commands.

In a paper written earlier than the one under discussion Adams distinguished between having knowledge of values, which is independent of God's commands, and having knowledge of moral wrongness, which is not.[28] One assumes that he was relying on the same distinction in his later version of his theory. In his earlier paper he argued that we can have knowledge that cruelty is bad and loving is good independently of God's commands, but we cannot have knowledge that cruelty for its own sake is morally wrong independently of knowledge of what a loving God commands. But why could we not have such knowledge? It would seem that one could easily infer that if something is an act of cruelty for its own sake is bad, then it is morally wrong. Consider the following argument:

(1) Cruelty is bad.
(2) Act A is an act of cruelty for its own sake.
(3) If cruelty is bad and act A is an act of cruelty for its own sake, then Act A is morally wrong.

---

(4) Therefore, act A is morally wrong.

The argument is certainly valid. Premise 3 seems analytic, true by the definition of the moral terms that are involved. Adams admits that one can have knowledge of premise 1 independently of knowledge of God's commands. Further, premise 2 is not an ethical statement; one can have knowledge of 2 independently of the knowledge of God's commands. For example, one can know that 2 is true by determining the motive or intention of the actor. It seems to follow that one can have knowledge of whether an act is wrong without knowledge of God's commands. Thus, it is difficult to see how Adams can maintain the distinction he wishes to make between moral knowledge based on God's command and moral knowledge not so based. One can have knowledge of what is morally wrong *without* knowledge of God's commands if one has, as Adams seems to allow, knowledge that cruelty is bad and that certain cruel acts are performed for their own sake.[29]

In addition, Adams's theory inherits many of the problems of the other divine command theories. The conceptual problem remains of how a transcendent being, a being that is nonspatial and on some accounts nontemporal, could make commands. We also have the problem of how a nonspatial and nontemporal being could be loving since a loving being entails loving action and loving action involves a body. Furthermore, Adams explicitly relates moral wrong to what God commands rather than to what God wills. This, he correctly argues, assumes a theory of revelation. He suggests several theories of revelation but he does not even attempt to answer the questions that can be raised against such theories. Finally, Adams admits that his theory has the apparently paradoxical implication that no action would be ethically wrong if there were no loving God. He attempts to dispel the apparent paradox by maintaining that if there were no God, people would still use the word "wrong." People would still call certain things "wrong." They might even call the same things "wrong" as we do. Indeed, he says that people might even express the same psychological state by saying "Cruelty is wrong" as we express by using these words. Unfortunately, none of this dispels the paradox. For, in his view, it would be true that if God did not exist, nothing would be wrong. Although, if God did not exist, people might correctly say in some sense "Cruelty is morally wrong," cruelty would not *really* be wrong. Any theory with this paradoxical implication is prima facie unacceptable. This, combined with other problems with the theory, gives us good grounds for rejecting it.

Conclusion

The variants of the Divine Command Theory examined here have serious problems. Since Christianity does not entail this theory of metaethics, its failure does not entail that Christianity is false. However, since the theory does follow from Christianity when it is combined with certain assumptions about the nature of God—assumptions that many theists accept—the failure of the Divine Command Theory entails that either Christianity is false or these assumptions are mistaken.

NOTES

1. For example, see Paul Helm, "Introduction," in *Divine Commands and Morality*, ed. Paul Helm (Oxford: Oxford University Press, 1981), pp. 2–5, for a brief historical discussion of the theory.

2. See Kai Nielsen, *Ethics Without God* (Buffalo, N.Y.: Prometheus, 1973), p. 1.

3. Elsewhere I have argued that atheism is not committed to moral anarchy in all versions of the Divine Command Theory. See Michael Martin, *Atheism: A Philosophical Justification* (Philadelphia: Temple University Press, 1990), Introduction. I have also maintained that those versions of the Divine Command Theory that entail that atheism is committed to moral anarchy are implausible. In my criticism of the charge that atheism is committed to moral

relativity I also claimed but did not argue there that even if atheistic morality is relativistic, the Divine Command Theory has equally serious problems. Although this theory purports to provide an absolute analysis of ethical discourse, in practice it does not. Although one is supposed to follow the commands of God, there is wide disagreement over what God commands and there seems to be no rational method to reconcile them.

4. According to Helm, Ockham held a view similar to this. See Helm, "Introduction," in *Divine Commands and Morality*, ed. Helm, p. 3.

5. For a contemporary statement of this theory see Roderick Firth, "Ethical Absolutism and the Ideal Observer," *Philosophy and Phenomenological Research* 12 (1955): 317–45. See also Richard Brandt, *Ethical Theory* (Englewood Cliffs, N.J.: Prentice-Hall, (1959), pp. 173–76.

6. For example, I have elsewhere argued that it is logically impossible on one standard concept of God for God to experience the emotions of hate or greed or envy since God is morally perfect. See Martin, *Atheism: A Philosophical Justification*, chap. 12. However, this concept of God is not the only one that theologians have accepted. According to this standard concept of God, it is assumed that God necessarily would not experience hate, greed, envy, and so on, because these are morally forbidden emotional states. But, as we shall see, in many versions of the Divine Command Theory it is doubtful that God has any essentially moral nature. In these versions of the Divine Command Theory, God could make any emotional state morally permissible.

7. Phillip L. Quinn, *Divine Commands and Moral Requirements* (Oxford: Clarendon Press, 1978).

8. Ibid., p. 30.

9. See Richard Price, *Review of the Principle Questions in Morals*, partly reprinted in Richard B. Brandt, *Value and Obligation* (New York: Harcourt, Brace and World, 1961), pp. 330–41.

10. The view that everything is morally permitted if there is no God is advocated by Smerdyakov in Dostoyevsky's novel *The Brothers Karamozov*.

11. For a defense of this theory against the criticism of R. M. Adams found in "Moral Arguments for Theistic Beliefs," *Rationality and Religious Belief*, ed. C. F. Delaney (Notre Dame, Ind.: University of Notre Dame Press, 1979), pp. 116–40, see Charles Taliaferro, "The Divine Command Theory of Ethics and the Ideal Observer," *Sophia* 22 (1983): 3–7.

12. See Thomas B. Talbott, "Quinn on Divine Commands and Moral Requirements," *International Journal for the Philosophy of Religion*, 13 (1982): 194–98. See also John Chandler, "Is the Divine Command Theory Defensible?" *Religious Studies* 20 (1984): 443–52.

13. Quinn, *Divine Commands and Moral Requirements*, p. 31.

14. See Talbott, "Quinn on Divine Commands and Moral Requirements," pp. 201–2.

15. This problem was first raised in Plato's *Euthyphro*. The question

posed was whether a pious or holy thing was beloved by the gods because it was pious or holy, or whether it was pious or holy because it was beloved by the gods. The latter thesis suggests that anything can be pious or holy if it is beloved by the gods. See Helm, "Introduction," in *Divine Commands and Morality*, ed. Helm, p. 2.

16. Quinn, *Divine Commands and Moral Requirements*, p. 58.

17. Ibid.

18. This is why possible cases are often used to make a clear moral point. See Talbott, "Quinn on Divine Commands and Moral Requirements," p. 205.

19. Quinn, *Divine Commands and Moral Requirements*, p. 60.

20. Ibid.

21. A theory along these lines is developed by Baruch A. Brody, "Morality and Religion Reconsidered," in *Divine Commands and Morality*, ed. Helm, pp. 141–53.

22. Richard B. Brandt, *Ethical Theory*, p. 17.

23. The Old Testament is full of various alleged commands of God that seem morally dubious. A few famous examples are: Death for unchastity (Deut. 22:20, 21), death for straying near the tabernacle (Num. 1:51), and death for blasphemy (Lev. 24:16).

24. For a criticism of aspects of Brody's theory not considered here see Robert Young, "Theism and Morality," in *Divine Commands and Morality*, ed. Helm, pp. 156–60.

25. Robert Merrihew Adams, "Divine Command Metaethics as Necessary A Posteriori," in *Divine Commands and Morality*, ed. Helm, pp. 109–19. This is extracted from Adams's paper, "Divine Command Metaethics Modified Again," *Journal of Religious Ethics* 7 (1979): 71–79.

26. Robert Merrihew Adams," A Modified Divine Command Theory of Ethical Wrongness," in *Divine Commands and Morality*, ed. Helm, pp. 83–108.

27. Adams, "Divine Command Metaethics as Necessary A Posteriori," in *Divine Commands and Morality*, ed Helm, pp. 116–17.

28. Adams, "A Modified Divine Command Theory of Ethical Wrongness," in *Divine Commands and Morality*, ed. Helm, pp. 109–19.

29. For a related critical point see Robert Young, "Theism and Morality," in *Divine Commands and Morality*, ed. Helm, pp. 160–64.

Appendix 2
THE ATONEMENT

The reason why Jesus came to earth, died, and was resurrected is only hinted at in the New Testament.[1] For example, in Matthew it is said that "the Son of man came not to be served but to serve, and to give his life as a ransom for many" (20:28). Also in Matthew, Jesus, at the Last Supper, is reported to have referred to "my blood of the covenant, which is poured out for many for the forgiveness of sins" (26:28). In John, John the Baptist proclaims of Jesus: "Behold, the Lamb of God, who takes away the sin of the world!" (1:29). In Romans it is asserted, "we also rejoice in God through our Lord Jesus Christ, through whom we have now received our reconciliation" (5:11). In Hebrews it is stated that Jesus was once offered "to bear the sins of many" (9:28). In 1 John it is maintained that Jesus is "the expiation for our sins, and not for ours only but also for the sins of the whole world" (2:2).

Vincent Taylor, a New Testament scholar, attempts to summarize and synthesize what the New Testament teaches concerning the Atonement in the following way:

> (1) The Atonement is the work of God in restoring sinners to fellowship with Himself and establishing His Kingdom in the world; it is the reconciliation of man and of the world to God. (2) It is the fulfillment of His purpose for man and the final proof of the greatness of His love, both revealing that love and expressing it for time and eternity. (3) The Atonement is accomplished in the work of Christ, whose suffering is vicarious, representative, and sacrificial in character; it is on behalf of men, in their name, and for the purpose of their approach to God. (4) The vicarious nature of Christ's ministry is one of the clearest elements in New Testament teaching, but its true content can be discerned only as its representative and sacrificial aspects are more closely defined. (5) The representative character of His death is disclosed by the fact that, in the greatness of His love for men, He identified Himself with sinners and in their service was completely obedient to the will of the Father, entering into and enduring in His own person the consequences of sin and the rejection and gainsaying of men. (6) The sacrificial significance of his death is suggested by the frequent use of the term "blood," by a limited use of analogies found in the ancient sacrificial system, by references to cleansing, redemption, and expiation, by allusions to the idea of the Suffering Servant, and by eucharistic teaching sacrificial in

character. (7) The Atonement is consummated in the experience of men through faith–union with Christ, through sacramental communion with him, and in sacrificial living and suffering.[2]

Obviously, the passages from Scripture quoted above and even Taylor's summary leave many questions open. For example, how by dying on the cross did Jesus take away the sins of the world? And why in any case would God save sinful humanity through the death of his son? Taylor is certainly correct that the representative and sacrificial aspect of Jesus' ministry needs to be more clearly defined if he means by this that what is needed is some explanation of why Jesus was sacrificed as a representative of sinful humanity. In the centuries that followed Christian thinkers have wrestled with these issues. In attempting to explain why Jesus died on the cross they created a variety of theories of the Atonement. Although a systematic critique of all of these would require a book-length treatment, let us briefly consider some of the historically most important types and their major problems.

Major Theories of the Atonement

THE RANSOM THEORY

For approximately the first thousand years of Christianity's history the most popular theory of the Atonement was the ransom theory. In the crude version held by early Christian thinkers such as Origen (185–254), the theory assumes that the devil is in possession of humanity and that his rights of possession cannot be ignored. God consents to pay a price, the death of his own son, for the release of humanity. The devil accepts the bargain because he believes that he will have the Son of God as his prize. However, the devil is tricked by God. God knows when he offers the devil the bargain that the devil will be unable to keep the Son of God as a prize. Consequently, the son escapes the devil's powers and is reconciled with his father. In later, more sophisticated versions of the theory, for example Augustine's, the devil is deceived not by God but by his inordinate pride. So the devil is justly overcome. Since the devil is not defeated by God's might, God's justice and righteousness are emphasized.[3]

There are obviously many problems with the ransom theory. First, crude versions explicitly attribute to God qualities of character that are unworthy of a divine being. If God is morally perfect, he does not deceive anyone, not even the devil. Second, even the more sophisticated versions make implausible assumptions, for example that the devil would be so blinded by pride that he would believe that he is more powerful than the Son of God. Third, the very idea of a devil, especially one that has gained a right of possession to human beings because of their sins, a right that God must acknowledge and honor, strikes many modern readers as bizarre and implausible. Why would God believe that the devil has any moral claim on his creatures? After all, the devil is one of his creatures, one that has disobeyed him and sinned against him. Fourth, it is unjust for God to sacrifice his son for this ransom especially when it is unclear that other alternatives did not exist. Since God is all-powerful and can do anything that is not logically impossible, God could surely have found other ways to achieve his ends. Finally, it is unclear why, in order to be saved, human beings must have faith in Jesus. Since, on the ransom theory, after Jesus' death and resurrection human beings were out of the devil's clutches, it would seem that the way to salvation would simply be to follow a life free from sin so as not to fall under the devil's control. What has faith in Jesus got to do with this? The ransom theory supplies no answer.

THE SATISFACTION THEORY

Although the satisfaction theory was anticipated to some extent by earlier thinkers, it was developed in an explicit and sophisticated way by Anselm in the eleventh century.[4] Anselm argues that God must save humanity and do it via the incarnation and death of Jesus. To offer God his due, according to Anselm, is to follow his will. However, he argues that when God's creatures sin this is precisely what they do not do. The sins of God's creatures insult God and detract from his honor. There is, then, an obligation to restore God's honor and to undo the insult. This is satisfaction. However, only the death of the God–Man, Jesus, can give proper satisfaction. Only the God–Man is able, by his divinity, to offer something that is worthy of God and, by his humanity, to represent humankind. A mere human would be unable to give the proper satisfaction, since this latter must be in proportion to the amount of sin, and the amount of sin is infinite.[5] Furthermore, the death of the God–Man is not unjust since the Son of God died completely voluntarily in order to restore God's honor. Those who accept Jesus' sacrifice are saved.

There are as many problems with this theory, whose argument

turns on assumptions that are questionable, as with the ransom theory. First, it is certainly not obvious that the sin of humanity is infinite. The idea seems to be that since God is infinite, any insult to God occasioned by not following his will is an infinite wrong. But this would seem to mean that if only one person committed one small sin, an infinite wrong would have been inflicted and an infinite satisfaction would be necessary. This seems absurd. One also wonders: if not following God's will brings about an infinite harm, then would following God's will bring about an infinite good? If this is the implication, it seems mistaken. For one would have supposed that only God himself can bring about an infinite good.

Second, it is unclear why, if the wrong brought against God by humanity is infinite, it could not be properly satisfied by simply inflicting punishment on sinners for eternity. The Incarnation would not be necessary. Third, the death of Jesus, even though voluntary, seems unjust. Justice surely demands that at the very least the guilty party provide as much of the satisfaction as he or she can. Furthermore, a perfectly good person would not permit a completely innocent person to provide satisfaction on a voluntary basis even if the guilty party could pay nothing. Indeed, the very idea of God's pride being so wounded and demanding such satisfaction that the voluntary sacrifice of his innocent son is required, assumes a view of God's moral nature that many modern readers would reject.

Consider the following example from everyday life. Suppose the proper satisfaction for Smith's wrong inflicted on Jones is for Smith to pay $1,000 to Jones. But Smith is able to pay only $100. Evans volunteers to pay the entire $1,000 to Jones although Evans has done no wrong to Jones. Thus, Smith ends up paying nothing. Justice has surely not been served. At the least, Smith should have paid as much as he could. Furthermore, a saintly person would not even accept Evans's offer. Such an individual would swallow his or her pride and would take an amount less than that which is due. But in Anselm's account, humans do not provide any part of the satisfaction that is due God and God shows conspicuously unsaintly behavior by accepting vicarious satisfaction from his innocent son.

Fourth, it is inexplicable why there has been only one incarnation and death of the God–Man and why it took so long for even this one event to happen. The birth and death of the God–Man is supposed to provide satisfaction for the dishonor that human beings have inflicted on God by sinning. But this satisfaction does not mean that people will no longer sin. In fact, Christians believe that since the birth and death of Jesus almost everyone has sinned. It would seem that the logic of this theory would necessitate at least one more incarnation and death of the God–Man in order to provide new satisfaction for the infinite wrong brought against God from the death of Jesus up until the present time. In fact, as history progresses it would seem that an indefinite series of births and deaths of the God–Man would be necessary to provide the satisfaction for the wrongs against God that occurred since the last incarnation of the God–Man. Furthermore, why did the son of God wait so long in order to sacrifice himself in the first place? After all, sin existed for tens of thousands of years before the coming of the God–Man.

Fifth, it is not clear why the *death* of the God–Man is necessary for satisfaction of an infinite wrong against God's honor. Why would not some other punishment suffice? If God's honor is infinitely wounded by human sin, why could it not be appeased by the eternal punishment of the God–Man, Jesus? Why the death penalty? It would seem much worse to punish Jesus for eternity than to kill him after only relatively little suffering. Even if one argues that death has a harshness that no punishment can match, it is important to recall that Jesus was dead for only a short time. It would have been a much harsher death punishment if Jesus had *remained* unresurrected.

Finally, it is unclear why those who accept Jesus' sacrifice are saved. Even supposing that Jesus' sacrifice provides satisfaction for the past damage done to God's honor, why should faith in Jesus *now* save anyone? And why should believers, but not nonbelievers, be rewarded?

THE ACCEPTANCE THEORY

Theologians in the Middle Ages were greatly influenced by Anselm's satisfaction theory but some of them developed the theory in ways radically different from his. Consider the views of the thirteenth-century philosopher Duns Scotus. Whereas Anselm emphasized the necessity of the incarnation and death of Jesus for the salvation of humanity, Scotus argued that all satisfaction derives from the arbitrary choice of God. The Incarnation was not necessary, according to Scotus, but was caused by the free choice of God. Neither human sin nor the satisfaction that brought about the death of Christ is infinite. It only becomes so by God's arbitrary choice. Although Jesus as a man only experienced finite suffering, God freely decided to accept this as satisfaction for the sins of humanity.

Scotus's theory of satisfaction—sometimes called the Acceptance Theory since the Atonement depended on what God freely accepts— certainly solved one of the main problems of Anselm's theory: the difficulties of explaining why God acted in one way rather than another. But it has problems of its own. It fails completely to account for the Incarnation, death, and Resurrection of Jesus. There is no apparent reason why God chose the way of salvation that he did choose. God might have accepted any, or even no, satisfaction. Indeed, he might have chosen to save humanity via an angel or a man who was not divine.[6] Indeed, it seems that the way that God did choose can be criticized on moral grounds. If there were alternatives open to God, it would seem that he should not have let his son sacrifice himself. But he did.

In sum, instead of providing us with an explanation of the Incarnation, the Resurrection, and salvation this theory makes them seem arbitrary and morally problematic.

THE PENAL THEORY

In the Reformation theologians such as Martin Luther (1483– 1546) and John Calvin (1509–1564) stressed the utterly sinful nature of humanity much more than did medieval thinkers. Justice, they argued, demands that sin must be punished and full compensation must be given to the injured parties. Thus, the attitude of a just God toward sinners can only be that of wrath. Only Jesus, the Son of God, who as a man represents sinful humanity, can take on the infinite sins of the world and can be punished for these sins. With Jesus' punishment justice is satisfied and God's mercy toward humanity can be manifested. Jesus suffers as our substitute making us righteous and free of sin. With faith we can grasp Jesus' victory over sin and be saved. Some Reformed theologians such as Calvin combined these ideas with that of the elect. Those who have faith in Jesus and are, therefore, saved are the elect of God. Their faith comes as a gift of God through the Holy Spirit and those who are saved through this gift were predestined to have this gift bestowed upon them.

The punishment theory has problems that are very similar to those of the satisfaction theory. Indeed, most of the criticisms of the satisfaction theory can be easily translated into criticisms of the punishment theory. For example, it is certainly not obvious that the sins of humanity are infinite and that only the son of God can vicariously be punished for them. The only basically novel aspect of this theory is the Calvinist doctrine of the elect, which seems especially morally repugnant. Since faith in Jesus is an arbitrary gift it seems grossly unfair that only the elect should gain the Kingdom of God.

THE GOVERNMENT THEORY

The government theory, which is usually associated with the seventeenth-century thinker Hugo Grotius (1583–1645), is in some respects a variant of the punishment theory.[7] However, in this view God is not the administrator of some absolute and unchanging rules of justice. He is not bound by an ideal of justice or obligated to provide full compensation to injured parties. What is important, according to Grotius, is that God administer a good world government and this entails preserving public order. If in order to do this the rules of justice need to be relaxed, God has the right to do so. Divine punishment should be judged by its deterrent effect in bringing about public order. Jesus' punishment was justified on these grounds. Although it was not necessitated by the demands of absolute justice, it was necessary for preserving public order and good divine government.

But why was it necessary even for this purpose? It was necessary, says Grotius, in order for God to show his hatred of sin as well as his clemency. Jesus' death on the cross vindicated his hatred of sin but at the same time mercifully offered humanity a way of salvation through belief in Jesus.

There are several problems with this theory. First, Grotius seems to assume that God could not have preserved public order in any other equally effective way. But this assumption is dubious. Since God is all-powerful it would seem that he could show his hatred of sin, give clemency to sinners, and mercifully offer humanity salvation in alternative ways that could have brought about public order just as well. Furthermore, alternative ways certainly seem preferable on grounds of justice since the way God chose involved the innocent suffering and death of his son. Finally, the facts of Jesus' death and resurrection would help preserve public order and good government only if they were known. However, before Jesus the world was ignorant of them. Why did it take God so long to make his message clear? For centuries after Jesus most of the world remained ignorant of them. Why did not God arrange things in such a way that the deterrent value of these facts was maximized? God's failure to communicate Jesus' death on the cross is hardly what one would expect of an effective governmental administrator interested in the deterrent effect of Jesus' example.

THE MORAL THEORY

Although a moral theory of the Atonement was hinted at by earlier writers, it was first developed explicitly by Peter Abelard in the twelfth century.[8] He argued that the cross is the manifestation of the love of God that inspires love in the hearts of human beings. But to love is to be free from sin and to be reconciled with God. Thus, Jesus by his teaching and his example of love taught us and redeemed us from sin. Another important advocate of the moral theory of the Atonement was Faustus Socinus who in the sixteenth century rejected the traditional idea that one is saved through Jesus' suffering and death. According to Socinus, Jesus was sent by God to human beings so that he would "set forth to them the will of God Himself, and might establish an agreement with them in His name."[9] In this view the main function of Jesus is prophetic. He taught humanity the promise of God and gave them an example of a perfect life. The death of Jesus on the cross and his resurrection is important mainly as the completion of his perfect life. Without his death in obedience to God his life would not have been able to stir human beings to follow his example. Further, when God resurrected Jesus from the dead and exalted him to a position at his right hand, Jesus became a high priest who offered freedom from sin and immortality in proportion to people's imitation of his example.

This theory suffers from problems as serious as those of the theories examined above. First, if God is all-powerful and all-good, it would seem that he could teach humanity to love in a way that did not involve the innocent suffering of his son. Why would the ethical message of Jesus have been less effective if he did not suffer and die on the cross? Even if present psychological laws make this impossible, God could have created different laws. Second, it is unclear why Jesus' death and resurrection were a necessary completion to his perfect life. Many ethical and religious teachers have stirred people to follow their example without dying in the dramatic way that Jesus did. Buddha, for example, has been an ethical inspiration for millions. Furthermore, Jesus could have been exalted to a high priest who offers freedom from sin and immortality in proportion to people's imitation of his example without his undergoing suffering and death. Finally, this theory provides no account of how people who have never heard of Jesus could be inspired to love, be free from sin, and obtain immortality.

Thus, this theory provides no explanation of the Christian doctrines of the Incarnation and the Resurrection, and it calls into question the goodness of God by making it difficult to understand how people who have never heard of Jesus could be able to gain freedom from sin and to achieve immortality.

THE CHRISTUS VICTOR THEORY

In his influential book *Christus Victor*, Gustaf Aulén (1879–1978) presents what he calls the classical theory of the Atonement, which he says can be found in the New Testament and the writings of the Fathers of the ancient church.[10] According to his analysis, the ransom theory seems to be merely a variant of the classical theory that should not be confused with the classical theory itself. The essence of the classical theory is the dramatic victory of Christ over the evil powers to which humanity has become enslaved, especially sin, death, and the devil. In this victory God through Christ not only frees humanity from death, sin, and the devil but is reconciled to himself.

However, although this theory does not have some of the obvious problems of the ransom theory, a crucial question is not answered. Why was victory achieved by means of the sacrifice of the Son of God? An all-powerful God could have "defeated" sin, death, and the devil without this sacrifice. An all-good God in a battle with evil should have followed the rules of just war. In just-war theory one should choose a means to victory that has the least unjust results. The defeat of evil presumably could have been achieved without the sacrifice of his son. Why then did he choose to sacrifice him? Since this sacrifice seems objectionable on moral grounds one wonders whether it is compatible with God's moral perfection. Furthermore, it is unclear why in order to defeat sin, death, and the devil the Son of God must be incarnate in a human being. Surely an all-powerful God could accomplish this without being incarnated.[11] In addition, there is the problem of why faith in Christ is the only means or even a means to salvation. Aulén maintains that the saving victory of Jesus over sin continues into the present, indeed that it is an eternal victory.[12] But why? It is certainly not obvious why or how Christ's victory could be eternal unless God arbitrarily willed it to be. But in that case God could have arbitrarily willed the defeat of sin, death, and the devil without either the Incarnation or the Resurrection.

THE MYSTIC THEORY

Mystical interpretations of the significance of Jesus' death and resurrection go back to Paul who declared "I have been crucified with Christ; it is no longer I who live, but Christ who lives in me" (Gal. 2:20). Some of the early church fathers such as Irenaeus in the second century, although explicitly embracing the ransom theory, also spoke of Jesus making men one with God.[13] In the Middle Ages philosophers such as Aquinas, although explicitly holding a form of the satisfaction theory, used mystical language to explain the union of Christ who was the head of church with the church's members. "The Head and the members are as it were one mystical Person, and so Christ's satisfaction pertains to all the faithful as to His own members."[14] Reformed thinkers such as Calvin, although advocating the penal theory, spoke of a mystical union of Christ with the members of the church. "He, in short, has deigned to make us one with Himself, therefore do we boast that we have fellowship in righteousness with Him."[15]

These and other Christian thinkers who could be cited wished to maintain that an essential part of the Atonement is a mystic identification or union with Jesus' death and resurrection. Does this supplement to the traditional theories help solve their problems? On the contrary, it may make the problem of these traditional theories more acute.

There is a problem with the mystic union itself. What epistemological status does it have? Can we even make sense of the paradoxical language of mysticism? What could it possibly mean to say that we and Jesus are one? If we put these problems aside, however, and accept the meaningfulness and epistemological legitimacy of such experiences,[16] there are still other problems.

Mystic identification with Jesus' suffering and death hardly helps the ethical problems faced by the theories discussed up to this point. The problem of the injustice of God inflicting pain on his innocent son remains despite a mystic union with Jesus. Indeed, the union should bring it home in a most poignant way. In our union with Jesus *we* would feel directly the injustice of his suffering and death since we would be one with him.

Nor does the mystic theory account for another problem of these other theories: Why did God choose to operate in the way he did when other alternatives were not clearly ruled out? If mystical union with God is important or even necessary for salvation, why does this union need to be achieved with the incarnated, crucified, and resurrected Son of God? Why not a mystic union with God directly? But if mystical union with the incarnated Son of God is necessary for salvation why must he suffer and be resurrected? Why could we not simply have a mystic union with an incarnated Son of God who did not suffer and die?

The idea of mystic union does not help the arbitrariness found in some theories. The need or desirability of a mystic union of humanity with an incarnated, crucified, and suffering God is on the acceptance theory still determined by the free arbitrary choice of God. God could have chosen to have the path to salvation not depend on any mystic union and, indeed, he could have made it essential for salvation that one *not* have such a union.

The mystic theory does not help explain why a mystic union is essential for teaching people to love. Even if present psychological laws make loving incompatible without a mystical union with God impossible, God could have created different laws. Furthermore, even if we follow Socinus in believing that Jesus was exalted to a high priest who offers freedom from sin and immortality in proportion to people's imitation of his example, a mystic union with him does not seem necessary for this imitation and, hence, for salvation.

Finally, the problem of salvation for non-Christians becomes even more acute on the mystic theory. Non-Christians have a hard enough time being saved by believing in the Incarnation and Resurrection of Jesus. However, if a mystical union with Jesus' suffering and death is also essential, non-Christians could not possibly fulfill the requirements.

Conclusion

All of the historically important theories of the Atonement have serious problems. In particular, they either fail to explain why God sacrificed his son for the salvation of sinners or else make the sacrifice seem arbitrary. Thus, they do not provide an adequate explanation of the Incarnation and death of the Christ. Not only are the doctrines of the Resurrection, the Incarnation, and salvation problematic in their own right, there is no known theory that plausibly accounts for them.

NOTES

1. See Alan Richardson, *An Introduction to the Theology of the New Testament* (New York: Harper and Brothers, 1958), chap. 10; William J. Wolf, "Atonement," *The Encyclopedia of Religion* (New York: Macmillan, 1987), vol. 1, pp. 495–96.

2. Vincent Taylor, *The Atonement in New Testament Teaching*, p. 182 quoted in William J. Wolf, *No Cross, No Crown: A Study of the Atonement* (Garden City, N.Y.: Doubleday, 1957), pp. 90–91.

3. L. W. Grensted, *A Short History of the Doctrine of the Atonement* (London: Manchester University Press, 1920), chap. 3. Some commentators argue that Augustine did not hold even a sophisticated ransom theory. See Joseph M. Colleran's introduction to Anselm, *Why God Became Man and the Virgin Conception and Original Sin*, trans., introduction, and notes by Joseph M. Colleran (Albany, N.Y.: Magi Books, 1969), p. 44.

4. Grensted, *A Short History of the Doctrine of the Atonement*, chaps. 4, 5, 6.

5. Colleran in Anselm, *Why God Became Man and the Virgin Conception and Original Sin*, pp. 44–45.

6. Grensted, *A Short History of the Doctrine of the Atonement*, pp. 161–63.

7. Ibid., pp. 292–302.

8. Ibid., pp. 103–5.

9. Ibid., p. 287.

10. Gustaf Aulén, *Christus Victor: An Historical Study of the Three Main Types of the Idea of Atonement*, trans. A. G. Herbert (New York: Macmillan, 1967).

11. Aulén says that the Incarnation is a "necessary presupposition" of the Atonement but he gives no argument for this contention. See Aulén, *Christus Victor*, p. 151.

12. Ibid., p. 150.

13. Grensted, *A Short History of the Atonement*, p. 58.

14. Ibid., p. 156.

15. Ibid., p. 219.

16. Michael Martin, *Atheism: A Philosophical Justification* (Philadelphia: Temple University Press, 1990), chap. 6.

BIBLICAL INDEX

Page numbers appear in boldface type.

GENERAL INDEX